PLEASE THROW
TWO CARROTS
AT YOUR
MOTHER

COMIC AND CURIOUS CLIPPINGS
FROM THE LEGENDARY THEATRICAL PAPER

THE ERA
1880-1890

COMPILED BY

JULIA D ATKINSON

THERE is a certain class of idiots that infests stage doors to worry actresses with silly attentions. To this class must belong the individual who has been recently haunting the Crystal Palace, and who the other day left at the stage door of the Theatre the following original epistle for a certain pretty and clever actress, who is engaged in the Pantomime. Here is the precious document: –

"Norwood. – Please do not be cross at my taking the liberty of writing to you, dear Miss ------. I have been wanting to for ever so long, but could never make up my mind. You are so awfully lovely, and I have fallen in love with you. Don't laugh, please. It is quite true, and very silly of me, I know. We go to the Pantomime nearly every day, but scarcely ever look at any one but you. If you are not cross at my writing this, will you please throw two carrots at your mother (you know who I mean) in the scene where you find yourself at home? Do please. Ever yours, SILLY. P.S. – You have seen me before with my sister, near the stage door."

The Era, 29th January 1881

CONTENTS

ACKNOWLEDGEMENTS

Many thanks to the British Newspaper Archive for making *The Era*, and many other fascinating vintage newspapers, available online.

The cover was designed by Maduranga Sampath of MSN Art Studio.

The back cover image is a photograph by Henry van der Weyde of Richard Mansfield in the title role of *Dr Jekyll and Mr Hyde* (1887). The photographer died in 1924, so this work is in the public domain in its country of origin and other countries where the copyright term is the author's life plus 80 years or less.
This work is in the public domain the United States because it meets three requirements:
1)it was first published outside the United States (and not published in the U.S. within 30 days),
2)it was first published before 1 March 1989 without copyright notice or before 1964 without copyright renewal or before the source country established copyright relations with the United States,
3)it was in the public domain in its home country (United Kingdom) on the URAA date (January 1, 1996 for most countries).

1
1880
HAD YOU SEEN THE CABBAGE BEFORE?

FIELDING'S "Diorama of the Zulu War" was freely advertised on the walls of Chester, to open at the Music Hall on Saturday (27ᵗʰ). In addition to the above mode of advertising, a local band, in a hired brake, moved round the town to announce the entertainment. The doors were thrown open at 7.30, and the area of the hall was soon comfortably filled by an eager and expectant audience. The hour of eight arrived, at which the business was announced to commence, but it was not until much later, when, after signs of considerable impatience had been manifested by the audience, an announcement was made from the platform by one of the company to the effect that, in consequence of a mishap, the entertainment would not be given, but, on application at the box-office, all moneys would be returned. Upon the receipt of this intelligence there was an immediate rush; but imagine the disappointment and disgust of the audience on learning that the box was empty, and that the fair creature who had so nicely taken their money was *non est*. This was *too* much! The public waxed furious, and returned rampagious to the interior of the Hall, where they commenced smashing everything they could lay hands upon. Whilst this was going on at one end of the room an interesting incident occurred in the vicinity of the platform, where a warm member of the company was attempting to explain matters. His speech was, however, interrupted by a voice from the middle of the Hall exclaiming "Behead him!" Instantaneously, and as if by magic, another rush was made for the platform, the broad sheet of white calico, which was the only apology for scenery, was torn down, and before the member had half finished his explanation, he was seized and carefully rolled up in the sheet, and, with a one! two!! three!!! was pitched among the furious audience, who gracefully received him with open arms and played at football with him. Another of the company was spotted, but he made a dash for the back door, which he succeeded in reaching just in time to escape a vicious kick from a small hob-nailed boot, and was afterwards seen making tracks for the railway station. Happily, at this juncture, Inspectors Farrell and Lindsay, accompanied by a couple of detectives, entered the Hall in time to stop further damage being done, and cleared the building.
4/1/1880

TO THE EDITOR OF THE ERA.
Sir, – From a dozen bills of some of our best Provincial Theatres, and from notices in *The Era*, I glean that the Pantomimes are produced under the "personal supervision," or "close superintendence," of Mr So-and-so, the energetic and courteous Acting-Manager; while the Stage-Manager, who arranges the business of the piece, with many hours a day of long, wearying rehearsals, gets very little of the credit, and in many cases none at all, as that is all accorded to the A.M., "who is to be highly complimented for his untiring energy."

As far as the actual production is concerned, what would he do without the Stage-Manager? What does he do? He leans majestically on his umbrella, suggesting that half a dozen supers would be more effective down R instead of L; while others are better passive than active, &c., &c.; often causing unnecessary delay and rearrangement – the whole amounting to the value of Pecksniff's happy knack, who, when his articled pupil had made an architectural plan of a building, put some insignificant window and his name to it, thus claiming credit for another man's work. C.G.W.

WANTED, to Purchase, for Side Show (No. 3). HAIRLESS HORSE, Giant Pig, or any really good Living Novelty. Send particulars and lowest price to JAS. WM. BOSTOCK, Royal Agricultural Hall, Islington, London. Open to purchase a Light well-painted Set of Park Swings. Must be in good order and have truck to carry them.
11/1/1880

AN accident of a rather alarming nature occurred at the Alhambra Music Hall, Hull, on Friday (9th inst.). A spectator in the top balcony, whilst attempting to reach a light from one of the gas chandeliers, overbalanced and fell into the pit. The man himself was uninjured and able to walk home; but two persons were somewhat seriously hurt by his falling upon them, and had to be removed in a cab.
18/1/1880

ON Tuesday night, during the performance of the Pantomime of *The Sleeping Beauty*, at the Holte Theatre, Birmingham, a singular fatality occurred. The stage is illuminated by an electric light. The wires which transmit the electric current runs along the passage leading to the orchestra. Attached to these wires are two brass connections, which are placed underneath the stage. Between eight and nine o'clock the members of the band left the orchestra for a short time. Mr Augustine Bierdermann (or Mr Bruno, as he was professionally known), the euphonium player, as he went out placed his hands upon the connections, presumably to try the effects of an electric shock. Unhappily, as the lights were out, the full force of the current was in the wires. The result was that immediately Bruno's hand touched the wires he fell back insensible and unable to move. He was lifted up by some of his colleagues, but before medical aid could be procured he expired. For a time the occurrence was kept from the audience, but when it became known it caused much sensation, and great sympathy was expressed. Bruno, who was an Italian, was much respected. The Coroner's inquiry was opened on Wednesday, but was adjourned after evidence of identification had been taken.
25/1/1880

A Filthy Patron of the Drama.
ON one or two occasions lately complaints have been made by visitors to the pit of the Princess's Theatre in Main-street, Glasgow, that some persons in the balcony were in the habit of spitting over on those underneath. With a couple of sharp detectives such as Flotsam on the stage, in *New Babylon*, and Sinclair, of the Southern Division, in the front of the house, it was not to be expected that such a filthy practice would long go unchecked. On Tuesday night (20th ult.) a person, dressed like a gentleman, was observed sitting in the balcony, and occasionally annoying people underneath by spitting over. Detective Sinclair and another officer drew the attention of the lessee, Mr Beryl, as instructed, to the matter, but as the curtain was about to fall it was resolved not to interfere till the interval. The party referred to then came out, when he was informed that he would not be allowed to return to his seat. He admitted having been guilty of the offence, and promised to behave better if allowed to sit out the play; but Mr Beryl very properly told him that a man who could conduct himself in such a manner was out of his place in the balcony of the theatre. He then began to be noisy, and Sinclair ordered him to leave the building. This, however, he would not do, and as soon as the officers tried to remove him he struck them. He was then taken into custody on a charge of assault, and at the police-station gave the name of John Hamilton.

He had to appear at the bar of the Southern Police-court to answer the complaint. He pleaded not guilty, but the charge was found proven, and Bailie Waddell fined him two guineas, with the alternative of fourteen days' imprisonment.

FOR SALE, Cheap, the finest PORCUPINE PIG in England alive, with First-class Den, Letter, Cloth, and Booth; price £4 the lot; also a Duck with Four Legs, alive, for Sale. Address, ROBERT RAWLINGS, Agricultural Hall, Islington, London.
1/2/1880

ON Monday last the Queen's Theatre, Manchester, was the scene of an occurrence without precedence in theatrical history. Mr Emm, the popular comedian, and his travelling company, were announced to make their first appearance here, and soon after the doors were opened the gallery overflowed. Consequently the doors were closed leaving a large number on the outside. A contingent arriving from Salford and finding the portals shut, climbed to the top of some adjacent property and thence to the roof of the Theatre, where, lifting the tiles over the gallery, they gained an entrance free. Others, witnessing the successful climbing proclivities of their venturesome predecessors, quickly followed, and it was not before about a hundred had obtained admission through this novel entrance that the officials connected with the Theatre were able to check the unwelcome influx. Beyond a few hats that were smashed by the intruding visitors dropping in, as it were, from the skies, no particular harm was done, and when the scaling party had settled down the performance proceeded without interruption.
7/3/1880

AT the Birmingham Police-court on Monday, before Messrs J. Lowe and and W.M. Ellis, William Mitchell, a rough-looking fellow, about twenty years of age, a tube-drawer, living in Icknield-street East, was charged with assaulting Miss Jenny Hill, an actress at the Prince of Wales' Theatre, on Saturday night, a little before ten o'clock, by throwing a cabbage at her. The case created a great amount of interest, several members of the Theatrical Profession being in court.

Detective Mountford, addressing the Bench, said – The prisoner is charged with assaulting Miss Jenny Hill, an actress at the Prince of Wales Theatre, on Saturday night, a little before ten o'clock, by throwing a cabbage, which struck her as she was performing on stage. Some two or three weeks ago he had complaints about roughs levying blackmail on the actors and actresses. An application was made to Major Bond to investigate the matter, and Sargeant Van Helden, myself, and other officers have been engaged to protect the artists going home. On Saturday night when Mr Kinghorne, who plays the Emperor, came upon the stage, the blackmailers hissed him, and a cabbage was thrown which struck Miss Hill. While I was investigating the matter, someone pointed the prisoner out to a policeman as the man who threw it. We have evidence to prove that he went out on purpose to fetch the cabbage.

Miss Jenny Hill said – On Saturday night I was upon the stage with several of the company, when a cabbage was thrown, from what part of the house I do not know, and struck me on the left eye.

Mr Gem (Magistrate's Clerk) – Did it hurt you at all? Was it sent with any force?

Witness – No particular force, and the injury was slight.

Had you been received with any marks of disapprobation? – Yes; there were several marks of disapprobation towards Mr Kinghorne every night.

He was on stage with you at the time? – Yes; I stood next to him.

Had there been any marks of disapprobation expressed concerning yourself? – Never.

Did you ever see this young man at all? – No, never.

Charles Barker said – I am a tube-drawer, and on Saturday night was in the right-hand side of the gallery. I saw the cabbage thrown by the prisoner.

Mr Gem – How near were you to him when he threw it? – About three or four yards from him.

Did he stand up or sit down when he threw it? – He stood up.

Then you could see him plainly? – Yes, sir.

Had you seen the cabbage before? – Yes; he came walking down with the cabbage in his hand.

Did he say anything when he had it in his hand? – No, sir.

Do you know where he bought it? – No. All I saw was the prisoner throw it. He came up to the right-hand corner of the gallery and then threw it.

Did you see it strike Miss Hill? – Yes, sir; it was not meant for her, though.

It was meant for someone near her, perhaps? – Yes.

How do you know it was not meant for her? – Because it was meant for the Emperor. They said so.

Who said so? – A good many of them.

Why don't they like him? – I don't know, I am sure.

It is this particular Emperor they don't like, and not Emperors in general, is it not? – Yes, sir.

Emperors are not very comfortable in many places. Why did they throw it at him? – Because he would not give them beer or "summut".

It seems, then, that he is an Emperor who does not behave like a Prince. Had you ever been by when they asked the Emperor to stand anything? – No, sir.

Mr Lowe – Had you known him before? – Yes.

He was a companion of yours? – Yes, he used to be.

Martin Loughlan said – I was in the gallery on Saturday night, and was near the prisoner. I was the one he asked for a penny to buy the cabbage with, but I would not give it to him.

Mr Gem – Where was it? – In the right-hand side of the gallery.

Who bought the cabbage at last, when you would not give him the penny? – He went out and fetched it.

Did you see him throw it? – Yes; I saw him with the cabbage, and saw him throw it.

Whom did he throw it at? – It was meant for the Emperor.

But it struck Miss Hill? – Yes, sir.

Have you ever heard him ask the Emperor for anything – No, sir.

Prisoner offered no explanation of his conduct.

Mr Ellis, after consulting with his colleague, said – This is a most rascally proceeding, and I am sure that Mr Lowe and every other Magistrate on the Bench will do everything they can to protect actors from the annoyance they seem to experience. I am very sorry we cannot give you more than two months for this offence. You will have to go to the House of Correction for two months with hard labour.

TO THE EDITOR OF THE ERA.

Sir – In the fall of 1867 and the rise of 1868 I had the honour of being a member of Mr James Rodger's company in "the toyshop of the world." At that time my position as an artist might be described as hovering between "second heavies" and "walking gentlemen;" but, by virtue of a previous connection with the newspaper Press, my services were secured to rewrite and adapt a Pantomime that proved highly remunerative and generally successful.

From the latter circumstance, I suppose my friends the "layers-on" in the gallery became particularly attentive to me, first in the way of unsolicited applause, and, secondly, as attendants at the stage-door every Saturday evening after performance. Up till a certain time I was so foolish as to throw them sixpence occasionally. Certain members of the company, however, paid regularly a fixed sum; and the latter fact has contributed not a little to the growth of the evil. I hope I am not misunderstood. The blame could not be attached to the actors and actresses or to the Manager, except in that they submitted to a vile state of things which had been a long time in existence at the older house – the Theatre Royal – before Mr Rodgers began his highly creditable career in Birmingham. Nor can Mr Mercer Simpson be to blame. If blame there can be for a system which is imperative in France, we must be tender now in bringing it home, for its author (in Birmingham), a most estimable gentleman, is now in the grave, and your columns but lately have contained an appeal on behalf of the loved ones he has left behind.

The disgraceful system has only now culminated in the Police-court. The ventilation must completely abolish it, one would think; but, in case anything should be required to prove the extent of the evil and its venerable age, I shall, if you can give me space, relate two incidents that will, I hope, have a salutary effect.

There is a lonely way from Broad-street into Navigation-street, in Birmingham, a part of which is called the Aqueduct. One night Mr Charles Walsh – a member of the Prince of Wales' company – who had persistently refused to pay the "Lay-on boys," was attacked in this dark and lonely thoroughfare by the youths who had threatened him, and one of his eyes was completely knocked out by the aid of a knuckle-duster, or other similar instrument. The eye was lying on his cheek, and nothing but skill and good fortune prevented its loss. Incident number one.

Incident number two was a personal one. The Pantomime was past, and one of the first stars to visit was the late amiable and accomplished Mdlle Beatrice. She had no company then of her own, and her speciality was *Marie Antoinette*. I played the person who spoke the first line in the piece – a certain Viscount. On Monday night my friend the king of the gallery waited upon me at the stage-door and asked for money. On this occasion I refused. He said, "Then we'll 'goose' you tomorrow night." Observe the intimate knowledge of the professional slang term. "Goose away," was my reply. I need not say that, at that time, I held the opinion of the majority of an audience in thorough contempt because they had not yet discovered the wonderful genius I believed myself to possess.

The following night came. A splendid overture was played – the prompter's bell rang. After so many "bars" the act-drop rose and the whole stage was perfectly vacant. The scene represented – I think – a Hall in the Palace of Versailles. [...] On this occasion no sooner had I made my appearance than the "Lay-on boys" yelled, hooted, and hissed. The rest of the audience, perfectly understanding the cause, cheered, and I, being ridiculously indifferent, proceeded. That was not the end of the affair, however.

At the time I speak of the stage-door was in a side street. That night I came along the stone-paved passage, followed by a young lady – a member of the company – with whom I was desperately in love. I "never told my love," however, and she is the pride of a certain London Theatre now. At the street door the chief of the blackmailers met me and said, "Won't you pay us now?" I refused angrily, and added something more expressive than elegant. My friend went on in a perfectly business-like way to inform me that in that case he would "take it out of me." Having heard terrible tales of Brummagem prowess in mortal combat, my heart fluttered, but my enchantress being behind, I could not show the white feather. Therefore, throwing aside my carpet-bag, "I hit him on the nose," having seen it on record that "the first blow is half the fight." I think that saying must be true, as I came out the victor, and my opponent was a young giant with "bones of brass and muscles of steel." In justice to his companions, I must say that they saw fair play in the strictest way. I was about giving in when my antagonist cried "I've had enough." When I gazed upon his manly brow I found his two "optics" curtained, as the Baron O'Grady would have said. Then I "treated the crowd," and ever afterwards became the recipient of the most uncalled for and undeserved applause, without paying a farthing for it. They respected, as your young brute will, the better animal – the animal who could punish.

If the authorities do not now put down the despicable system some of the young athletes in the Profession should amuse themselves by beating the cowardly ruffians who threaten women and children. The mother of a child-actress at the time I am speaking of was afraid to miss paying the *claquers*. Afterwards we heard that they used to waylay her. It often struck me as being very odd when some young lady had spoken a most beautiful and pathetic speech in the midst of appreciative silence to hear a coarse voice shout suddenly, abruptly, sharply, "Lay on." Highly flattering, thought many novices to "Brum." But when the demand for payment came every actor and actress of my acquaintance became as disgusted as, Yours faithfully, ERIC ST. C.K. ROSS, Park-villas, Lower Broughton, Manchester, March 10th, 1880.
14/3/1880

MISS GENEVIEVE WARD is the possessor of a pretty little dog whose name is "Teck." "Teck" was the other night banished from the presence of its accomplished mistress while she was receiving due homage paid to her ability by H.R.H. the Prince of Wales and the Duke of Teck. Their compliments having been rendered, they turned to leave, and had not proceeded many yards when the canine favourite thought himself at liberty to approach. "Teck, Teck, get in the basket!" called Miss Ward playfully, and little thinking of what was to follow. The Prince caught the words, informed "Teck" – his companion, not the dog – that he was wanted, and, upon receiving explanation from the admired actress, once more took his leave, enjoying the mistake immensely, laughing heartily, and jokingly telling the Duke to "get in the basket."

BRANDY, IF YOU PLEASE. For God's sake, darling, come and see me before I go, if only for five minutes; this suspense is killing me. Bad news from your Brother. For address, see Companies' page; or, call Cuxton's, for letters.
28/3/1880

A CONTRAST to the Oberammergau Passion Play, which is to be performed again this season, is thus described by a well-known Shakespearian authority in a letter to a friend: – "Years ago I saw a Passion Play in Spain which was sublimely national. After the Magi had presented their gifts to Mary, who was seated beside a pasteboard manger surrounded by pasteboard oxen, with a great deal of genuine straw about, at the tinkle of a little bell ballet girls in short skirts and pink tights darted from the side scenes, and pirouetting around the group, finally struck an attitude with their hands over the cradle, and their elevated toes pointing to the audience. When the curtain went down there were vociferous calls for the actors and Christ appeared, leading Joseph and Mary, and bowed his thanks. It was deeply religious to the people, and many women wept."

A VERY melancholy case of suicide occurred in Dunfermline on Thursday morning, 1st inst., when Arthur Weston, who is better known as "Signor Boz, the conjurer," strangled himself in his lodgings in Randolph-street. The act was a most determined one, deceased having wetted a silk pocket handkerchief, tied it round his neck, and used a poker as a tourniquet. He must have been dead several hours when found, as his body was quite cold. Deceased was a native of West Brighton, about thirty years of age, and married.
11/4/1880

BALLOON ASCENTS. Mr T. WRIGHT, the Crystal Palace Aeronaut, can arrange for Balloon Ascents with his Owl shape Balloon. This Balloon has proved a great attraction many times at Crystal Palace, Germany, Belfast, Dudley, Cheltenham, Edgbaston, Leamington, Gainsboro', &c. Ordinary Pear shape Balloons, if required. Send for Posters and Photos of Owl. Address, Aerial Villas, Howard-road, Plaistow, E.
9/5/1880

THE chief attraction at a gala at the Arboretum* on Monday was the ascent of the great owl balloon. As the hour of six o'clock was approaching the crowding at the gates was immense. The Robin Hood Rifle band entered, and played the very appropriate air "Up in a Balloon," during which time the bird was struggling for wing. As the sand-bags were liberated one by one the owl made efforts to get free, and at length flew away beautifully, carrying with her Mr Wright, the pilot and owner, Mr Mosley, and Mr Jones, landlord of the Milton's Head Hotel. After a splendid trip of thirty-seven miles, the balloon descended in safety.
*In Nottingham.

WANTED, a Gentleman to Play MONKEY and make himself useful in other Ballets, for the Continent. Must be short active man that can tumble and knock about. Apply, A.B.C., 50, Bath-lane, Newcastle-on-Tyne.
23/5/1880

CONSIDERABLE amazement was caused in the Small Debt Court, Aberdeen, on Thursday, 20th inst., during the hearing of a dispute between the members of a travelling theatrical company which had been giving performances at Woodside. Thorpe Chadwick, now residing in Brechin, sued Henry Douglas Hicks, Proprietor of a Theatre at Woodside, for 17s. 6d., as the salary of pursuer and his wife for three days. The pursuer conducted his own case, while Mr David Stewart represented the defendant.

It was alleged that at the performance in defender's Theatre on a certain night the pursuer was very drunk, and not only blundered on the stage, but made a disturbance behind the scenes; so that, according to the defender's account, the drama was turned into a farce, and the farce into a tragedy. The pieces played were *The Dumb Man of Manchester* and an Irish comedy entitled *His Last Legs*. In the former the pursuer represented the Lord Chief Justice, and he, it was said, made a sad mess of the part, going on to the stage two or three minutes too soon, and shouting "silence" instead of saying what he should have done. He went away on the following day without defender's leave, thus violating his engagement, and in consequence of his conduct Mr Hicks had refused to pay his salary. Pursuer indignantly denied that he was intoxicated, averred that the derangement of the play was caused by the "cue" not having been given him at the proper time, and declared that the disturbance was created by the defender challenging him (the pursuer) to fight, and calling him a craven-hearted, broad-shouldered, fat-bellied coward. The Sheriff held that the defender was justified in refusing to give pursuer his wages, his Lordship jocularly remarking that the pursuer had plainly been too much intoxicated to perform his duties, and particularly those of a Lord Chief Justice. He, therefore, gave judgement in favour of the defendant, and allowed him expenses.

AN extraordinary accident occurred at the Queen's Theatre, Manchester, during the performance of *Henry the Fifth* by Mr George Rignold and his company. All went well until the last act, when the stage was filled with joyous citizens. When the King presented himself, seated upon his white charger, the vast audience joined heartily in the shouts of satisfaction, and the scene was one of tremendous enthusiasm and success. Whilst the cheering was at its height the curtain descended, but so gratified were the spectators with the magnificence of the spectacle, and so thoroughly did they enter into the joy and satisfaction of the moment, that they vociferously insisted upon once more beholding the victorious monarch and his steed, which seemed to share the pride of his rider, and which excited the admiration of the audience as he tossed his head aloft, and advancing nearly to the footlights seemed to acknowledge the plaudits of the multitude. When, in answer to the call, the curtain again ascended, the horse and the king were seen emerging from an arch, and as they advanced the cheering became most vociferous.

Suddenly the animal stumbled, and there was fear that either Mr Rignold or the horse would be hurt, and the excitement of the moment was not relieved when it was found that the animal was unable to recover itself. The fear became more intense at it was perceived that a trap in the centre of the stage had given way, and that the horse's off hind leg was in the hole. Mr Rignold behaved with consummate coolness. The audience were becoming alarmed, but he calmed them. Kneeling behind the animal, he looked down the hole which the now wholly open trap had formed, and, after asking a question of those below, called for a rope. Before anything could be done, however, the horse made another effort to recover itself and as a consequence it began gradually to slip into the trap, and, finally, it overbalanced and disappeared altogether. Then the drop-scene was lowered. Presently Mr Rignold appeared, and announced that neither he nor the horse was injured.

WANTED, a Respectable BOY of COLOUR to wait in a handsome Bazaar at the Seaside. Address, E. HART, 4, Victoria-terrace, Coatham, Redcar, Yorkshire.
30/5/1880

TO THE LADY CLOG DANCERS – Who is the Champion? Great Contest for the Championship, August 2nd, at the PRINCESS'S PALACE, LEEDS. First Prize, Championship Belt, Value Twenty Guineas; Second, Gold Medal; Third, Bronze Medal. Forms on application to J.H. WOOD, Mechanics', Hull.
6/6/1880

IN the neighbourhood of Tunbridge Wells, the other day, a bill was placed in our hands announcing, among other matters at the local Skating Rink, and for the benefit of Mr William Vol Becque, "A purse of silver to the best comic singer – each competitor to sing while standing on his head." This was described as "real fun."

FOR SALE, PHONOGRAPH, or Talking Machine, in good order. Has been worked lately; also Brown Tame Bear, young, performs a little, and very tractable and quiet. Could be learned easily; also large Monkey. Apply, JOSEPH KELLS, 81, Morrison-street, Glasgow.
13/6/1880

APROPOS of the London notices on Madame Sarah Bernhardt's rendering of Adrienne Lecouvreur, the *Evénement* says: – "The summing-up of *Messieurs les Critics* is this – 'Yes, it is a triumph, but far below that which Rachel obtained under similar circumstances.' Well, it is there that they make a mistake. Rachel played Adrienne Lecouvreur twice in London, and of the performances thus wrote a most unbiased critic, Léon Beauvallet – 'The piece was rendered in an odious fashion. The stage properties were not forthcoming, the cues were forgotten; Mdlle Rachel – yes, Rachel herself – did not know a word of her part. She omitted, she chopped, she mutilated, right and left, the unfortunate dialogue that fell to her share; and, worse still, she was five minutes – a terribly long time at the Theatre – late in her entry in the third act. For once in a way Raphael rode the high horse, and seizing the occasion, proved that directorial power could assert itself by fining the great *tragedienne* one hundred francs, the fine being inscribed upon the Green-room card, where even the call-boy could see and impart the astounding fact to his friends and acquaintances. As a fitting finish to this deplorable evening, Randoux, who played Maurice de Saxe, entangled himself, on his entry in the fifth act, in an iron curtain-rod, and fell full length upon the stage, with his head nearly in the prompter's box.'"

A BOGUS BOUCICAULT.
Dundee boasts a Poet whose name is McGonagall. According to a local contemporary, he, many a time and oft, has soared up beyond the moon on wings of faith and hope only to come down again by the run in double quick time. For months past, he has been waiting with a patience worthy of a better cause "for something to turn up." After the favourable reception he lately received from the public, and the flattering decision passed on his talent as a poet and an actor, he did expect that some tangible recognition of his genius would soon be forthcoming. Judge then what were his feelings when, on Wednesday last (9th inst.), the postman brought him a letter headed "Theatre Royal," and subscribed "Dion Boucicault."

The contents of that precious epistle were to the effect that the renowned dramatic author had heard of McGonagall's talents as an actor and a poet, and after reading the account of his late *levee* which appeared in the *Weekly News*, he had come to the conclusion to offer him an engagement as a leading actor in one of the travelling star companies. The letter concluded by requesting McGonagall to meet the writer at Straton's Restaurant at twelve noon that day, where they could have luncheon and talk the matter over together. Such a letter from such a quarter was enough to send McGonagall flying up to the seventh heaven and a storey higher. Here was "the silvery dream" of his life about to be realised at last. First, there was the immediate promise of a good beef dinner, and a prospective engagement in a London Theatre at a good weekly "screw." Such a chance was not to be met with every day.

Punctual to the hour named in the letter, the Poet called at the restaurant, and inquired for Mr Boucicault. The attendants started at the Poet, but a "friend" of the Poet's, who just at that precise moment chanced to drop in, came to the rescue and offered to take him to the gentleman, who, he said, was patiently awaiting him in the smoking room. Following his *soi-disant* friend upstairs, he was led into the presence of a middle-aged man, with a flowing black beard streaked with silver. His face was commonplace enough, and his "togs" were rather seedy, and the Poet thought he had not the "smell" of an author or an actor about him. However, the Poet's officious friend introduced the bearded gentleman as Dion Boucicault, and the latter shook hands with the Poet, and expressed the pleasure he felt at meeting with one whose fame had spread over the whole habitable globe. McGonagall thanked Dion for his flattering compliments, and assured his new-found friend that he was delighted to make his acquaintance.

The formalities of introduction over, McGonagall was requested to take a seat, and Dion went straight to the business on hand. He said he had been led to the conclusion that if he and the Poet could make arrangements for a dramatic tour through the Provinces it would tend to their mutual benefit. The Poet "would be most happy." "What are your terms?" promptly inquired Dion. This was to the point, and meant business. The Poet scratched his "pow," and thought for a minute. It would not do to sell his talents for an old song. A guinea a night might do in Dundee, but travelling was expensive. Taking all things into consideration the Poet finally came to the conclusion that £2 a night was a moderate salary to begin with. "O, you are very reasonable," replied Dion. "Of course we don't want to kill you right off, and we propose that you shall only appear four nights in the week, and more if necessary." Here the Poet's friend stepped forward and suggested that Mr Boucicault should just conclude to give him £20 a week, pay the first week's salary in advance, and give him £5 towards the expenses of his outfit. To this arrangement Dion at once agreed, but when McGonagall insisted that the arrangement should be written out and mutually signed, Dion jumped to his feet and retired to the other end of the room, and left the Poet staring in astonishment at his eccentric patron. While the interview was in progress a number of the Poet's friends and admirers dropped in, and seated themselves within earshot of the Poet and actor. To this group Dion now attached himself, and joined in the conversation with all the familiarity of an old acquaintance.

The conversation of the party naturally turned on the Poet's versatile powers, and it was suggested that he should recite some of his "effusions" by way of a sample to his new patron. McGonagall would be highly delighted if Dion would condescend to hear him. "Bannockburn" was suggested, but the Poet was not in costume. "O, never mind that at present," said Dion, "your stick will do for a sword, and here is my handkerchief, you can extemporise it into a waist belt." Thus equipped, with the red cotton "hanky" round his waist, and his trusty oaken cudgel hanging by his side, the Poet launched forth into "the depths of his grand historic piece." The audience applauded to the echo, and Dion declared that if he gave that in London he would bring down the house. "Forget me not" and an "Address to the Moon" were subsequently called for, and at last the Poet sank on a chair completely exhausted. Some one suggested that refreshments should be provided for the Poet, and, after some discussion as to what he would take, a glass of beer and a sandwich was called in. The Poet looked askance at the scanty bill of fare, but, as half a sandwich and a glass of bitter was better than no dinner, he restrained his feelings, and partook of the bread and beer. Then Dion retired, without even shaking hands with the Poet, and one by one the rest of the company followed his example, and left the Poet alone in his glory.

A faint suspicion now began to dawn in the Poet's mind that the whole affair was not exactly "up to dick," and this idea was further strengthened when, by the advice of some friends, he called, in the evening, on the Acting-Manager of the Theatre Royal. Mr Hodges listened with great interest and sympathy to the poor Poet's story. On being shown the letter he informed him that it was a spurious

production, that Dion Boucicault never penned such an epistle, as he was not then and never had been in Dundee. We understand that the Poet has put the matter in the hands of the authorities, who are busily engaged investigating into the circumstances; and we can assure the authors of this heartless hoax on a poor struggling genius that they may yet be called upon to stand the Poet a good dinner to compensate him for the one he was so shabbily cheated and deprived of.
20/6/1880

TO THE EDITOR OF THE ERA.
Sir, – Referring to your article in last week's *Era*, headed "A Bogus Boucicault," permit me, through your columns, to tender my best thanks to Mr Dion Boucicault, who has not only generously sympathised with me, but has also in practical manner evinced the warmest interest in my position by forwarding me, through Mr Hodges, the Acting-Manager of the Dundee Theatre Royal, the handsome contribution of five pounds (£5). A kindness which I shall ever remember.
I am, Sir, yours truly, WILLIAM McGONAGALL, the Dundee Poet. Dundee, June 23rd, 1880.

ANY Person Knowing the Address of BEN BOORN, Circus Manager, will oblige by sending the same to his wife, at 21, Little Europa-place, Bridge-road, Battersea. Alfred, your mother is in great distress.
27/6/1880

WANTED, through incompetency, a FIRST VIOLIN, with Good *Repertoire* of Music, for the steamboat Scarborough, to join at once. Terms, shares. Address, F. WILKINSON, 43, North-street, Scarborough.
4/7/1880

ON Monday night Mr Charles Cooke and his dramatic company gave their farewell performance in Tralee, after a stay of three weeks. The ball-room was crammed with a respectable and appreciative audience, it being the largest we have yet seen gathered within the walls of the Theatre. *Lady Audley's Secret* was the piece selected for the evening, and was performed with the company's usual good taste and ability. At the conclusion of the drama Mr L.A. Lyons recited in character "The Derby," and was repeatedly encored. Mr Lyons then came in front of the drop-scene, and while acknowledging his hearty reception, a bouquet was thrown to him by one of his lady admirers, and unfortunately it struck one of the oil lamps used as footlights, and upset it. The burning oil was spilled on the stage, and but for the timely interference of some of the spectators the flames would have caught the carpet and scenery. Most of the audience became excited; ladies screamed and fainted on all sides, and a general rush was made for the doorway, which got blocked up, exit becoming almost impossible. A bucket of water thrown on the oil suppressed the flames for a moment, but again they leaped up stronger and fiercer than ever. However, after a short time, some of the company succeeded in extinguishing the flames by means of a tarpaulin and a liberal supply of water, and a greater part of the audience having returned to their seats, the performance was proceeded with.

IF MR THOMAS BATTY, of Batty's Circus, do not send his Address to his Mother, 112, Radcliffe-street, Liverpool, he may lose the amount of £700, if not seen to without delay. MARY BATTY.
11/7/1880

A SHORT time ago a party of friendly Zulus gave an exhibition at Chesterfield, and one of the band, who assumed the *role* of the "Zulu Queen," became so enamoured of the place, or the crooked spire, that "her Majesty" desired to remain and declined to accompany the rest of the party to "pastures new." An enterprising innkeeper, with an eye to business, engaged the "Zulu queen" as barmaid at 6s. per week and rations. Whilst serving in this humble capacity, the Zulu appropriated a sum of money and a gold watch belonging to the landlord, and during the investigation with reference to the misssing property left the house. The "Queen," who was subsequently found at another inn, understanding that an offence

against the English law had been committed, took to flight. A chase ensued, and "she" was captured; about £14 and the watch being found on "her" person. It was thereupon discovered that the "Zulu Queen" was a man, and that, although he went by the name of Ungami Wallah, his real name was Thomas John Wilson, alias George Williams. The landlord had all along thought that Ungami was a woman.
25/7/1880

AN extraordinary robbery was committed at St James's Hall, Brighton, on Tuesday afternoon. The Royal Handbell Ringers left the Hall, and on returning discovered that their bells, fifty-three in number, and their music, in all valued at £50, had been stolen. Consequently, no performance could take place, as a fresh set of bells, though telegraphed for from London, could not be obtained in time.
1/8/1880

NO little excitement has been caused in Runcorn owing to a human skull having been found in an ashpit. There is, however, no mystery now attached to the affair, as at first conjectured, for it seems that the said skull has often appeared before the public as "Yorick," "a fellow of infinite jest." About three years ago a Mrs Rowles had several actors connected with the local Theatre lodging at her house, who, after a time, suddenly and rather hurriedly departed without making their landlady any recompense for their maintenance, but leaving behind them a box. The box remained as its owners had left it until recently, when, thinking she would never see her professional friends again, Mrs Rowles broke it open and found among a few other trifling items poor Yorick's headpiece. She threw it into the ashpit, and forgot the circumstances until it was recently unearthed.
15/8/1880

A NUMBER of accidents, some of them fatal, have lately occurred in various parts of the country showing the perils associated with "swing-boats" and "merry-go-rounds," and in more than one case the need of regulation and vigilance has been urged. Another case is reported from Liverpool, where an inquest was held on Monday on the body of Sarah Tapley, twenty years of age. On Thursday evening, the 12th inst., she and a young man named Duggan went to the swing-boats at Islington, and engaged one to hold two persons, and swung by the occupants by means of a rope. Duggan worked the rope, and Tapley told him not to go any higher, and he sat down. The deceased, who was holding by the rods of the swing, let go to pin her shawl, lost her balance, and fell back out of the swing. Her feet remained in it, and she was carried twice up and down, her head striking the ground each time. She was taken to the Royal Infirmary in an unconscious state, and died on Saturday morning. The Jury returned a verdict of "Accidental death," adding the following presentment: – "That swings for public recreation, such as the one in question, ought to be under the inspection of the authorities, with a view to their safe construction and working."

WANTED, MDLLE JULIA RICHARDS and MONS WILLIE RICHARDS (Equestrians), Children of the late Davis Richards, who was killed in the year 1867, while riding in Mr Renz's Circus at St. Petersburg. If they will communicate with ALFRED S. BISHOP, 35, Gibson-square, Islington, London N., they will hear something to their great advantage.
22/8/1880

DURING the engagement of the *Rescued* company at the Theatre Royal, York, last week, an occurrence took place which might have ended fatally. In the last scene of the play most of the company were clustered in a group around Count Ruscor, who, finding himself thwarted on all hands, attempts the life of his accomplice (Widdikoff) by firing a pistol at him. The barrel exploded with a tremendous report, dividing into six pieces, leaving only the stock in the Count's hand. It was found that Miss Bessie Russell and Mr T.A. Tyndall were both struck by pieces of the pistol, but, beyond being greatly alarmed,

they suffered no ill consequences, whilst the remainder of the company escaped unhurt. Mr Owen Johnstone had a narrow escape, his face being only a short distance from the pistol. Had the weapon been fired point blank instead of high in the air many of the company would have been injured.
19/9/1880

ROYAL YACHT OSBORNE, COWES, ISLE OF WIGHT, SEPTEMBER 3rd.
To the Manager: –
Sir, – Having sung "The Beautiful Baby on Dr Ridge's Food" before the whole of the Royal Family, and lately before the Prince and Princess of Wales and Family, I shall feel obliged if you could send me a copy of the words and music, as I learnt it years ago from one of your pamphlets, and should like a copy to correct myself if not accurate in the music. I have sung it here over five years and elsewhere. I saw reference in *The Standard* during the wedding tour of the Duke and Duchess of Connaught. It is very popular with Royalty. Sorry to trouble you. I am, Sir, yours, &c., HERBERT PALIN, Seaman, R.Y., Osborne.
P.S. – Also before the various crowned heads during our travels. (ADVT)
26/9/1880

TO THE EDITOR OF THE ERA.
Sir, – In a report of the Church Congress, held at Leicester, I see that the Rev Gordon Calthrop read a paper attacking the Stage. The bigotry of the address was so extreme as only to proceed from a parson. I am informed, and it is an interesting fact connected with the Rev G.C., that he has been for some years accustomed to take his family to witness the Pantomime at Sydenham every Christmas. Evidently, therefore, the rev. gentleman considers that there is no harm in a representation given at the Crystal Palace, which, if held in London, would be deadly poison. This is only another instance of people (especially parsons) not practising what they preach. I am, Sir, your obedient servant, PLAYGOER.

MR J.P. MOORE, of *The Danites* company, having finished his performance at the Theatre Royal, Coventry, on the 29th ult., proceeded to the dressing-room, and was in the act of washing his hands when suddenly that part of the floor upon which he was standing gave way beneath him. He attempted to clutch at a beam across the ceiling but failed, and fell back head first down the aperture. In the descent he providentially clutched part of the remaining floor with his left hand, and hung in a perilous condition until some one came to his rescue. Had he not clutched the flooring, he says, he must have fallen through on to a flight of stairs and broken his neck. The cause of the accident was the snapping of a four-inch beam (which could be crumbled between the finger and thumb like bread), on to which the flooring, which was in the same state of decay, was nailed. There were four gentlemen in the room at the time, and they say it was a miraculous escape.
10/10/1880

WHO IS BROWNE? We can answer that query only by saying that he is an individual boasting the possession of an amazing amount of impudence. Browne during the past week wrote to the Manager of a well-known and highly popular Theatre in these remarkable terms: "73, Atlantic-road, Brixton. – Sir, I am informed that when a new piece is put on, you often find it desirable to give free passes to ensure a good house. Should an opportunity of this kind occur I shall be pleased to hear from you, as I can attend with two ladies in evening dress. I enclose stamp-directed envelope, and believe me to be, Sir, yours obediently, J.W. Browne." We hope the Manager referred to followed the example once set by Mr Hollingshead, who, on receipt of a similar communication, forwarded to the applicants passes for the gallery, bearing the words "*evening dress indispensable.*"
24/10/1880

A DETACHMENT of the Salvation Army, under the leadership of the local captain, recently took up its stand opposite the Theatre Royal, Cardiff. The campaign against the devil and his victims, theatre-goers particularly, was opened by a young man who has not yet attained the Salvation "pitch" of eloquence. He could "roar as gently as" a bull of Bashan, but there was an utter lack of the true canting ring. He was followed, however, by the leader himself, a man of stentorian voice, with legs and arms of almost unequalled acrobatic eloquence. He "dealt damnation" with great gusto on the hundreds of people who flocked to the Theatre, and no doubt slept that night the sleep of the just man who feels that he has made a great number of wicked people miserable. We looked into the Theatre some time afterwards, says a correspondent, and were shocked to see an audience which literally packed every part, roaring and laughing at *Crutch and Toothpick*, as if the vengeance of Captain Bull Bashan, of the Salvation Army, had not consigned them to perdition. Even the worthy Mayor of Cardiff was convulsed with laughter.

A GENTLEMAN wishes Instruction in the Pronunciation of Difficult Words, Vowel Sounds, Change of Voice, &c., between Two and Four o'clock in the Day, and within about Two Miles of City. Terms must be moderate. Also name of good Dramatic Club. Address, with full particulars, to C.M., care of Housekeeper, 8, Old Jewry, E.C.
31/10/1880

WANTED, PROPERTY BIRDS, Robin, Fly, Fish, Beetle, Linnet, Owl, Lark, Rook, Bull's Head, Four Crows. Perfectly Moulded to Fit Children; also Two Basket Horses, Wolf's Mask and Dress complete. Managers having same for disposal, or Modellers who can supply them, address, F.W. PURCELL, Opera House and Theatre, Bury, Lancashire.
7/11/1880

THE Lyceum curtain, made of costly plush of dragon's blood hue and used to enhance the surprise and delight of the spectators made by the sudden and revelation of the striking tableaux in the *Corsican Brothers*, has been admired for its elegance by all who have seen it. It has also been parodied in a Gaiety burlesque. Now we learn that it has been the cause of some amount of tearful lamentation among about five hundred footmen. We hear that more than one thousand yards of plush were used in its manufacture. One thousand yards of plush, it has been estimated, would make five hundred pairs of flunkeys' breeches. The flunkeys have it that plush was invented for breeches and not for curtains, and that when that intention is frustrated the market price of breeches must inevitably rise. Hence these tears.
14/11/1880

EXPLOSION AT HER MAJESTY'S THEATRE.
On Saturday afternoon, the 13th inst., Gounod's *Faust* was performed at Her Majesty's Opera, and attracted a large audience. The performance went on very satisfactorily until the middle of the last act, when every one was startled by a terrible explosion behind the scenes. Mdlle Widmar, who had been playing Margherita, went on singing with wonderful *sang froid*, and was emulated by Signor Runcio, but the general alarm and confusion were so great that the performance was stopped. The conductor, Signor Le Calsi, called out that there was "no danger," and the Stage-Manager came forward and explained that the explosion had been caused by an accident to the limelight. Several persons quitted the Theatre, but the opera went well and smoothly to the end. The gas was temporarily extinguished, but was soon relighted, and the only difficulty resulting from the explosion was that experienced in the final "apotheosis" of Margherita, the group of angels ascending in *chiaroscuro*, instead of in the celestial beams usually shed by the limelight.
21/11/1880

IN the midst of such marvellously good acting as may now be seen at the Prince of Wales's Theatre*, it is deeply to be regretted that such a performance – or rather non-performance – as that of Mr Eric

Bayley should utterly destroy the effect of an interesting and and otherwise artistic scene. Mr Bayley is, we understand, a gentleman of fortune, and, therefore, there is not the same excuse for his shortcomings that there would be in the case of a young, struggling artiste, just endeavouring to make his way on the London stage, and failing through want of experience. We firmly believe Mr Eric Bayley can never hope to become an actor. He does not appear to have the slightest comprehension of an actor's duties, and while there are so many capable artistes in want of engagement his place should be filled by a really competent actor, not only for the credit of the Profession, but also for the sake of a powerful drama, which suffers greatly through such utter incompetence.

*In A New Trial *by C.F. Coghlan.*
26/12/1880

2
1881
HE OFFERED TO FIGHT THE WHOLE AUDIENCE

MR W. TERRISS* is now killed twice nightly at the Lyceum. His first *quietus* he receives in the character of Sinnatus at the hands of Mr Irving, as Synoris, in the Poet Laureate's new play *The Cup*. Here he represents virtue, and wins our sympathy. When next Mr Irving kills him it is in *The Corsican Brothers*. The virtue then is on the other side, and no tear of pity falls to his share.

WANTED, Engagement for a FAT GIRL. Stands a Yard high, and weighs Twenty-three Stone in weight. She is one of the heaviest girls now travelling. Her last Engagement Two Years with Mr F. Norman. Address, Mrs BLAND, Post-office, Cardiff.
8/1/1881

AN extraordinary scene was witnessed in the Leicester Theatre Royal on the 14th inst., just before the close of the performance of the Pantomime of *Cinderella*. In the second gallery, it appears, a woman had attracted some attention by her strange conduct, but nothing very remarkable happened until she was seen to throw her muff over the front of the gallery on to the floor of the Theatre. This attracted general attention, and, to the alarm of the house, the woman was seen attempting to jump clear of the gallery herself. She caught against the brass railings, and, amid the shrieks of the audience, she fell over and landed with a heavy sound on the reserved stalls in the first gallery below. It was exceedingly fortunate that she did not clear the reserved gallery, or she must have been killed on the spot, and in all probability seriously injured those on whom she must have fallen. The reserved seats on which she fell were luckily vacant. When picked up she was found to be seriously injured. It is stated that she was under the influence of drink, and was suffering from *delirium tremens*.

A SHORT time ago Dr Hyrtl, the eminent Austrian anatomist, celebrated the seventieth anniversary of his birth surrounded by some of the best-known gentlemen of the medical profession in Vienna. During the banquet given in honour of the occasion, the *savant* spoke of the experiences of his long life, and amongst other interesting anecdotes related one incident which, though it had occurred thirty years ago, had left a deep impression upon his mind.

The story is a simple but touching one. It turns upon a ballet dancer's shoe. In 1850, when Dr Hyrtl was Professor of Anatomy at the Vienna School of Medicine, he was lecturing one day on the formation of the foot, and the injury done this member by ballet dancing and pirouetting on the tips of the toes. To bring his remarks home to his hearers by practical demonstration, he exhibited a ballerina's shoe, and was expatiating on its prejudicial effects for the wearer, when a little rose-coloured billet dropped from it. The professor, surprised, picked it up and read it with deep emotion depicted on his countenance, and the shoe with its billet became a mystery much talked of in Vienna for a time, Dr Hyrtl being credited with having received a love letter from some operatic *danseuse* who had maliciously concealed it in the article in question.

The billet, however, contained no tender love message, but was traced by the hand of a dying girl named Wanda, with whom the doctor had become acquainted some months previously under painful circumstances. Wanda was one of the best pupils of the Imperial Dancing Academy, and was intended for the stage. The contortions to which she had to twist her feet brought on a malady in the right one, and inflammation supervening a consultation was held to decide whether the foot should be amputated. Dr Hyrtl took part in the consultation; his two colleagues were of opposite opinions, and he had the casting vote. Before pronouncing his verdict, he repaired to the sick girl's room to examine the diseased member once more, and the inspection satisfied him the foot must be cut off. But just as he was leaving the room his eyes met those of the patient, and the mute terror and entreaty he read in them unmanned him. He proposed that a delay of twenty-four hours should be allowed; this was conceded, but when it had expired mortification had set in, and the poor child was given over. Some days after the doctor received a small parcel. It contained the dead girl's shoe, and it was the same shoe he had used in the course of his lecture. The rose-coloured billet in it, which had escaped his notice, was written on her death bed. It expressed her gratitude to the man who had wished to spare her humiliation, and begged him to keep the little shoe in remembrance of Wanda.
15/1/1881

MR EDITOR: Sir, – In your impression of the 15th inst. you favourably mention a performance given at the People's Palace, Peckham, by Harrold, Davis, and Tiny Tim, in which you mention the last-named as being a droll, dwarf-like individual. As the credit of your criticism is due to our dwarf comedian, Little Jim, and not Tiny Tim, we shall feel obliged by your correcting the error. Yours respectfully, HARROLD, DAVIS, and LITTLE JIM.
22/1/1881

THERE is a certain class of idiots that infests stage doors to worry actresses with silly attentions. To this class must belong the individual who has been recently haunting the Crystal Palace, and who the other day left at the stage door of the Theatre the following original epistle for a certain pretty and clever actress, who is engaged in the Pantomime. Here is the precious document: –

"Norwood. – Please do not be cross at my taking the liberty of writing to you, dear Miss ------. I have been wanting to for *ever* so long, but could never make up my mind. You are so *awfully lovely*, and I have fallen in love with you. Don't laugh, please. It is quite true, and very silly of me, I know. We go to the Pantomime nearly every day, but scarcely ever look at any one but you. If you are not cross at my writing this, will you please throw *two carrots* at your mother (you know who I mean) in the scene where you find yourself at home? Do please. Ever yours, SILLY. P.S. – You have seen me before with my sister, near the stage door."
29/1/1881

LAST Saturday, before Mr Raffles, Stipendiary Magistrate, at the Liverpool City Police-court, a rough-looking young fellow named Peter Ragan was charged with assaulting Henry Rushton, an assistant at the Gaiety Temperance Theatre, Camden-street, and also with assaulting Police-constables 326, 537, and 933. It appeared that the prisoner on Friday evening, 28th ult., went into the pit of the Theatre in a hilariously drunken condition, and whilst the performance was in progress he suddenly conceived a dislike for some person who was sitting in the balcony, and tried to "get at him." Upon some of the persons near him remonstrating with him upon his disorderly conduct he offered to fight the whole audience. When Mr Rushton went to him to try and eject him he "butted" him with his head, and threw him down. He "scattered" every one around him, and varied his amusements by tearing down a partition. The whole Theatre was in an uproar, and eventually it took the three constables who were

called in, assisted by several of the audience, to secure the prisoner. He had to be carried "like a frog" between four constables; but he struggled so violently on the way that his clothes were torn into shreds. It was not until he was safely locked up in the cell that he acknowledged himself beaten. The prisoner had nothing to say, except that "he was quite sober," and that the police had attacked him and abused him shamefully. Mr Raffles committed him to gaol for three months with hard labour.
5/2/1881

HEREWITH we offer a warning to those members of the profession who take part in morning performances. A new method of obtaining goods under false pretences has sprung up; and there are just now prowling about a few dishonest rascals who evidently would feel no remorse did their nefarious practices result in leaving the most impressive of our tragedians or the most mirth-moving of our comedians without, say, a second pair of unmentionables in which to encase their legs. The plan is this: While Jones is playing at Drury-lane, or Brown at the Lyceum, or Smith at the Adelphi, one of the rascals referred to, having discovered their private addresses, waits upon Mrs Jones, or Mrs Brown, or Mrs Smith, or upon all three, and, representing himself as the worthy man's messenger, pours into the ears of the sympathising wife the story of an accident, by which the said worthy man's clothes have been torn, and which necessitates the immediate dispatch of a second suit or part of a suit. Or perhaps the story takes another form, and to the, this time, unsympathetic wife is unfolded a story of a sudden invitation to dinner or supper, where dress clothes will be absolutely necessary. Ladies are not given to suspicion in these little matters as a rule, and in more than one case recently coming under our notice their confidence has resulted in a sad diminution of a husband's wardrobe. Here, then, is the danger. The remedy we must leave to the ingenuity of those who would not willingly have their wardrobe reduced to infinitesimal proportions.

A FEW nights ago several young fellows, of highly respectable parentage, occupied a private box at the Prince of Wales's Theatre, Birmingham, and during the evening they amused themselves by a liberal distribution of bouquets to the actresses of the company. As time progressed they became more hilarious, and at length one of them took his hat – an ordinary sort of "deerstalker – and threw it on to the stage, striking the young lady who plays Boy Blue in the face. The husband of this lady, who happened to be on the stage at the time, was exceedingly wrath at the indignity to which his wife was subjected in full view of the audience. Addressing himself to the box where the young blackguard was sitting, he said the owner of the hat would have to apply for it at the stage door, a remark sufficiently significant to cause the sudden disappearance of the entire party. The husband of the lady imparted a somewhat comical aspect to the otherwise painful and discreditable occurrence by jumping on the hat in a fit of anger before the audience, the Pantaloon afterwards assisting in the demolition of the "deerstalker."
19/2/1881

A GLASGOW SHOWMAN IN TROUBLE.
AT the Eastern Police-court on Monday, before Bailie Farquhar, a man named Andrew Stewart was remanded for forty-eight hours on the charge of having obtained by false representation the sum of 2s. 6d. in pennies from thirty children. He announced an entertainment to take place on Saturday in the Public Hall, Charles-street, Bridgeton, and he distributed yellow tickets of admission, for which he charged a penny, admission without these being threepence. According to the advertisement "His Right Royal Highness Julep De Sing would appear in the gorgeous costume as worn at the Court of his Royal Father, King Amdel Rush, of the Loadstone Mountains, introducing the Celestial Palace of Magic and Fortune-telling, with Jack the Giant Killer and the Babes in the Wood." The whole was to conclude with a laughable extravanganza. The performance, however, consisted only in the disappearance of a half-penny in a handkerchief, and after keeping the audience, which was composed of children, some time he

suddenly dismissed them. The children informed the police of the occurrence, and Stewart was apprehended.
1/3/1881

TWO Young LADIES want Engagements at a Good Provincial Theatre, or on a First-class Tour. They have hitherto only played with Amateurs, but have prepared for the Professional Stage under the best masters. They can Fence, Dance, Sing, play the Piano, and act in French if required. As they chiefly desire Practice, they would undertake any kind of parts, and would begin with a small Salary. Highest references given. Address, E.C.M., Music Depot, 211, Strand, W.C.
19/3/1881

DR SPARK, the Leeds borough organist, who was announced to give an organ recital in the Victoria Hall on Tuesday afternoon and play a selection of Russian music *apropos* of the late Czar's death, received an anonymous letter warning him that, if he did, "Evil would come to him." In consequence, great precautions were taken; but the performance passed off without anything unusual occurring.
2/4/1881

AT the Small Debt Court, Glasgow, on Monday, before Sheriff Mair, William McDevitt, residing in South Wellington-street, sued John Dunlop, residing in the same street, for the sum of £3 10s., being the fees for five months' dancing instruction between October and March for the defender and two ladies, at the rate of 4s. per month for the latter, and 6s. per month for himself. The claim was repudiated entirely.

The pursuer, being first put into the witness-box, said he was not a professional teacher of dancing, but he sometimes devoted his spare time to it. The defender came to him and said that he wanted to learn some steps, as he was going to a marriage.

The Sheriff – There are often very serious steps taken in going to a marriage.

Witness – He also wished his sister and another girl to get lessons, and arrangements were come to for commencing practice in the house of the defender. At the close of five months the pursuer said he would only charge for three, and the defender told him that he had been greatly complimented for his dancing at the wedding. He was quite willing when they came to settle up to make a reduction, but they could not agree. Witness sometimes took up an assistant or two to help in carrying on the practice.

The Sheriff – Had you a violinist?

Witness – I had different instruments. I am not a good violin player. I had sometimes a concertina and sometimes an accordion, and I had another gentleman dancing while I was playing. He considered his charge a fair one.

The Sheriff – How do you charge less for girls?

Witness – Well, their feet are less seen, and they do not need so much attention as gentlemen in their steps.

In reply to the defender, the witness said he was willing to take 7s. 6d. for him, just to save trouble.

A young man who assisted at the practice said he sometimes acted as a partner, and was sometimes the musician too.

The Sheriff – But you cannot play and waltz?

Witness – Oh yes, I can. You put your arms round the lady's waist and play the accordion at her back.

The Sheriff – Well, that is an accomplishment. It will require some skill for that.

After two youths had been examined, a girl named Campbell was called for the defence, and said they got no instructions of any value from the pursuer, who insulted her about her style of dancing. She did not know what a waltz or circle dance was.

Mrs Dunlop, another of the defenders, gave some very amusing evidence, and said she believed the whole thing was got up for fun. The pursuer could not dance at all, and she denounced him, amidst considerable laughter, as an impostor.

The Sheriff – Are you a judge of dancing?

Witness – I have seen as good dancing at the end of the house when I was young. It's just a farce altogether.

The Sheriff found that the defender had not undertaken to pay for the girls, and, as to the instruction given to the defender himself, he would allow the pursuer 15s., with expenses.
9/4/1881

ON the last night of *The World* at Drury-lane, in the hotel scene, when Mr Macklin, as Martin Bashford, was seen crawling along the carpet to chloroform Mr W. Rignold (the Clement Huntingford), a man in the gallery was so excited and carried away that he shouted to the latter to "look out." The house, of course, roared, and roared again when, the handkerchief being over Mr Rignold's face, he again called out, "There, I told you so!"
30/4/1881

OF theatrical nuisances there is no end. We have denounced a great many of them – from the harpy who picks the pocket of the playgoer to the persistent chatterer, who will neither listen to the dialogue of the piece presented nor permit his neighbours to listen. At the Royalty, on Wednesday, a hitherto unexpected nuisance cropped up. Among the occupants of the pit was a rude fellow, who thought to combine business and pleasure, without regard to the comfort or convenience of others. He was armed with a number of stiff, sharp-pointed cards, bearing on one side an inscription recommending a trial of somebody's boots; and these – the cards, not the boots – he, between the acts, sent flying about the house, putting the eyes of those present in considerable peril. If this enterprising individual should turn up at any other Theatre to recommend a trial of boots, it is to be hoped the trial will be made on his own person, and that he will be unceremoniously kicked into the street.
7/5/1881

ON Monday last as Mr W.H. Patterson, the Manager of the Winona Company, upon his arrival at Preston was passing from the station to the Theatre, and leading by a chain his performing dog Wallace, they were assailed by a large dog, half bloodhound, half mastiff, which, rushing madly from side to side, his mouth covered with foam, instantly buried his fangs in the neck of Wallace, who was unable to defend himself, being muzzled*. Mr Patterson and a soldier who was passing succeeded in separating the dogs, but the hound returned again and again to the attack. Mr Patterson in attempting to shield his dog was dashed upon the pavement, the bloodhound then seizing Wallace in the centre of the street. Mr P. again rushed to save his dog, and the hound now turned upon him, and a dreadful fight ensued, Mr P. raining blows with his clenched fist upon his adversary. They were at last separated by the spectators, who drove the dog off with various missiles. Mr Patterson performed his part of Hawkeye at the Theatre in the evening, but it was evident that he was severely shaken. On Tuesday he was confined to his room, suffering from internal injuries received in the struggle. The hound had been in the hands of the police for some days, and had only escaped that morning. The owner has not yet been found.
Wallace survived his ordeal and resumed his stage career.

WANTED, Managers to Know that MR W.H. PATTERSON will be compelled to relinquish all present Engagements, owing to severe internal injuries he has sustained from the furious attack of a Bloodhound in the streets of Preston on Monday last. The "Winona" Company will be disbanded, and all Engagements be cancelled for present dates.
14/5/1881

DEATH of CHARLES COOPER, Pantomimist; also of his eldest daughter, ROSINEA, aged sixteen years, both dying within a few hours of each other of consumption; both buried in one grave last Wednesday at Tooting. Having no means to meet the expenses, I appeal to his kind friends for a little assistance,

however small, for myself and child. Address, MRS CHARLOTTE COOPER, 91, Wickham-street, Tyre-street, Lambeth-walk.
21/5/1881

THE attendants at the Theatre Royal, Birmingham, were a little surprised the other night by the visit of a singular patron. While *The Colonel* was in full swing a fat little man, smoking a short pipe, walked deliberately along the entrance hall, past the ticket gate, and was just about entering the dress circle, when an astonished attendant gently reminded him that he had forgotten the preliminary of paying for his ticket. "Oh," said he, "I wanted to see what was on first," but as the officials refused to enter into an arrangement on the pay-as-you-are-pleased system, he marched out of the Theatre with the nonchalant air with which he entered.

WANTED, by VOCE, the Marvellous and Mirth-Provoking Ventriloquist, with his Six splendid Life-sized Mechanical Figures – Mr and Mrs Chirrup, Johnny Casey, Jeremiah Winter, Little Snowball, and his dog Spot – and Engagement for Twelve Nights, June 13th, and Twelve Nights, July 11th. Address, Museum Concert Hall, Wolverhampton.
4/6/1881

TO THE EDITOR OF THE ERA.
Sir, – Will you permit me as a frequent playgoer to draw your attention to the nuisance of cab touters at the doors of the Theatres. The other night I was coming out of the Lyceum, and was almost prevented from reaching my own conveyance owing to the persistent efforts of sundry cab touters, who could not be made to understand that I neither required a hansom nor a four-wheel. There was a dilapidated four-wheel at a short distance from the Theatre doors, and it appeared to be the object of these noisy fellows to get me into that vehicle whether I liked or not. In addition to the annoyance caused by this, one is not always certain that hailing a cab is the sole business of these persons. Some of them have simply a desire to earn a trifle, no doubt; but may there not be an excuse also for the light-fingered gentry, who, making the cab business their excuse, may dispose of our watches or purses, or any other property of a portable kind. That in some cases it may be useful to have a civil, intelligent man to get a vehicle when from the midst of a crowd for a nervous visitor we grant; but when half-a-dozen at once clutch the playgoer and pull him first one way and then another it becomes a great nuisance. They are often dirty, coarse fellows, and frequently they are intoxicated. Some we know would rather give them "the price of a pint" to get rid of them; but most visitors to the Theatres would only be too glad if the police told these cab touters to "move on," for owing to their pertinacity it is by no means easy for the playgoer to do so. What makes it still more annoying is that one is frequently abused when declining to fee these persons, who really hinder rather than help the visitors in getting to their vehicles.
I am, Sir, your obedient servant, A WORRIED PLAYGOER.
18/6/1881

AN amusing incident took place during Mr Henry Irving's recitation at Sir Julius Benedict's concert on Wednesday at St James's Hall. Mr Irving was reciting a poem entitled "The Uncle," and when he came to the line "My uncle took me on his knee and said" – a stentorian voice from the court at the back of the Hall called out "Strawberries, fine strawberries." A smile was seen on every face, including that of the popular actor, who finished his recitation without further interruption.

WANTED, through unprincipled conduct, DOUBLE BASS. Must be thorough Musician. Long Engagement. Join at once. Lowest terms. J. GATHERCOLE, Temperance Hall, Fochabers.
2/7/1881

DISGRACEFUL ATTACK ON AN AERONAUT.
ON Saturday July 2nd, a fete was held on the Manchester Racecourse Grounds, in aid of the funds of the Railway Servants' Orphanage. Mr Adams, giving his services free, made an ascent in his balloon "Jupiter." After sailing through cloud-land for twenty-five minutes, he descended safely at Bradford. In less than two minutes he was assailed by several hundred roughs, who cut and hacked his balloon fearfully. Some few friends helped him to pack the balloon and to get on to a cart; but the roughs again pulled him off and cut his head, and he was obliged to have a doctor to dress his wound before he could proceed home.

THE Oxford Agamemnon Company*, who, having fondly imagined that all London was eager to see them play *Romeo and Juliet*, took the Imperial Theatre for four nights during the past week, must have been undeceived on the first evening when they found only their friends in the stalls and the Great British Public represented by a soldier and his sweetheart in the gallery. It is only fair to the soldier to say that he seemed more appreciative of the charms of his adored one than of the merits of the actors.
The amateur company was led by F.R. Benson, whose first performance as Romeo at the Imperial received derisory reviews. He later became a leading Shakespearean actor and was knighted in 1912.

SOME consternation was caused in Briggate, Leeds, on the 29th ult., by the appearance, within a well-appointed trap, of two well-dressed bears – one as black as midnight, the other white as snow – one handling the ribbons in a very capable manner, and the other deporting himself with the seemly dignity which all well-behaved bears assume in public. The fun was caused by a practical joke played by Mr H. Burton, who is fulfilling an engagement at the Leeds Theatre Royal, and Mr Scouler, the Acting-Manager. The gentlemanly bears were soon surrounded by an amused crowd, and were obliged to take refuge in a neighbouring hostelry, where refreshments were served to Messieurs Bruin amidst general astonishment, and to the particular dismay of one individual who expressed violent surprise at the visit of the animals. Afterwards the bears drove through the town to the Flower Show, and were everywhere received with the consideration and and kindly welcome which such well-conducted animals are entitled to.
9/7/1881

FOR SALE, Life-size WAX HEADS, Correct Likenesses Warranted, of LEFROY*; also Mr GOLD, the latter, modelled from the dead as found after the murder, with the wounds on the head. Address, the Works, Victoria Lodge, Brookfield-road, Victoria-park, London.
Percy Lefroy Mapleton murdered Isaac Frederick Gold in a railway carriage on 27th June, 1881. He was executed on 29th November.
23/7/1881

MR FREDERICK NEEBE, of the Theatres Royal, Bath, Exeter, and Weymouth, has received the following characteristic letter: –

"Mr Neebe, Manager of the Theather, Exseter, Devon. – sir, – could you ingage me to learn the Acking on The Stage. I have not the Slites Ida a Bout it, But I am very quick to learn and very willing Trusting you will Ingage Me as Forseen commpinnichins has Induce Me to get My on leaving Their for Place Rite by the Return of Stating Fwll Petuclars and wether every thing Found and so Much a Week or what as I do Not Know anything about it and I should Interly to Depand on get ing My Leaving Please dont Fail to Rite to ISABELLA PYM, care of The Revent P-----d Y-----c, Vicarage, near Chard, Somerset."
30/7/1881

WANTED, for the established Cheltenham Town and Promenade Band, EUPHONIUM, Piccolo, and Second Cornet. Good salary. No unprincipled old soldiers and incompetent men need waste paper. A

legitimate Harpist may apply; no self-taught fireworks. Address, J.H. THOMAS, R.A.M., Richmond Villa, St. Luke's, Cheltenham.
13/8/1881

OUR Birmingham correspondent says: "The unique spectacle was witnessed last night of the occupants of the pit of the Theatre Royal here turning round *en masse* to and hissing the occupants of the gallery. The rebuke was richly deserved, for a grosser display of rowdy behaviour has rarely taken place in a Birmingham place of amusement. Owing, we suppose, to the melodramatic attractions of *The Black Flag*, the gallery was densely crowded, but from the first there appeared to be a settled determination among a certain section to interrupt the performance. The place was a perfect Babel of cat calls, yells, and shouts of "Hor-der" from those who were themselves the liveliest cause of disorder. […]

When the curtain rose there was not a chance of a word spoken by the actors being heard. The first two acts of the play were conducted in dumb show. Whole scenes were gone through without a syllable even of Mr Gould's powerful voice rising superior to the discordant din of the "gods." Hats were thrown into the pit, women screamed and fainted, many of the occupants of the front row amused themselves by spitting down into the projecting part of the dress circle. Some ladies sitting below them were obliged to retreat to a seat further back in order to escape this persistent and disgusting baptism. In the third act the monotony of the disorder was varied by an exciting free fight in the gallery, and then a policeman became visible in the upper regions, and, after he had been pushed over the seats once or twice, the greater symptoms of excitement were allayed. It was not, however, until the fourth and last act of the play was reached that any of the dialogue could be heard, and then it was impossible for anyone who did not know what the play was about to understand the drift of that which he did hear." The Management here is, as a rule, most exemplary; but in this instance rowdyism appears to have been too much for it.

AT midday on Tuesday, just after the performance on the great organ in connection with the Foresters' Fete at the Crystal Palace, a gentleman named George Ogborn, of Joy Cottage, Bramley, near Guildford, who had been sitting in the orchestra, was making his way down to the central transept, along the side of the gallery, when in some way he mistook the canvas over a large refreshment stall for flooring, and leaped over the railings to get upon it. The canvas at once gave way, and he fell through upon one of the large coffee urns with such force as to break his back. He was at once removed to Guy's Hospital, where he died on Wednesday morning.
27/8/1881

TELEPHONIC OPERA.
A visitor to the Paris Electrical Exhibition describes an early attempt at live broadcasting from the Paris Opéra and Theatre Francaise:
ROOMS have been fitted up in the galleries, each with a number of pairs of telephones. Two rooms are devoted to the Opéra and two to the Theatre. The former is the more interesting, for there the actions and features of the performers are of less importance. You enter the room in groups of, perhaps, ten at a time. Each one advances to a wall and seizes a pair of telephones, which he places to his two ears. Each of these is connected with a microphone on the stage of the Opéra, one to the right, the other to the left of the prompter and inclined towards the singers. The microphone to the right of the prompter is connected with the telephone at our right ear, the one to his left is connected with that at our left ear. Thus, while the singer moves to right or left, the sounds increase or diminish in the right or left ear; when they advance or recede the sounds increase or diminish in both, and thus we are able to appreciate their movements and it becomes difficult to believe that the performers on the stage are not directly behind the wall which we are facing. So soon as the telephones are applied to the ears the glorious voices of the finest singers in France are heard by us undiminished in purity, beauty or force by the strange means which have carried them to us over the distance of a mile. […]

There are a few defects, but these are of minor importance. The orchestra is a little too much subdued; a crackling noise is sometimes heard (but very rarely), which comes from the microphone; and there are special notes which seem to be reinforced by the instruments and to be heard with undue loudness. These defects are, however, hardly noticeable, and as a rule, the deepest bass and the highest soprano can be listened to and heard through all their most delicate changes as accurately and almost with as great pleasure as at the Opéra itself.

ONE evening last week, during the performance of *Oliver Twist* at the Prince of Wales's Theatre, Chester, shortly after the Dodger (Mr Sheridan) had grandiloquently installed Oliver (Miss Bessie Thompson) as a pupil of old Fagin's, he introduced the well-known comic song "He's a pal o'mine." Just at that moment a black cat, which haunts the house, and is a hanger-on of the drama, made an unexpected appearance, and sauntered leisurely across the stage into the orchestra. Oliver seemed somewhat taken aback at the sight of this feline intruder, but the Artful Dodger coolly observed, "It's all right, he's a pal o'mine," a clever little bit of "gag" which saved the scene. It was received with much laughter and applause. We believe this is the identical cat which, some time ago, completely spoiled the celebrated combat scene in *Macbeth*, by inopportunely appearing between the combatants, the exhausted Thane of Cawdor receiving his death blow amidst roars of laughter.

A NEW method of illuminating the tanks at the Royal Aquarium, Westminster, was shown on Thursday evening by means of the "Faure" electric battery, and which, so far as it went, was of a successful character. The lights shown were, to the number of six, submerged in the tank at the foot of the west staircase with excellent effect, showing up each fish and plant with great distinctness, a result impossible to obtain under the old system of gas illumination. One of the great advantages of the electric over the gas lighting system is that the fish do not seem to mind in the least the close proximity of the incandescent lamps, while at the same time they do not suffer from the noxious emanations evolved during the combustion of gas. Under Mr Faure's system a steady light of almost any intensity can be obtained, while the engines, which can be run without cessation during the whole of the twenty-four hours of the day, effect a great saving by their power of storing the electric energy, while at the same time they obviate the danger of a sudden accidental extinction of the other light employed. The electricity used on Thursday was generated in Woolwich and carted down to the Aquarium, where it arrived but a short time before it was used.

Defective articulation. WANTED, the Address of a Gentleman thoroughly competent to detect the cause of the above, and, if necessary, to perform an operation. Kindly address, "SPEECH," 41, Gillespie-road, Highbury, N.
3/9/1881

TO THE EDITOR OF THE ERA.
Sir, – Babies are nice little things; "precious pets;" "sweet tiddy-ickle sings," their mammas call them, and I don't object. I'm a crusty old fogey; still I own that at times I have said "ketchy-ketchy", "upsadaisy," and other such nonsense to the little people, and I must confess I often pity them when I reflect upon the possible sorrows, disappointments, and troubles they may have to endure. Still there are times when the charm of babyhood fails to move me, and when the harsh cry of the gallery to "throw it over" appears almost justified. Fancy a little mite, having just found its tongue, calling out when the Ghost in *Hamlet* revisits the glimpses of the moon, "Dadda! Dadda!" Isn't it enough to make the actor "give up the ghost" altogether? I shall be called hard and unfeeling, I suppose, if I say that I would "put my foot down," as Lincoln used to say, and refuse babies admission.

I know that there are "good" babies. Ask their mothers if ever there was a bad baby? There are some who really conduct themselves admirably at the Theatre – who coo at the chandelier, open their round

eyes at the triumph of the scene-painter, and even make an occasional gurgle when the principal performers have done something out of the common way which might almost be taken for applause. Still there are babies of another sort – babies that are fractious, babies in their first dissatisfaction of getting their teeth, who, doubtless, find that crying is some sort of relief. There are babies who sleep all the day and are "eager for the fray" whenever there is anything going forward. There are babies who won't sit still for two seconds in any position their mammas may place them; and there are babies also who will insist on clutching everything that comes near them. It may be the feather on a lady's hat, or a walking-stick, or a watch chain, or a shirt-pin, or even the "Piccadilly weepers" of a youthful swell, who dares not complain lest the mamma, in an undertone, calls him a brute and hopes "*he* will never be a father*.*" These are some of the little inconveniences one suffers from babies; but all their playful little eccentricities are nothing compared with the horror of a thorough good squall in the midst of a pathetic scene in a good play. And this is the reason, Mr Editor, why I write these few lines to *The Era* on the subject of babies, in the hope that Managers will take the subject into serious consideration. There must be babies, of course, and delightful little creatures they are, no doubt; but, with all my admiration for them, I think I could get on better without them when I go to the play. I am, Sir, your obedient servant, AN OLD BACHELOR.
24/9/1881

A VERY handsome donkey played an important part on the first night of *The Foundlings* at Sadler's Wells. He was introduced in the third act, and was so tickled by the novelty of the situation that he laid down, stared at the audience, and then, turning on his back, kicked up his heels with evident delight, the voices of the actors being drowned in the uproarious laughter of the spectators, which continued until the animal was put on his legs again and led from the scene.
15/10/1881

ON Saturday evening a case of sudden death occurred in the Bath Theatre. Miss Linda Dietz's company was representing *The Ticket-of-Leave Man*, and just at the close of the first act one of the supernumeries, named Frederick Evans, while assisting in the arrest of Bob Brierly, fell dead.
22/10/1881

TO THE EDITOR OF THE ERA.
Sir, – Will you kindly allow me to make an appeal on behalf of the family of an old actor, Mr George Howard, which has been sorely tried of late? As your representative at Warrington, I have known the family for several years. The following are the particulars of their latest misfortune. On Monday last a serious accident happened to Alfred Howard, aged sixteen. The lad was about to descend from the work-room, in which he was employed, when his foot became entangled in a piece of wire, and he was precipitated down the whole flight, breaking his right arm and severely bruising himself. This is the third accident the poor lad has met with during the last two years, each time breaking his arm – twice the left arm, and now the right. The consequences of this accident are very serious to his family, as his earnings, of which he is now deprived, were almost the sole support of three younger brothers, a sister, and his father (George Howard), who is an invalid, and for many months past has been unable to follow his Profession, or earn anything towards the support of his family.

Those charitably disposed may send the smallest donations to me, and I will undertake to see them properly distributed.
Yours truly, JOS. POTTER, Guardian office, Warrington.

LUNATICS AT LADBROKE HALL.
Mrs Darby – a lady who, we understand, professes to instruct pupils for the Stage – added something to her income on Monday evening last by giving what the bills called a dramatic performance at the Hall which, by a misuse of terms, is styled a Theatre, and which is situate almost directly opposite the

railway station at Notting-hill. We were invited to be present, and sorry indeed we were that we accepted the invitation. The Hall was tolerably well-filled; and, as nothing less than a shilling was charged for admission, a pretty good sum must have been netted for an entertainment which, judging by the first half of it that we had the patience to sit through, would have been enormously dear at sixpence – we mean sixpence among the whole of the audience – for the privilege of being present.

The business began with the farce entitled *The Turned Head*, and we may say at once that, with all our experience of amateurs, we have never yet seen anything more contemptible than the exhibition presented by the young, ambitious, and incompetent people who appeared in this. There had, we are inclined to believe, been no effort upon anybody's part to master the words of the farce, which, adequately rendered, has so often proved amusing; the prompter was busy from beginning to end, and not only repeated the lines, but called out the names of the characters who had to speak them; every minute or two there was an awkward pause, and the performers stood there and grinned at each other like so many idiots; there was plenty of stamping, pushing, and rough horse play, but in vain did we look for the slightest evidence of ability and the faintest notion of fun. Oh, yes, there was Mr Alfred Ellis. He evidently *is* a humorist – in his own estimation, and doubtless thought he was doing something remarkably clever when, in the character of the man-servant Dick, he with his fingers essayed to wipe the nose of the lunatic who imagined himself to be a pump. His fun by most decent-minded people would doubtless be voted nastiness. […]

It will hardly be credited, by those who do not know as much of amateur impudence as ourselves, that the young men who had showed such astounding incapacity actually at the end of the farce made their appearance before the curtain. We noticed at the back of the Hall there was stationed a policeman. Had there been in existence a law against people making fools of themselves the representatives of the male characters in *The Turned Head* would most certainly have been "run in."

Our card of admission had promised us a concert; we found it supplied in the singing by Miss Jennie Halwell of the popular old Irish ballad of "Thady O'Flynn." Miss Halwell seemed to regard this as something sacred, and so dragged it along with terrible solemnity. Some slight applause which followed she regarded as the expression of a desire to hear more of it, and we had to submit. […]

And now we prepared ourselves for some genuine fun, for the programme announced a "Comic Lecture on the History of the World," by Professor Moonstone. The lecture, like the lecturer, proved to be an imposture. There was nothing comic in either. Our only regret in connection with this matter is that we are not in possession of the real name of the offender, who, if the fathers, husbands, and brothers present had done their duty, would have been hooted from the stage before he had occupied it ten minutes. This Professor Moonstone had a few pictures in front of him affording opportunity for fun of a harmless character to anybody possessed of brains. Professor Moonstone proceeded to atone for a plentiful lack of wit by a supply of indecent suggestions, using Holy Writ for his ribaldry in one instance, by associating the dove of the deluge with the "soiled doves" of St John's-wood, and in another trying to raise a laugh by a reference to the "little dears" who are to be seen outside "The Criterion," and who are too "dear" for him. Let it be remembered that these allusions were made in presence of a mixed assemblage, consisting to a large extent of young respectable girls, and we shall be pardoned for saying that our blood boiled with indignation, and that, following the example of several ladies and gentlemen in our immediate neighbourhood, we left the Hall in disgust, fearing lest we should be tempted to commit a breach of the peace by publicly denouncing the fellow who, while pretending the comical, had furnished little but the coarse.

Mrs Darby we presume it was who was busy at the entrance looking after the tickets and the money. Consequently she could have known nothing of the unpardonable utterances of this Professor Moonstone, and must not be held responsible. *The Miser of Oakwood* was announced to complete the bill.

5/11/1881

JOSE AUSTIN, a Mexican member of Messrs. Tayleure's Circus, was killed in the Forest of Dean a day or so ago. The Circus, after performing at Cinderford on Saturday night, was proceeding to Coleford, and Jose assisted, when ascending a steep hill, by blocking the hind wheel with a large stone. The latter was crushed, and the wheel ran back, crushing also the life out of the man. Among the *troupe* much sorrow is felt, as Jose was much beloved by his comrades. He was reputed one of the most skilful performers of the *troupe*, of which he had been a member since boyhood.
12/11/1881

TO THE EDITOR OF THE ERA.
Sir, – At the St James's Theatre, even at the pit entrance, one would imagine that the male portion of the crowd would show a little consideration in endeavouring to shield the ladies from being crushed during the struggle for admission.

Not so, however, was the case on Saturday night. Ladies who had waited patiently for their turn were suddenly displaced from their vantage ground by a vigorous rush made by gentlemen with black coats and tall hats, who, thinking only of themselves, hustled, struggled, and pushed with the rude roughness of navvies.

One of the ladies, thus suffering, was, I think, quite justified in her muttered protest of "The brutes! What would they do in a shipwreck?" I am, yours obediently, A SPECTATOR.
26/11/1881

THE WRECK OF THE CLAN MACDUFF.
MR LEWIS J. WARD, the actor, a member of the ill-fated dramatic company who were journeying to Bombay on board the Clan Macduff, arrived at his home in Birmingham on Thursday, and gave a number of interesting details concerning the painful wreck by which the members of the company were drowned. A peculiarly distressing phase of the disaster is that the actress, Miss Ada Lester, the daughter of a London wine merchant, was seen sitting up in the small boat in which she left the vessel, having been battling with the heavy seas nearly two days. In this perilous position she had drifted to within a couple of miles of shore, but the sea was running so high that it was impossible to render her any assistance from land. The statement is incorrect that Miss Lester was lashed to the boat. When found upon the rocks her body was still warm, and she held in her death-grasp a large fragment of the broken boat. The lady's sister, who also lost her life in this dreadful shipwreck, was not a professional actress, but being in delicate health was recommended a sea voyage by her physician, and her father accompanied her. All three were drowned. Mr Ward mentions as a curious coincidence that the last piece the company appeared in before embarking for Bombay was *The Tempest*.

Mr Ward also has with him a photograph of the mutilated remains of the stage-manager of the company, Mr J. Turner, washed ashore at Bandon, the day after the shipwreck. The photo was taken for the purpose of identification, and it is a noteworthy fact that the finger on which there was a valuable ring is missing. Both Mr Turner and his wife were drowned, and it seems that before the storm had lashed itself into its greatest fury Mrs Turner had a presentiment that neither she nor her husband would escape. On entering the cabin some time before the order was given to launch the boat, Mr Ward found Mrs Turner on her knees, imploring one of the women to see if anything could be done for her children. It is satisfactory that already a very handsome subscription has been raised to provide for the unfortunate orphans. [...]

Mr Ward does not think the captain was precipitate in the orders he gave for the lowering of the boats, as there were indications that the ship was going down every minute. To add to the dangers and discomfort to which the survivors were subjected, they were forced in their confusion to leave the vessel without any provisions during the twenty hours they were tossed about in their tiny craft. All they had to sustain their strength was a small bottle of brandy, which Mr Ward threw down as he leaped from the vessel. This gentleman gives a very graphic description of their long suspense and imminent peril. After leaving the ill-fated steamer, during the dreary vigils of the night, when every eye was on the look-out for a passing ship, there was seen at frequent intervals a glimmering light, which they too hopefully proclaimed to be signals from their approaching rescuers, but gradually it would die out again until it was too apparent that what had attracted their notice was only a phosphorescent gleam of the storm-tossed sea. The few survivors have all suffered more or less from the shock to their nervous system.

TO THE EDITOR OF THE ERA.

Sir, – Will you kindly grant me space to call attention to a very impudent attempt at blackmail practised upon myself last week. I am playing Henry Huntingford, in *The World*, and part of my business consists in falling down a trap, nightly, on to a bed, which, in this instance, was surrounded by four men, appointed to see that I did not miss the bed and fall into the cellar. On Thursday night as I fell, one of these men hinted to me – in a tone half bullying, half cajoling – that he should expect something for himself, adding, with a touch of grim humour, that the cellar was thirty feet deep. On Saturday night, as I fell, the same man saluted me with the demand, "Now, then, where's that half dollar you are going to give us?" – thus kindly fixing the amount of the bribe for me. I stepped out of the trap and said, "I've got a shilling for you, lads, who shall I give it to?" when the aforesaid ruffian brought matters to a climax by saying, "If you don't give it to me I'll drop you into the cellar next week." I at once returned the coin to my pocket, expressed my opinion of the man and his abominable threat in the most forcible terms at my command, and laid a formal complaint before the management. I am bound to add that I received every courtesy from Mr Anderson (manager) and Mr Hastings (stage-manager). The man was relieved from his duties in connection with me, and has, no doubt, since regretted giving utterance to what, in his defence to the management, he said was spoken "in chaff," but which sounded remarkably like an attempt to extort money by threats.

I should not have troubled you with this incident but that it seems to me to open up the whole question of blackmail, and no time could be more appropriate to ventilate it than the present. The pantomime season is close upon us, when nine-tenths of the theatres will be under the sway of the Lord of Misrule; when star-traps, vampires, and harlequin leaps will will be in the ascendant, and when the lives and limbs of many of my brother and sister artists will be at the mercy of more or less conscientious stage men. It is a well-known fact that many pantomimists have to purchase safety by weekly instalments of "beer money," *alias* blackmail. The remedy is simple. It only needs a little co-operation between manager and artists to put an end to this system of blackmail at once and for ever. In the first place, I would ask every manager to post a printed notice behind the scenes to the effect that any workman demanding money from artists engaged would thereby subject himself to instant dismissal. This plan has, I am told, been already adopted with good effect by Messrs Conquest and Merritt at the Surrey Theatre. Secondly, I would ask every actor to pledge himself to meet any demand for blackmail with a direct refusal and at once to point out the man who made it to the management. Were these two rules strictly acted upon we should soon hear the last of such cases. The British workman is, in the main, a shrewd, sensible fellow, and when he finds that "beer money" is an equivalent for loss of employment he will carefully eschew it, and rest content with his legitimate wage.

I am, Sir, yours faithfully, FREDERIC DOBELL, Grand Theatre, Leeds, November 29th, 1881.
3/12/1881

THE theatrical sensation of the week has been the appearance of the "professional beauty" Mrs Langtry*, at the Haymarket. We were unable to discover any of that histrionic ability that fashionable friends and fashionable toadies have given her credit for, and if it be true that the lady proposes to adopt the stage as a profession "society" and the curious will, perhaps, for a time flock to see her; but it seems to us doubtful whether intelligent and impartial playgoers will be ready to endorse the approving verdict that was born of flattery on Thursday afternoon.
Despite her limited ability Mrs Langtry had a lengthy career as an actress and theatrical manager.

ANOTHER of those painful events, which demonstrate the uncertainty of human existence in such a striking manner, occurred at York on Monday last. We refer to the awfully sudden death of Mr Charles King, acting-manager for Messrs. Holt and Wilmot in connection with their *New Babylon* company, which commenced an engagement at the Theatre Royal, in that city, on the same day. From what we can learn, Mr King was in his usual health on the arrival of the company in York, and, during the afternoon, determined to have a warm bath, for which purpose he proceeded to the public baths in St George's-fields. On leaving the baths he complained of a chilly feeling, and thought it advisable to return to his apartments at the Castle Inn, Castlegate, where his appearance was noted by the landlady, who, feeling alarmed, went to his room shortly afterwards, and perceived that he was sitting in a chair, speechless. A surgeon was at once sent for, and on his arrival every effort was made to restore consciousness, but, as it proved, without avail, the doctor pronouncing life to be extinct. When the members of the company – most of whom were entirely ignorant of the sad event – arrived at the theatre, the news of Mr King's death caused the utmost consternation; indeed, at first the truth could hardly be realised; but when a full consciousness of the awful occurrence dawned upon them, expressions of regret at their loss, and sympathy with the deceased gentleman's relatives in their bereavement, were heard on every side. An inquest* was held on Wednesday afternoon, when the jury found that death was caused by exhaustion, produced by too long an immersion in water. The funeral was fixed for Thursday afternoon at the York cemetery.

At the inquest it was revealed that Mr King had spent two hours in a very hot bath, eventually losing consciousness.

EDWIN BOOTH'S COMPANY IN A FIX

A member of the company describes what happened at a theatre in Waterbury, Connecticut, when their props and costumes failed to arrive in time for the performance:

"Horatio appeared in the first scene in a monkey jacket and round felt hat, while Hamlet, in a cutaway coat, apostrophising his father's ghost, who was clad in light tweed trousers and stand-up collar with a bold face, was something to remember. Miss Bella Pateman, as Ophelia, appeared in a dark brown travelling dress, embellished at the last moment with a cloud of white lace purchased at a neighbouring store. Laertes wore a blue pilot suit, and looked like the captain of a river steamer, while Polonius looked eminently clerical in a black frock coat, and, for lack of the necessary requisites, appeared without his traditional beard. There was no possibility of "making up" for the parts, and the King of Denmark, with a dark moustache and clad in a forty dollar sporting suit, looked like Bob Jackett, more on the spree than ever. The evening's entertainment concluded with *The Quiet Family*, in which the Royal Court of Denmark appeared under other names, but in the same costumes. From the applause with which the entertainment was received, it was evident that the audience did not share the distress of the actors placed so unexpectedly in a position both embarrassing and novel. Very few comparatively asked for the return of their money, and we leave the town richer by a thousand dollars, netted by a performance which, for originality, has perhaps not been equalled in this generation."
17/12/1881

FATAL ACCIDENT IN A MUSIC HALL.

ON Tuesday last a sad accident befell a lad in the Oxford Music Hall, Brighton. The concluding feat of Ling Look, a conjurer engaged, was, after swallowing a sword, to fire a cannon poised on the hilt. On the eventful evening, through misdirection of the piece, or from some foreign substance being in the weapon, a lad of some fifteen years, named Smythe, who was sitting in the front row of the gallery, had the top of his head blown completely away. The scene was most distressing, his blood and brains bespattering not only the audience, but the band below. Ling Look was immediately arrested, and the hall closed.

On the accused being brought before the magistrate, on Wednesday, the town clerk undertook the prosecution, and explained that the performance which brought about the melancholy event consisted in prisoner balancing a cannon on a dagger which he put down his throat, with the end only projecting from his mouth. Whilst balancing on this projecting point, the cannon, which was loaded with powder, was fired by prisoner's wife. Some attempt was made to clear the way in front of the cannon, but when it was fired the charge took effect on deceased, who was sitting in the gallery, 22ft. off, just in the line of fire, and the result was that the top of his head was completely blown off. The magistrates asked whether this was the first performance, but it appeared that a similar trick was performed on the previous night, whilst a solicitor who appeared on the prisoner's behalf stated that it had been performed in various towns, at different music halls, in England and abroad, without accident, and no one more deeply deplored the melancholy event than did the prisoner.

The cannon was produced in court. It was made of hard wood, cased in tin or zinc, covered with a black composition, and fastened together with nails. Its length was between 3ft. and 4ft., with a bore of about 3in. in diameter. The dagger which prisoner partially swallowed before balancing the cannon upon it was about 2ft. in length, and the hilt fitted a hole in the under part of the cannon. Evidence was given that deceased was sitting in the front row of the gallery, and that before the cannon was fired prisoner waved his arms as if to motion people away from the line of fire. When the light was applied to the cannon deceased fell back and rolled on his side. The top of his head was completely smashed, and the brains were scattered over the audience. A medical man who was called in found in the gallery a pellet, about the size of a hen's egg, made of paper, but compressed so tightly as to be as hard as wood, and this, from its appearance, had evidently been fired from the cannon and had pierced deceased's brain, as it was blackened by gunpowder smoke and covered with blood. Prisoner was ultimately remanded till Monday, the magistrate refusing to accept bail. His solicitor observed that he should venture to suggest that the occurrence was a pure accident.

31/12/1881

3
1882
"YOUR HERD OF ELEPHANTS CALLD AT MY SHOP"

THE PANIC IN A LEEDS THEATRE.
ON Monday, at the Quarter Sessions, Leeds, the Recorder passed sentence on Edward Martin, who at the last sessions had been convicted of maliciously injuring George Rylas and Margaret Davey, at the Theatre Royal, in the summer of that year. The Recorder said the facts would be in the recollection of everybody. As the prisoner was leaving the theatre he put out the gas on the gallery stairs and placed an iron bar across a doorway so as the obstruct the egress of the crowd at the close of the performance. The offence was a serious one, and the jury had found that the prisoner had an unlawful and malicious intention; but the recorder was willing to give the prisoner credit for not having anticipated the very serious results which happened. As he had been unable to find bail, the prisoner had been in prison three months, and therefore the sentence would be nine months, with hard labour.
14/1/1882

THE POLICE AND THE PANTOMIME.
ON Monday, January 23rd, proceedings against Mr Charles Hemingway, described as of Dawes-street, were reopened in the Borough Court, Town Hall, Bolton. The charge against defendant was that he did permit to be used words and expressions offensive to public decency...[...] On the 14th inst. the police visited the Temple Opera House, not quite on their own motion, but a complaint had been lodged as to what was said, and they went for the purpose of taking notes. [...]

Detective-inspector Ormrod was the first witness called. He said – On Saturday night, the 14th of this month, I went into Majilton's Opera House. A pantomime* was going on.

Mr Hall (prosecuting) – Did you hear any of the performers say anything?

Witness – I heard Princess Prettypet (Miss Louisa Crecy). Mrs Majilton here came forward, and was identified as "Miss Crecy." Princess Prettypet said:

There is a young gent
Sits down there,
It is a perfect riddle;
He has been to see us every night,
And he fancies her in the middle.

Mr Hall: – People should understand that this is not a day performance of the pantomime.
Witness – She also said:

If I tickle you and you tickle me,
And we both tickle one another:

But if I tickle you and you don't tickle me,
I'll go home and tell my mother.

One of the men, Baron Boosey (Mr A. Rivers), sang a song and whistled at the end of the verse. At the end of the verse he mentioned something about the old crinolines, and he added "You could almost see the darlings' ------," and then he whistled. […]

Mr Wharton (defending) – Will you swear that the words were not "He parts his hair in the middle?"

The witness did not seem willing to answer the question with a direct negative or affirmative, and it was only after some fencing between him and the barrister that he said he could not swear those words were not the words used. [...]

Mr Wharton – Now, in this whistling song of Baron Boosey's there is whistling in every verse? – Yes.

How many verses did he sing? – He has only sung two since. That about the "darlings' ------ has been omitted, and the tickling has not been mentioned since.

Well, I'll read it to you:

With the skin-tight fitting dresses,
Girls had better draw the line,
For they show us quite too much
Of the human form divine.
But their dear old crinolines
Were quite as bad as these;
For when they used to wear them
In a strong and roguish breeze,
They were blown about until
You almost saw the darlings' ------

...and then, you know, he whistled. The word ending the line before was "breeze," so instead of using a word which rhymed he whistled. Didn't he? – He did.

Well, can you tell me a single word that would rhyme with "breeze" that would be in any way indecent, except "knees?" – I cannot say that I can.

Detective Howcroft, the next witness called, corroborated Ormrod's statements.

At the conclusion of Detective Howcroft's evidence, the magistrates retired, and, after an absence of about a quarter of an hour's duration, they returned into court.

The Mayor then said – I may say, gentlemen, that the magistrates have been out to consider the case; and we have come to the unanimous conclusion that that the prosecution has failed in establishing the case, and we dismiss it.

Mr Wharton – Of course it is not necessary at all to say a single word about the case. I can only say I was instructed to go into the whole thing upon its merits, and we have ample evidence to show that there is not the slightest thing to offend anyone.

The court was then cleared.

*Cinderella.
28/1/1882

TO THE EDITOR OF THE ERA.

Sir, – In the interests of the dramatic profession, let me earnestly implore its members in the provinces to avoid Trowbridge. There has not been one single company, of the many that have acted there, that have covered their out-of-pocket expenses, and, as to any salaries, they are out of the question. Two companies, whose names I won't mention, within the last year came to Trowbridge; one consisted of nine members. Their expenses for rent of room, gas, and band were £1 16s. a night. They played five nights and took £8 1s. 8d. One evening they closed the doors, there being but 3s. 6d. in the house! The other company did equally badly. Let me tell all those who think to come here with a dramatic company that the result will be a certain loss. Yours obediently, A.F., 8th February 1882.

WANTED, by the CORNISH DWARF, Man with Four Feet and only Thirty-six Inches High, a Situation in Public House Bars or any other Entertainment. For terms and particulars, apply S. HILL, care of Mr Smith, 101, Byrom-street, Liverpool.
11/2/1882

VISITING the Alhambra during the past week to glance once more at the many attractions of *The Black Crook*, we discovered that one of those wonderful Indians introduced was suffering from a cold in the head. This, of course, was commonplace enough, but we were amused to find that Indian, like Mr Gladstone, fully prepared with "all the resources of civilization," for slyly from beneath his feathers he drew what no Indian wild could be expected to possess – a white pocket handkerchief. An Indian who is compelled to indulge in luxuries ought to have his salary raised forthwith, and we commend the noble savage with a cold in his head to the attention of the Board of Directors.
4/3/1882

IN the City of London Court on Tuesday, before Mr Commissioner Kerr, an action was brought by Mr Hayes, publisher, Royal Exchange-buildings, against Mr T. Cullen, accountant, Vigo-street, Regent-street, to recover two guineas for two theatre tickets supplied under novel circumstances. Mr Tirrell, barrister, appeared for the defendant.

It appeared from the evidence of the plaintiff that on the 31st of December last he received by telephone an order for two theatre tickets to be forwarded to the defendant at the above address, but when the account was sent in he refused to pay on the grounds that he accepted the tickets as complimentary ones.

His Honour – Who gave the order? – Plaintiff – Of course we do not see the people who speak to use through the telephone. We merely get name and number, and what is required.

Mr Tirrell – An important and material question to the public is involved in this case, because there is a strong suspicion that the use of the telephone is abused by designing and fraudulent people very frequently. The defendant received by post the tickets in question for a morning performance; and as he acts as accountant for several metropolitan theatres he naturally thought that they were sent to him as a present, and he accordingly handed them to one of his clerks. He never ordered them.

Plaintiff – Orders come to us in the same way many times a day.

His Honour – If you choose to give tickets away every day that is your business. You must try and find out who it is that defrauds you.

Plaintiff – It is absurd for any one to suppose that two tickets of a guinea each would be sent free from the box office of a theatre.

His Honour – Why not go to the telephone office and inquire whether any one had been playing a trick upon you?

Plaintiff – I am afraid it would not be of any use.

Mr Tirrell – Oh, yes, it would. If you go to the Telephone Exchange you will discover who gave orders for the tickets. I have done it myself.

His Honour – There are people in the world who are always ready to take advantage of any new invention for wrong purposes, and it may be so in regard to the telephone, so it is well that the public should be on their guard. I must find for the defendant, with costs.
11/3/1882

TO THE EDITOR OF THE ERA.

Sir, – The following incident will serve to show how deeply many members of the "Salvation Army" are imbued with the spirit of the master they profess to serve. At St James's Hall, Plymouth, the other night, during a performance in connection with Hamilton's well-known pictorial entertainment, a part of the gallery-front gave way and fell into the stalls and two-shilling seats, injuring several persons – one

gentleman seriously. The next day, Sunday, the people in connection with the Salvation Army, preceded by their leaders, were marching out, as usual, to the accompaniment of tambourines, concertinas, brass instruments and drums, making Sunday hideous with their awful noises. When they reached the front entrance to St James's Hall, the Captain called a halt, and the Christians – save the mark! – gave "three cheers for the accident!" which at that time was generally reported to be much more serious than it really was. Comment is needless. Yours truly, LINDON TRAVERS, St James's Hall, Plymouth.
8/4/1882

DAMAGING GUYS AT ALEXANDRA PALACE.
AT the Tottenham Police-court on Wednesday, before Messrs Nash and Howard, Henry Turner, of 25, Caledonian-street, King's-cross, was charged with wilfully damaging a guy, the property of Messrs Jones and Barber, lessees of the Alexandra Palace, to the extent of £1.

It appeared that an exhibition of guys took place at the Palace on the 5th of last November, and that the figures have since remained in the bazaar as an attraction, several additions – Jumbo, for instance – having been made to the original collection. About half-past seven on the evening of Easter Monday a large crowd was in the bazaar, and made an attack upon the whole of the guys. First that representing Mr Bradlaugh was thrown over, then Jumbo was pulled down, followed by Mr Gladstone, Mr Henry Irving, several members of the Salvation Army, policemen, Mr Parnell, and other celebrities, the only thing which stood firm being the representation of the Temple-bar memorial, with the griffin, and a huge figure of an African king. The prisoner was seen by Inspector Redstone to seize a rope to which a guy representing Lord Randolph Churchill was attached and pull the figure over. It fell on to the floor, and was greatly damaged by being kicked about and beaten with sticks. The inspector described the scene as an extraordinary one, and said that he had been instructed by Messrs Jones and Barber to request the Magistrates to make an example of prisoner, in order to prevent wanton destruction of property in future.

Mr Howard said it was a pitiable thing to find that people could not avail themselves of a public holiday without committing an outrage such as had been showed in this instance.

The prisoner assured the justices that he was perfectly innocent. He certainly was amongst the crowd, but took no part in overthrowing the figures. He was pushed against the rope in the confusion, and the guy came down, but not through any wilful act of his.

The magistrates, believing that prisoner's version of the affair might be true, and that, amongst so many people, the inspector might have made a mistake as to the prisoner actually pulling the figure down, only imposed a penalty of 5s., remarking that if they had been satisfied that prisoner had wilfully committed the offence with which he was charged they would have dealt very severely with him.

WANTED, DWARF. Must be very small and good-looking. Prince Mite may write. Rosinsky, 1, Rue Baudin, Paris.
15/4/1882

THE following curious epistle was recently received by Mr John Sanger* from a vegetable and fruit merchant in Sheffield – "Sir, – Your Herd of Elephants calld at my Shop & had their dinners of Coleflour & Curly greens to the amount of 11s. 6d. Would you be kind eneph to return it with the boy and Oblige yours G. TANFIELD." The elephantine account was, of course, duly settled.
A circus proprietor.
22/4/1882

A CORRESPONDENT writes: Having a delicate affair to transact on the following morning, Marwood came up to town on the evening before Dr Lamson's* execution, and resolved to pay a visit to "Pepper's Original Ghost and Spectral Opera Company," whose entertainment was being exhibited at the Beaumont Hall, Mile-end, and afterwards to go to Lusby's Music Hall to see "Winkle's Waxworks," &c. He was speedily recognised at the Beaumont Hall, but was able to stay the entertainment out. On going over to Lusby's, however, he created considerable sensation, and a "scene" occurred, wherein all doubts as to his identity were set at rest by his deliberately producing his card and handing it to one of the waiters and to several others. He was much interested in "Winkle's Waxworks," sitting in a box, and beating time with his fingers to the music. His cards were inscribed – "Marwood, Horncastle, Executioner." As he passed out of the hall he waved his hat, and said, "Servant to you all, gentlemen; like to meet you in the evening – not morning." The scene terminated by Marwood and his friends driving off in a cab to avoid being mobbed.

Dr Lamson was an American-born surgeon who killed his disabled brother-in-law with a slice of poisoned Dundee cake.

6/5/1882

SHOCKING DEATH OF A DRAMATIC WRITER.

ON Wednesday afternoon Mr George Collier, deputy coroner, held a long inquiry at the Bank of Friendship, Harford-street, Mile-end, touching the death of Mr Joseph George Saunders, aged fifty-five years, a dramatic writer, who was found dead in his room at 126, Oxford-street, Stepney, on Sunday morning last. Henry Greaves, a fireman at the London Docks, who refused to be sworn and was allowed to affirm, said he lived at 126, Oxford-street, Stepney, about nine months, and the deceased had occupied a room there about five years. He paid three shillings a week for rent, and was very retired in his habits.

On Saturday afternoon a telegram came for him, and witness's wife took it down to his room, and on knocking on the door could get no answer. On Sunday afternoon witness went down and knocked on the door, and, being unable to obtain an answer, burst it open. He then saw the deceased lying dead on the floor, with a part of his body under the bedstead. In his left hand he was holding his pipe, and his pen was close to his right hand, so there could be no doubt that he was in the act of writing when he fell. The room was filthy beyond all description. There was nothing in it but an old broken-down table, and a bedstead in the same condition. The stench was enough to "knock one down," and the vermin and filth about the room were something horrible to contemplate. The ceiling was literally darkened with cobwebs, which hung in festoons all over the place. It was a mystery to him how the deceased kept himself so clean, for he always made a respectable appearance. He never admitted anybody to his apartment. There were no signs of any food about the place. He was personally known to Mr Reade, the author, for whom he had done a deal of work.

Mr Edmund King, surgeon, of No. 23, High-street, Stepney, said the stomach was empty, and the condition of the intestines denoted an absence of food for at least several days. Death was due to the rupture of a blood vessel on the brain. The jury returned a verdict in accordance with the medical testimony.

20/5/1882

AT the Middlesex Sessions, on Thursday, Louis Keppel, aged forty-two, was indicted for stealing a goat, a dog, a monkey, and other goods, the property of Antoniazzi Guiseppe. Mr Gill prosecuted; the prisoner was undefended. Mr Albert interpreted the evidence.

It appeared that the prosecutor is an Italian living at 58, King-street, Hammersmith, and he stated that it was his business to teach dogs, goats, and other animals to perform various tricks. About eight o'clock on the night of the 23rd of May the prosecutor called at Brook-green-place, where the prisoner lived, and left in his care a performing goat, dog, monkey, table, and a pair of steps. The monkey was locked in a box, of which he had the key. At nine o'clock that night he returned from London, and on proceeding to Brook-green found that his goat, dog, monkey, and other things were gone, the monkey box having been broken open. Subsequently from information received, Police-constable George Carter, 111 K, in consequence of finding the prisoner with his animals in High-street, Romford, where their performance was going on, told him he would be charged with having stolen the whole of them from Hammersmith.

The prisoner was then taken in custody, and on being received at Barking Station, where the prosecutor was in attendance, and told that he would be charged with stealing a goat and other articles, the property of the prosecutor, he said that he had as much right to them as he had, that they were partners, and he told him he was going away, and should not return until Tuesday or Saturday with the things, and the goat was his property.

The prisoner, in his defence, said ten weeks ago he and the prosecutor left Hastings together, having with them two goats, a French poodle dog, and a monkey. They travelled together until they reached Croydon, when he asked the prosecutor to sell him a goat, and he did so for 7s., saying he gave 6s. for it at Falmouth. This was on condition that he should stay with him, as he had half the profits.

The jury held that the prosecutor and prisoner were partners, and returned a verdict of Not Guilty.

WANTED, GROTESQUE DANCERS, Gentlemen, not less than Eight Feet Nine Inches in height. A long Engagement to suitable parties. Must be prepared to go abroad if required. Apply, first by letter, to C. BAKER, 422, Battersea-park-road, London S.W.
10/6/1882

IT is reported that a boy, sixteen years of age, living in Jersey, has become insane through witnessing a performance of *The Man in the Iron Mask*. When he reached home from the theatre he fell under the hallucination that a masked man was in his room, and, seizing a weapon, would have done injury to one of the members of the family had he not been prevented. He had now been removed to a lunatic asylum.
17/6/1882

THE sympathies not only of their friends, but of the profession and community at large, will be with the Sisters Hortense and Elise Damain, who are as well known in London and Paris *salons*, for the drawing-room entertainments they so admirably organise, on the occasion of the affliction that has just fallen upon them. A young niece, Marie Damain, left her aunts' home about a twelve month since, and could not be induced to return, when a week ago the news reached Paris that the girl, and her friend Aline Renneville, had committed suicide with revolvers, at Vienna. No cause can be attributed to Mdlle Renneville's self-destruction; that of the other young lady is known to be the old, old story of unrequited love.

FOR SALE, Four PERUVIAN MUMMIES, just imported (Three Men and a Woman). They will be Sold very reasonable, and would soon earn the price asked for them. WM. CROSS, Importer, Earle-street, Liverpool.
24/6/1882

TO THE EDITOR OF THE ERA.
Sir – Having lately seen several of Shakespeare's plays performed by travelling companies of undoubted ability, I may, perhaps, be permitted to make a few observations in your valuable paper relative to the above subject. I would respectfully suggest that Shakespeare's lovely lines should not be spoken with what may be termed a drawing-room accent, and that the uttawly too-too style-of-thing in pronunciation sadly mars the most exquisite music of the Shakespearian language. Macbeth is not improved by saying "Is that a deggaw I see befaw me, the hendle tawds my hend," or Richard by saying "Now is the wintaw of our discontent, changed into glorious semmaw by the sen of York." Puck should by no means put a "gedle rand the earth in fawty minits," and the sweet south wind should not blow upon a "benk of vaalets," and so on *ad infinitum* and *ad nauseum*. […]

Pray let English actors and actresses beware ere they trifle with Shakespeare's English, which, well-spoken, is a concert in itself, and conveys to the grateful intellect such endless enjoyment that one mighty easily imagine that its luscious cadence formed part of the ideal music of the spheres. Yours truly, PAGANINI REDIVIVUS, Liverpool.

AN alarming accident occurred at Drury-lane on the evening of Wednesday last during the performance of *Macbeth*, Mr William Rignold, who was representing the guilty hero, receiving a serious wound in the side from the dagger wielded by Mr J.H. Barnes, the representative of Macduff. The surgical skill of Mr Arthur Dacre – the Malcolm – was happily at once brought to bear, and the sufferer was forthwith removed to his home at Hornsey, where it is probable he will be compelled to remain for some days. Mr Swinbourne's services were called into requisition under these sad circumstances, and at very short notice that able actor undertook to play Mr Rignold's part on Thursday.
8/7/1882

TO THE EDITOR OF THE ERA.
Sir, – Being particularly interested on the subject of costume, it is a constant annoyance to me on going to a theatre, which ought to be an authority on costume, to too frequently see the ladies on the stage dressed according to their own fancy, utterly regardless of the period, rendering the effect from the front absurd and unnatural.

For instance, the action of the play may suppose to take place about the beginning of the present century. I make no complaint of the costume of the gentlemen on the stage; they are generally dressed correctly. The characteristic points of fashion of the period being observed, naturally harmonise, and, therefore, their costume looks well.

Then see the ridiculous contrast too often made by the ladies on the stage – those, I am sorry to say, often who are taking the leading parts – who persist in wearing high heels and narrowed waists, and and sometimes high buttoned-up boots. Very little of George the Fourth remains, but a good deal of Victoria.

Who is responsible for this most inartistic effect? Has not the manager some power over this want of good taste? Surely the ladies ought not to be permitted to take such liberties with their dresses, for if they are allowed such licence we shall shortly see them introducing the horrible modern crinolette into every part entrusted to them, whether it dates back to George the Fourth or the Battle of Hastings.
Yours faithfully, WEEDON GROSSMITH, 82, Gower-street, W.C., July 29th, 1882.
5/8/1882

DEATH OF AN ACTOR FROM STARVATION.
ON Wednesday Mr Collier held an inquest at the Weavers' Arms Tavern, Baker's-row, Whitechapel, on the body of Guy Linton*, aged thirty-five, an actor, who died from starvation.

Police-constable James Cox, 122 H, stated that on the 24th ult. he was on duty in Hanbury-street, Mile-end New Town, and about ten o'clock at night he saw the deceased standing, with a crowd of people round him. The witness asked him what he was doing there, and he said he had only twopence-halfpenny, and wanted some more money to pay for a night's lodging. Some of the bystanders gave him some money, and the deceased attempted to walk away, but he was so weak that he fell to the ground, and appeared thoroughly exhausted. The witness felt certain that he was in a starving state. He procured a conveyance, and had the deceased removed to the Whitechapel Infirmary.

Eliza Hyde, nurse at the Whitechapel Union Infirmary, stated that deceased was in a very dirty and destitute condition, and he appeared only skin and bones. He told the witness that he had a wife and sister in America, and was a professional actor, and formerly held an engagement at the Pavilion Theatre.

A juryman here said that he knew the deceased well as an actor.

The witness, continuing, said the deceased never rallied, although everything that was possible was done for him, and he died on Sunday afternoon. He told her that he had earned a few halfpence by selling matches and envelopes.

Dr John James Ilott, resident medical officer at the Whitechapel Infirmary, said that when the deceased was admitted he had no shirt or hat on, and was in a very destitute condition. He was at once put to bed and food given him, but he was too far gone to rally. The witness had made a post-mortem examination, and found the lungs and brain diseased. The stomach and intestines both bore indications that the deceased had suffered greatly from want of food. The cause of death was serum of blood on the brain, accelerated by destitution and exposure.

The jury returned a verdict in accordance with the medical evidence.

The juryman above referred to then stated that the deceased was well known throughout the theatrical profession, and was on one occasion specially selected by Mr Hollingshead to play a leading part at the Gaiety Theatre. He also had a brother in the profession, and his aged mother resided in Glasgow.
Linton was a once-popular London music-hall artiste and songwriter.
2/9/1882

MADAME ALIAS* narrowly escaped a severe accident on Sunday evening last. She, with her husband, had been dining at the house of a friend at Canonbury, and towards the close of the evening some of the company strolled into the garden. Madame Alias followed, and, it being very dark, she did not notice an ornamental pond around which some wirework and flowers are placed; and, catching her feet in the former, fell head foremost into the water, which luckily is only three feet deep. Had she struck her head against the artificial rock-work in the centre a very serious injury might have been the result. As it was a severe shock and thorough drenching, which quite spoilt a velvet costume she was wearing, appeared to be the only damage. After a little rest and complete change of attire from Mrs Lurcott's wardrobe, M. Alias was able to take Madame home.
Sarah, the wife of theatrical costumier Charles Alias.
9/9/1882

MR HENRY VARLEY, an evangelist, at present on a visit to Edinburgh, delivered an address to men in the Free Assembly Hall, on Saturday evening, upon the subject of "The Social Evil." In the course of his lecture he referred to the influence of the theatre, and gave an instance of a fallen woman, whose first step into vice had been attending a theatre. Pausing suddenly, and stretching out his arms, he exclaimed, "Look at that miserable woman, Sarah Bernhardt!" The remark was received with a storm of hisses and cheers, whereupon Mr Varley said, "I have yet to learn that my countrymen are prepared to accord the position of honour to a woman who was a mother before she was a wife." A young gentleman at once sprang up in the gallery, and shouted to the lecturer, "You're a slanderer, sir." Cries of "Put him out" were raised, and amid considerable excitement the gentleman was ejected. He offered no resistance, declaring that he scorned to stay in a meeting where one of the most gifted of womankind was so spoken of.
16/9/1882

A REGULAR playgoer has been advising that managers, instead of buying antimacassars which get hooked on the coat tail buttons, and make people look ridiculous, should spend the cash thus wasted in the purchase of what he calls insecticide. He had evidently discovered that upholstered seats harbour lively things that make sitting still certainly unpleasant and almost impossible.
23/9/1882

MARY ANN BUTTERWORTH was charged at Henley Police-court on Tuesday with defrauding "General" Booth. It appears that in April last the Salvation Army hired a hall at Chesterton for services, but were unable to commence them on the night fixed. The prisoner, however, obtained possession of the hall, conducted a service, announcing herself as a "Captain" of the Army, and, after making a collection, decamped. Last Wednesday she appeared at the Army headquarters at Henley and posed as a converted tight-rope dancer, where she was recognised by one of her Chesterton victims and arrested. "Major" Fawcett, on whose authority she was arrested, not being present, the other "officers" – all females – seeing the difficulty of proving the case, withdrew the charge.

A SHOCKING accident occurred at Hull Botanic Gardens about ten o'clock on Monday night during a pyrotechnic display representing the bombardment of Alexandria. A three-inch mortar burst, and the pieces going among the crowd, wounded four persons, three being youths. One, named Meekin, had his entrails literally blown out, and he died shortly afterwards. Another, named Gillett, son of a Town Councillor, had a thigh taken off, and lingered till Tuesday morning, when he died. The third is seriously wounded, and one of the pyrotechnists, John Wilder, had a thumb blown off.
30/9/1882

OPERA BY TELEPHONE. – A very interesting experiment took place at the opening of the session of the London Hospital Medical College on Monday evening, when a *conversazione* was given to a large company. By permission of Mr W.S. Gilbert and the United Telephone Company, the anatomical theatre was placed in telephonic communication with the Savoy Theatre, and many of the audience heard distinctly, and with great pleasure, the aesthetic opera *Patience* by the telephone. The electric light used on the occasion was also a great success, Professor Cooke's incandescent lamps being adopted – for the first time at a public exhibition – driven by a Gulcher dynamo machine, the current from which is of so low a tension that no inconvenience whatever is experienced if the naked wires are accidentally taken hold of, while the crowded room was kept perfectly cool.
7/10/1882

DURING the rehearsal of the pantomime *Robinson Crusoe* at the Plymouth Theatre, on the 22nd inst., a funny incident occurred. The water surveyor, unknown to the manager or those inside the theatre, was trying the "service," and unwittingly turned on a wrong tap, which caused the "water curtain," which was created after the last fire at the theatre, to suddenly pour down a torrent on the stage just in front of the orchestra. The band beat a hasty retreat over the barrier into the pit stalls, while the actors and actresses, who were rehearsing, flew in all directions, one lady doing a very clever "header" into one of the private boxes. The damage exceeded £50.

ON Thursday night a novel experiment in bell-ringing took place in the City. The riders of bicycles have alarm bells fixed to their machines, the notes of which differ occasionally one from the other. This gave rise to a suggestion by a bicyclist that a couple of octaves should be provided, the performers having one or two bells affixed to their machines. The suggestion was carried out, the result being that the octaves met by the Mansion House, and started off up Cheapside, ringing out "The Bells". This was continued until reaching St Paul's-churchyard, when the musicians changed the theme, and gave the "Blue Bells of Scotland," "Auld Lang Syne," and "Home, Sweet Home," as they ran down Cannon-street, up Union and King-streets, and round the back of the Bank of England. After a rest of ten minutes, the musical bicyclists had another spin through the City, playing "Rule Britannia," the "March of the Men of Harlech," and "God Save the Queen."
30/12/1882

4
1883
UNBOILED RICE AND SILVER SPANGLES

WANTED, a SONG. – The Proprietors of a Celebrated Article of daily Consumption are wanting a good Song Written, introducing in the words of the Chorus the name of their Article. Send terms to E., 895, SELL'S Advertising Offices, Bolt-court, London, E.C.

WANTED, Proprietors of Hotels, &c., to know that Miss MINNIE GRANT, the American Stout Barmaid, is at Liberty for Bar attraction. Age, Twenty-Two Years; Measurement around the Arm, 30in.; around the Shoulders, 6ft.; and the Waist, 5ft.; weighing over 30st. Address, JOHN BLAND, Mitre Music Hall, Halifax. A genuine draw.
6/1/1883

THE Carl Rosa Opera Company opened at Rochdale on Monday night, with Madame Marie Roze as Fidelio, to a large audience, who, judging from the applause, fully appreciated Beethoven's opera. A most amusing incident occurred while Madame Marie Roze was singing her great aria in the first act. A dog belonging to the manager of the theatre twice walked on to the stage, crossing from P. to O.P. Side. Madame Marie Roze, however, did not lose her presence of mind, in spite of the general titter, but finished her aria amidst enthusiastic applause.
3/2/1883

MR EDITOR. – Sir, I must not complain of the kind attention paid to me in your issue of January 27th by your reporter at Greenwich, but, as he fancies that I sang of a "Launderee," pray let me say that the subject was a "Nunnery," which word I have tried to distinctly enunciate, and with which I will in future use even a greater effort to catch his kindly ear. Yours respectfully, HARRIET VERNON, Sun Music Hall, February 4th, 1883.
10/2/1883

A serious accident occurred on the 16th ult. at Plymouth Theatre, where the pantomime of *Robinson Crusoe* was being performed. In one scene a camel is introduced, and the keeper, William White, having in the course of the performance struck the camel across the legs while it was attempting to rise, the camel suddenly knelt on him, and remained in this position until another of the supernumeries came to White's rescue. It was then found that, besides having sustained other serious injuries, his thigh was broken. He was at once removed to the hospital.
3/3/1883

A STRANGE incident occurred at the Opera House, Bury, on Tuesday evening last, where Miss Forrester is fulfilling a six nights' engagement with her *Mazeppa* company. After the overture had been played the

audience were kept waiting about an hour and a half, that time being occupied in endeavouring to get the horse "Lightning" to ascend the rake and enter the theatre, which he persistently refused to do. By this time the audience, becoming very impatient, were addressed by Miss Forrester and Fred. W. Purcell, the resident manager, who explained briefly the cause of the delay, and who suggested that the play should proceed without the horse, and that everyone in the theatre should have a free admission the next night. Thousands of persons had assembled to witness the hopeless attempt to persuade the horse to enter the theatre, several local veterinary surgeons and horsey men taking an active part in the efforts without success. On Wednesday morning early, for several hours, efforts were renewed to induce the horse to enter the building, and it was discovered that the intelligence of the animal was not at fault, as a beam over the entrance was not sufficiently high, and caught his head on entering. The horse is now stabled on the stage behind the wings.
17/3/1883

AN amusing disturbance occurred at a Dublin theatre a few nights ago. A young "masher" wished to throw a bouquet to one of the dancers with whose charms he was smitten. Provided with a huge nosegay, and accompanied by his bosom friend, he made his way to a box which he had previously secured, and impatiently awaited the coming of the fair one. In the meanwhile his treacherous friend had quietly affixed a string to the bouquet, which was in due course thrown by its purchaser, with the result that when the fair recipient stooped to pick it up the "friend" pulled the string, and the bouquet returned to the box! A "set-to" between the gentlemen followed, and finally both were expelled by the manager.
24/3/1883

WANTED, by a Dwarf, a Situation as Waiter. Not experienced. Eleven Years' good character from last employer. Address, CHUCK, at Mr HADDOCK'S, Land's-lane, Leeds.
21/4/1883

FLORAL offerings are now so plentifully distributed when aristocratic amateurs come before the public that the recipients of those gifts hardly know how to dispose of them, but a plan adopted at the Gaiety Theatre on the occasion of Miss Walpole's matinée has, at least, the merit of novelty. Miss Walpole appeared as Helen in the play of *The Hunchback* on Tuesday afternoon, and her friends sat in the stalls and boxes ready with choice exotics to testify their admiration. However, these floral tokens were so numerous and so large that they were not thrown upon the stage as usual. When Miss Walpole appeared to receive the congratulations of her supporters the floral offerings were *wheeled across the stage in a barrow!*
28/4/1883

WANTED, Managers, requiring a GIANT for their forthcoming Pantomimes, to know that Mr C.H. FROME can work an invention by which he can appear from 12ft. to 15ft. high. Figure in proportion. Can refer Managers to a well-known firm of Engineers for this astounding invention. References and particulars from Messrs BLACKMORE, Sole Agent.
2/6/1883

TO THE EDITOR OF THE ERA.
Sir, – On behalf of Mr Charles King, clown and pantomimist, who met with a frightful accident while superintending a parade of the Royal Troupe of Clown Cricketers on Whit Monday at West Hartlepool, and is now lying in the Union Hospital, Sunderland, and will be an inmate for some weeks to come, I earnestly solicit the aid of his brother professionals to help one in the time of need who in his time has helped many. Any subscriptions sent will be duly acknowledged. Address, Mr Charles King, No. 2 Ward, Union Hospital, Sunderland. Yours respectfully, GEORGE RICARDO, Acrobat and Juggler.
9/6/1883

AN amusing incident took place the other night at Carlisle, during the performance of *Fighting Fortune*. In the last act the death of the villain, Leonard Harrington (played by Mr Herbert Dudley), is brought about by means of a falling rock, representing a landslip. So realistic is the mechanical contrivance used for this purpose that a gentleman, witnessing what he took to be a fearful accident, rushed on to the stage and, while reproaching the other characters for their heartlessness in "leaving a poor human being there," began to work with a will to remove the heavy mass. Having partly succeeded in this, he changed his tone to one of surprise as he asked, "Where is he?" The supposed victim was all this while at his side coolly smiling at his would-be rescuer.
16/6/1883

MR EDITOR – Sir, Your Darwin correspondent, in his very able notice last week, complains that he was unable to hear Miss Eleanor Reardon distinctly. Seeing the lady was in the North of Ireland at the time I can fully understand his inability to do so. Yours, &c., E.L. GARSIDE.
23/6/1883

AT Edinburgh Police-court on Friday nine students were remanded on the charge of creating a disturbance in the Theatre Royal on the previous night. From an early hour a large number of students in the gallery annoyed the audience and performers annoyed the audience by throwing peas, rotten eggs, and other missiles, until it was found necessary to drop the curtain. Eventually the police arrived, and, after some scuffling, took several of the rioters into custody. A card found on one of the accused indicated that the disturbance was pre-arranged.
30/6/1883

THE acting-manager of the Comedy Theatre was recently the recipient of a curious letter, of which the following is a copy: "Dear Sir, – Could you oblige me By telling me were I can get a Cheap suit of actors clothes and oblige yours obidend A. PEARSON. if you want to know the age 14 kind sir only me Brother warts to get me a suit of clothes to do trap ese Work in. Wig tights Pangle clothes and shoes if you know were I can get them will you send word."

MR E.C. DUNBAR, of the *Fun on the Bristol* company, had on Tuesday a narrow escape from being crushed by the wall of the London, Chatham, and Dover Railway at Ramsgate, the said wall being knocked down by a train which was not properly controlled.
7/7/1883

MR OSCAR WILDE, in his lecture at Prince's Hall on Tuesday evening, told his hearers that American theatrical audiences, when they did not take a play quietly, quitted the building and left the actors alone in their glory. This plan he thought better than the English one of of exhibiting hostility. As Mr Wilde's lecture far exceeded the limits announced, and threatened to become wearisome, not a few of his patrons acted upon the hint, and by twos, threes, and half-dozens, kept up a continual move towards the doors during the latter part of his discourse.
14/7/1883

THE suicide of Mr David Gaunt will be sincerely regretted by a wide circle of friends, and not a few of the playgoing public, who have learned to appreciate his abilities and to look forward to a promising career for a young actor who possessed decided talent. Mr Gaunt arrived at the Cambridge Hotel, Scarborough, last Sunday evening, and on Wednesday evening, at about half-past six, a cabman on the South Cliff stand saw him leap head foremost from the highest storey of the building. He found the deceased lying on the footpath, his head being absolutely battered in by the fall. It appears he had been in the bathroom, as he had no covering but a towel over his shoulders. The window was closed when he

made his terrible leap, with such force as to shatter the glass and framework. He struck the pavement with terrific force, and, horrible to relate, his brains were scattered about the roadway. As soon as the deplorable occurrence was made known to the inmates of the hotel, the deceased was carried in, and Dr Hutchinson attended, but of course without result, as Mr Gaunt must have been killed instantly. He had remained at Scarborough after performing with Maxwell's burlesque comedy company, owing to an attack of congestion of the lungs, and it cannot be doubted but that his brain was affected, as in one account of the lamentable affair it is stated that he exclaimed "I am mad!" before rushing to the window. The deceased had also acted with Mr W.J. Hill's comedy company, and but a few weeks since he played with very great success at a Gaiety matinée, his last performance being at the Spa, Scarborough.
Mr Gaunt was only twenty years old.
11/8/1883

ON Tuesday night much laughter was caused at the Opera House, Leicester, by a lady in the pit, who, being carried away by her feelings in the scene of *The Lights o' London* where Mr Armytage accuses his son of the murderous attack upon him, called out that "it was them two at the back who did it."

MR CHARLES HERMANN, the proprietor of the *Uncle Tom's Cabin* company, and manager of the Salford and Warrington Theatres, intends on touring a troupe of real Indian savages, introducing their war dances and mode of living in a startling sensational drama, *Buffalo Bill*. Mr Hermann has had most miraculous escapes. He was shot in the eyes with a revolver at Accrington, blown up at Lincoln with an infernal machine, and nearly torn to pieces by bloodhounds at Bury. Perhaps next he will be eaten by his own savages in their eagerness to show their "mode of living."

WANTED, MAN or LADY FISH, to perform in own tank. Apply, stating lowest terms, to Mr T. WHITELY, Allsop's Wax Work Exhibition, City Hall, Lime-street, Liverpool.
15/9/1883

THE opera of *Faust*, given by the Carl Rosa Opera Company at Manchester on Wednesday evening, was distinctly heard by telephone at Warrington, a distance of about sixteen miles.

WHEN in the Closet Scene of Hamlet, at the Prince of Wales's Theatre at Birmingham, on Monday evening last, Barry Sullivan as the Prince exclaimed, "A rat, a rat, dead for a ducat – dead!" and rushed off hastily as usual, a large black cat quickly bounded after him, evidently also intent on making it "rough on rats." Strange to say, the vast audience present did not even titter. The actor's "hold" must have been, indeed, firm.
22/9/1883

A MYSTERIOUS EXHIBITION.
ON Monday last Piccadilly Hall, lately the abode of Chang and the Midgets, was opened with what was grandiloquently styled "a highly refined and and entirely novel musical and illusionary entertainment, comprising the Tent of Medea, the Vocal Owls, and Wise Saws and Modern Instances," illustrated by Eckerell's Linearscope. We accepted an invitation to a "private view," as did three other unfortunates, the audience, with the man who kept the door, and the little girl who distributed programmes, thus numbering six persons.

About an hour after the time announced for the for the commencement of the proceeding there was a little fiddle scraping behind the scenes, and the curtain was lifted, giving us a view of a darkened stage, with in the background a picture of a castle and a bit of the moon. Presently a tall young woman, supposed to be Medea, came to the front, and having provided a prominent position for a couple of skulls and some cross-bones, gave forth an incantation in which the assistance of the midnight manufacturers of mushrooms was invoked. The lady concluded her address by by fixing her two eyes on the four representatives of the press, and by giving utterance to the following:

If for your crimes you would pardoned by,
By your indulgence set me free!

We cannot answer for our companions in distress, but we certainly were not conscious of any particular crimes committed on Monday afternoon. Nevertheless, we were perfectly willing to set the lady free. Unfortunately she showed no disposition to depart. She turned her attention to the skulls and cross-bones, threatening them with a stick.

Her curious antics had some effect, for in a short time there appeared from out the "cimmerian gloom" the "Elfin Moths," which were neither more nor less than a couple of pieces of paper waggled for the space of five minutes at the end of wires to the scraping of an unseen fiddle. When the "Elfin Moths" had taken their flight the centre of the stage was occupied by a huge vase, containing a fir-tree. This gave two boys – also unseen – an opportunity of singing "Know ye the land of cypresses and myrtle?" Nobody being disposed to answer the question, the vase gave place to a cage of love birds, addressed by the boys more or less tunefully as "Ye pretty warblers of the grove." Next we were introduced to Mercury, a scrubby youth, looking exceedingly uncomfortable and disposed to wink at the small company. After him came a mythical warrior who seemed to be saying "I don't want to fight, but by Jingo, if I do," &c., and he was succeeded presently by the boys, who, seen at last, extracted ear-torturing sounds from a violin and violoncello. Then there was shown a fountain, with Medea filling a glass, not to "wet her whistle," but just to show us it gave real *aqua pura*. Next, and still through Medea's threatening to beat the skulls, came a sculptor hammering at a statue – the winking, blinking, scrubby boy again – and finally we got a view of a skeleton. Where these things came from, and where they went, we do not know. Neither do we care. They did not interest us, and we were glad to be rid of them.

In the second part of the entertainment (!) we were introduced to the "Vocal Owls." Vocal howls would have been a more appropriate designation. A large cage was pushed to the front. It contained a couple of "properties" meant to represent owls, but which looked very much like a pair of poodles that had been tarred and feathered. Their jaws were made to wag, and then the boys behind the scenes started again with "When icicles hang by the wall;" "At midnight cold and dark and drear;" "The moping owl doth to the moon complain;" stopping between each selection to indulge in dreary jokes and pointless conversation. They were going on to "The farmer I knew," and "The farmer I know," when our patience being exhausted, we beat a retreat, leaving the "three more unfortunates" to make an acquaintance with "Wise Saws and Modern Instances."

We should say that the first part of this curious exhibition was divided into eight mysteries. We may supply a ninth in the questions – Why has such a show been put up at big prices in a West-end hall? And what do the promoters expect to become of it?

MR CHARLES LAURI is meeting with immense success at the Châtelet in Paris, where, as a monkey, he nightly runs round the dress circle as he did in the last pantomime at Drury-lane, adding to the fun by purloining a gentleman's hat, which is subsequently sent back to its owner from the stage-door. His engagement at the theatre named has been extended to next April.

MR SIMS REEVES gave the first night of his South Wales series of concerts on Tuesday night at the Drill Hall, Cardiff. Owing to a relaxation of the throat, the celebrated tenor substituted "My pretty Jane" for "Once again." In part second he did not readily appear in consequence of his objection to a noise caused by the stationary steam engines on a neighbouring mineral railway. He at length essayed to sing "Come into the garden, Maud," but soon retired, as the noise continued.

6/10/1883

ERRATUM. – Miss Alleyn, the clever young tragedienne, was last week by a curious slip referred to in our Lincoln report as an actress whose talents were of a mean order. The words intended were of course "no mean order."
13/10/1883

IN *A Sailor and His Lass*, at Drury-lane, the showers of spray in the wreck scene dashed over the form of Miss Sophie Eyre – and which the spectators believe so dangerously drench that actress while clinging to the foundering vessel – have raised a protest against the cruel realism of employing even lukewarm water for such a purpose. This admirable stage illusion is, however, nothing more, let us whisper in confidence, than an ingeniously blended mixture of unboiled rice and silver spangles.

FOR SALE, EIGHTY MUSHROOM DRESSES, for Pantomime or Ballet Children. Apply to Miss THOMPSON, Gaiety Theatre, London.
27/10/1883

MR HOWARD PAUL, lately in Philadelphia, hit on an ingenious idea of advertising Charles Wyndham.* Passing through the courtyard of the new public buildings, he saw the colossal head of a female with glorious upturned eyes and broad, expansive brow, that in a few weeks is to be placed on top of one of the edifices in course of construction. On interviewing the men in charge of this gigantic head, Mr Howard Paul found they were willing for a consideration to have a legend temporarily painted on her spacious forehead. The arrangement was rapidly negotiated, and now on that massive brow can be read by the thousands who pass daily through the courtyard "I'm wearily waiting for Wyndham "
**A distinguished actor-manager.*

AT the Bow-street Police-court on Wednesday, Mr William F. Thomas, lessee of Covent-garden Theatre during the Promenade Concerts season, and Police-constables Honor, 17 E B, and Smith, 28 E R, appeared to summonses charging them with assaulting Edward S. Seligman. There was also a cross-summons against Seligman, taken out by Mr Thomas, for an alleged assault. Mr Montagu Williams appeared for Mr Thomas.

Mr Seligman deposed that on November 10th he was at the Promenade Concerts, and some ladies asked him to treat them, and, as he "never refused to treat ladies, he complied," but some gentleman sitting near to him threw some ice and lemon at him. He did not know the gentleman, as he "had not been introduced, but with ladies it was a very different thing." Someone expressed surprise at him being in the company of the ladies in question, and he replied, "I am a bachelor, and I can do as I like, and do not want to be advised." He appealed to the defendant constables, and asked them if they were there to listen to the music or to protect him. At that time someone directed him to be ejected, and the defendant constables put him out. He complained at the police-station, and afterwards paid for readmission to the concert, when he was again ejected, and alleged that Mr Thomas had kicked him on the head.

In cross-examination witness denied that he was drunk, as he was "quite capable of drinking three bottles of Rhine wine just the same as a baby would milk; he was a gentleman, and that was quite sufficient."

Mr Vaughan – Have you any witnesses?

Witness – I am too short-sighted, and cannot see.

Mr Vaughan considered that the witness conducted himself in a very impertinent manner.

Police-constable Honor was called for the defence, and deposed that Mr Seligman had behaved in a very objectionable manner in the theatre. As he refused to desist he was ejected.

Police-constable Smith stated that Seligman was very violent, and shouted "Fire" in the theatre. No more force than was necessary was used in ejecting Seligman. [...] Mr Vaughan characterised complainant's conduct as being wicked in the extreme by shouting out "Fire!" and expressed his opinion that the object was to cause a panic. The summonses would be dismissed.

Complainant – I shall appeal to the Prince of Wales tomorrow.

Mr M. Williams mentioned the cross-summonses, but Mr Vaughan said that in the present excited state of the complainant, who seemed to be hardly master of himself, he (Mr Vaughan) thought it was hardly worth while mentioning it.

Mr Williams said that after such an expression he would not press the charge.

24/11/1883

"PATIENCE" AND THE NOTTINGHAM AMATEURS.

TO THE EDITOR OF THE ERA.

Sir, – In a paragraph in last week's *Era* referring to a piratical performance of *Patience* at Nottingham, the following statements are made:

"The Manager stepped forward and announced that just before eight o'clock that night a telegram had been received from Mr D'Oyly Carte, forbidding the performance of the opera." *** "The Manager stated that permission had previously been obtained to play the piece, and it was not until the eleventh hour, when the hall was filled with an audience waiting for its production, that they received any intimation to the contrary; and then they could not break faith with the Nottingham public." *** "A crowded audience," I learn, "received the performance with the utmost demonstrations of approval."

Will you permit me to say that the statement that I ever gave any permission for the performance is untrue? A Mr Garratt wrote to me from Nottingham some months ago asking for permission to give a performance of *Patience*. I replied, refusing permission. Further pressure being put upon me, I then named terms, which I presume were not approved, as Mr Garratt replied stating that the idea was abandoned. However, unless I am mistaken in supposing that Mr Garratt wrote to me on behalf of the same persons who gave the performances of November 28th, 29th, and December 1st, the idea appears to have revived accompanied by the inspiration of dispensing with permission.

Not one performance only, but three, it seems, were given. The promoters of the affair hid their light under a bushel successfully during two days, but on the third the matter came to my knowledge, and I promptly telegraphed to stop them. I pay a large yearly sum to Mr Gilbert and Sir Arthur Sullivan for the sole right of performance of their operas, and it is, therefore, conceivable that I might object to have performances of these pieces given without my consent, seeing that such performances might seriously prejudice the receipts of my own regular companies.

The high-handed manner of the Nottingham amateurs in dealing with other people's property, the assumption by the manager of a noble and public spirit in insisting upon going on with his illegal act, and the reception of all these proceedings by the public, suggest considerations on which I may ask you to allow me to address you later.

I may scarcely say that I have instructed my solicitor to take proceedings against everyone concerned.

I am, Sir, yours faithfully, R. D'OYLY CARTE, Savoy Theatre, December 14th, 1883.

15/12/1883

MADAME PATTI'S diamonds are almost as famous as those of Mdlle Georges, the celebrated French actress, who generally displayed all her jewels when playing before provincial audiences, no matter what her role was; and the announcement that Mdlle Georges would appear in the piece "with all her diamonds" was a regular feature in the bills. Patti, who usually appears before her New York audiences with something like £50,000 worth of jewellery when she sings in *Traviata*, it is said, never ventures to take her treasures with her to the theatre. About half an hour before the theatre doors open four men, well armed, in charge of a casket, may be seen leaving her hotel. They are detectives specially told off by the authorities for this service. They never lose sight of her while she is on the stage, and one of them

is constantly stationed at the door of her dressing-room. When the performance is over she carefully puts back the jewels in their case and hands them to her body-guard to take back to the hotel.
22/12/1883

5
1884
DEAR SIR, I LOVE YOU TONIGHT

ON Boxing Day, at the Portland Hall, Southsea, during the morning's performance of Gounod's *Faust*, a most amusing incident occurred, and is thus described: – In the lovely duet in the garden scene between Faust and Marguerite, suddenly a large collie dog broke from his chain in the hotel adjoining the hall on hearing his master's (Mr Faulkner Leigh) voice, rushed through the hall, dashed over the orchestra on to the stage, and began most affectionately to caress him. That gentleman and Madame Cave-Ashton could not maintain their gravity; but the latter artist led this most musical dog off, and on her return to the stage the duet was continued (amidst loud applause), and was splendidly rendered by the artists above-named.

THAT a pantomime should ever become capable of being recommended as a vehicle for lessons in elocution would seem to be impossible of belief, yet a better illustration of the value of tone and emphasis could hardly be afforded than the topical duet so amusingly rendered by Mr Harry Nicholls and Mr Herbert Campbell as the two elderly sisters in the Drury-lane comic annual of *Cinderella*. In about a dozen verses these acting vocalists show that fifty different significations may be imparted to such a simple phrase as "I beg your pardon." With a slight change of facial expression and a little alteration of emphasis, the words convey on each repetition quite a different meaning, and the varying inflexions of tone are worth studying by all who would wish to master the full capability of the human voice in the expression of a particular thought.
5/1/1884

IN the representation of *Whittington and His Cat* at the Theatre, Winter Gardens, Southport, Mr Herbert Budd, assistant stage-manager, who plays the old merchant, recently met with a heavy fall in a tussle with the Cat (Master Frederick Liebert), and with great difficulty succeeded in going through his remaining scene. This endeavour aggravated the injury, which, at first thought to be a severe sprain, turned out to be the fracture of a small bone of one leg, and the patient was put both in splints and in bed. The Sunday intervened, but on the Monday night Mr Budd, nothing daunted, chartered a cab to the theatre, and had himself dressed with his leg made up as an immense gouty package, and then and since has nightly played the part upon a pair of crutches. It is needless to see that this display of pluck met with a hearty reception from the audience, and his novel reading of the part has turned into quite a success.

A GRIM joker has compiled the following terrible record: – Mr Barry Sullivan, during the course of his dramatic career, has committed 17,000 murders, and has been killed in battle, slain in a duel, poisoned, or fatally stabbed 9,000 times. Mr Henry Irving's record is not quite so full of blood, but our great tragedian has taken 15,000 lives, and on 7,000 occasions has been violently done to death in the full glare of the footlights. Mrs Bancroft has been foully betrayed or abducted 3,200 times; Mr Henry Neville has 3,100 times been ruined in consequence of the treachery of his friends; Miss Ada Cavendish has been betrayed, deserted, or abducted 5,600 times, and is still suffering similar misfortunes; Mr Charles Warner has 2,000 times been killed by ardent liquors, and has nearly as often perished by accidents on sea and land; Mrs Kendal has been 2,000 times deserted or betrayed, and has besides been otherwise basely treated 1,100 times; Mr Kendal has 900 times fallen dead suddenly; and Mr John Clayton – to his honour be it spoken – has nobly befriended 1,800 miserable and deserted women, and has subsequently married about half of them. As for Mr Charles Wyndham, he has been divorced from 2,800 wives, and is now in America, where he is continuing his disgraceful and heartless conduct to crowded houses.
12/1/1884

FRIENDS have informed me of your goings on on January 18th. I have full evidence for a divorce, but I shan't try it on. Once bit two times shy; very much, Mary Ann.
8/3/1884

AN ANGRY AMATEUR.
In noticing an amateur performance of *Moths* at Ladbroke Hall we last week remarked of Miss Elise Elbert, who had been entrusted with the part of Lady Dolly, "Her talents do not lie in the direction of the stage; she had neither the voice nor the appearance that are necessary to success, and her assurance is largely in excess of her intelligence." We have discovered now that if there is one thing more than another in which Miss Elbert excels it is the art of polite letter-writing. The following is the latest specimen of her style:

"To the Gentleman who wrote notice of *Moths* at Notting-hill on March 3rd.
Sir, – I have just sufficient intelligence left to enable me to write and thank you for that 'bray' of yours in *The Era* about the performance of *Moths* and my part of Lady Dolly. I used when a little child to possess a donkey, and so I fortunately understand their stupid and spiteful propensities, and, perhaps, like the aforementioned animal, you are worse when your thistles have disagreed with you; therefore it may be that after all you were on that fatal evening suffering from an attack of indigestion. Your attempt to be funny, too, is, in my idea, quite a failure, and, probably, the picture of a gentleman in a muddy hat was but a reflection of your own sweet self in your looking-glass when you retired to rest. My assurance also leads me to believe that the report of the performance is the result of nightmare brought on by the nasty thistles. Should you desire a *further* proof of my assurance you can make any use you please of this letter, but my last gleam of intelligence had vanished, and I can only subscribe myself,
Your much obliged, ELISE ELBERT, 23, Townshend-terrace, Richmond, Surrey, March 8th."
15/3/1884

PERFORMING ELEPHANTS IN A CELLAR.
The usually quiet neighbourhood of Kentish-town was on Sunday afternoon the scene of extraordinary excitement. The well-known estabishment of Messrs Sanger and Sons had been advertised to give performances at Agincourt Park, leading out of the Mansfield Road, which unites Gospel Oak village with Lower Hampstead. A special train conveying the troupe of artists, a portion of the large equestrian establishment, and four of the five performing elephants arrived at the Kentish-town Station of the Midland Railway at 1.45 p.m. The artists having left the train at the passenger platform, the trucks containing the horses and elephants were drawn round to the cattle platform.

These trucks were ranged alongside the platform; but it being necessary for the elephants to be taken out at the end of trucks, some sleepers were laid down between the end of the carriage and the yard, over which the two elephants, known by the names of Jim and Rose, which were in the nearest trucks, safely walked, and were quietly ranged in the station yard, getting a welcome supply of water after their journey. The sleepers were then removed to form a passage-way between the first and second trucks, so that the two elephants in the latter (known as Palm and Ida) could cross over and be landed as the first were. They had reached the front carriage, and preparations were being made for their disembarkation by removing the sleepers that had been placed between the trucks to the end of the first carriage, as before.

Whilst this was being done one or more of the sleepers was accidentally thrown, and the noise of the fall so frightened the two elephants that were waiting that they leapt over the intervening space – some four feet – rushed through the open gateway in the yard to the front gates, which were closed, in their headlong flight knocking down one of their keepers, named Charles Miles, whose collar-bone was dislocated. These front gates are very massive and heavily framed, but as Ida, followed by Palm, charged the gates these gave way instantaneously, and broke off from the solid hinges as if made of matchwood. As soon as they reached the open they started along the Highgate-road, knocking over an unfortunate pedestrian who had not time to get out of the way. Happily he was more frightened than hurt, as he was seen to get up and run away, leaving his hat behind him. Pursuing their course along the Highgate-road, they presently left the main thoroughfare, turning to the right by the Vine public house, which is close to College-lane. Here there was a knot of people, and in their hot haste to get out of the way, one of the party was knocked down and trampled on, not by the elephants, but by his friends, with the result of a broken collar-bone, it is said. The lane which the elephants had strangely selected for their route is very narrow, and terminates at the Highgate-road Baptist chapel in Carroll-road. Here Palm and Ida attempted to get over the chapel boundary wall. In this they were foiled, and rushing along the commencement of the Carroll-road, they turned to the right into Twisden-road, knocking down a child, who is reported not to have been seriously hurt. Coming out from Twisden-road they proceeded up Chetwynd-road, and when they reached the top, which leads into Dartmouth-park-hill, they crossed over to a fence, which encloses a private road, Cathcart-hill. This fence they soon cleared, and at the bottom of Cathcart-hill proceeded along Junction-road until they arrived just opposite the tramway stables, when they turned down Francis-terrace.

This is a *cul-de-sac*. At the bottom, however, there is a closed passage which leads into Pemberton-terrace, between nos. 29 and 31. The boarding of this passage, in width about 6ft., was got over, and on their arrival at the other end they continued their course until they reached a flight of steps, which gave way under their weight, precipitating first Ida and then Palm into the cellar. Here they were stuck fast, and a large crowd, as may be supposed, soon assembled. The other two elephants – Jim and Rose – were sent for to draw them from their place of confinement, and in the meantime, after about one hour's working, the pavement was removed, and an incline made from the cellar. When this was completed, the keepers had provided themselves with a supply of bread, which they broke up and gave to the elephants, who quietly walked up the incline and allowed themselves to be coupled by the chains which they wore. They were then led four abreast to the camping ground at Agincourt Park.
22/3/1884

A PRINTER'S error may prove expensive. A pianist and composer of New York has brought a suit against Chickering and Son, the piano makers, to recover $10,000 damages, because in a concert programme he was described as "the milkman pianist," the word "milkman" being a misprint for "well-known."
19/4/1884

ONE of the greatest difficulties managers of theatres have to contend with is the practice indulged in by gentlemen of smoking cigarettes between the acts. Mr John Huy, the acting-manager of the St James's Theatre, is the latest victim of the violation of the rules set down for public safety. A few nights ago, after the first act of *The Ironmaster*, a gentleman who, in spite of numerous remonstrances, insisted upon smoking, flung Mr Huy to the ground, and severely injured his knee joint. Mr Huy is now under the doctor's hands, and is confined to his room unable to walk. It is likely that he will be disabled for several weeks.

THE latest form of complimenting a composer who produces a successful opera is to present him with a wreath. This was done on Monday night at Drury-lane, when Mr Villiers Stanford produced *The Canterbury Pilgrims* for the first time. Wreaths are all very well, but what can a composer do with them? Here was a wreath big enough to cover a dining room table, or to make a wheel for a wagonette, or it might have been worked up for a tricycle, or used as the fly-wheel for a steam engine. But Mr Stanford evidently wished the wreath at the bottom of the sea, with all its fluttering ribbons.
3/5/1883

MR OTTLEY, the late lessee of the Theatre Royal, Darwen, was to have taken his benefit a few nights since, and the play of *Hamlet* was to have been performed. The curtain rose upon an audience of seven persons, scattered about in various parts of the building, and Mr Ottley requested them to concentrate themselves in the centre boxes, so that he might see them. When they had done so he proceeded to address them, and said that he and his company had been performing at that theatre for a week without having anything like the semblance of an audience. He had, therefore, been studying the placards upon the walls of the town with a view to learn what sort of amusements the people of Darwen patronised, and he had noticed that these consisted chiefly of temperance and religious meetings. There was also a circus announced, which might possibly offer some little attraction. On looking further he found that the town was about to be honoured by the visit of an educated pig, and that, too, might interest some portion of the inhabitants. He had only one thing to suggest about the pig, and that was, so far as the taste of the people of Darwen were concerned, the pig's education had been thrown away, and that an uneducated pig would have suited them quite as well. "This," says a local writer, "is rather hard hitting, but it is only fair to this rising young actor, Mr Ottley, and also to the good people of Darwen, to state that the hands were on strike, and that the most intellectual and respectable townspeople could not leave their homes in safety."
10/5/1884

THE following "special notice" was recently issued from the Royalty Theatre, Glasgow: – "As certain Glasgow papers have expressed their disapproval of the gentlemen's evening-dress worn by the ladies who impersonate the 'Mashers' in *Silver Guilt*, Mr Cowper begs to announce that he has procured some kilts, which will be worn in addition to the trousers complained of."
31/5/1884

WANTED, a Large DOG, Must be young, thoroughly trained for Dog Pieces. State qualifications and price. A Newfoundland Dog preferred. Must be well up in the business. Address, SULLIVAN'S Coloured "Merry Moments," Winter Palace, New Brighton.
7/6/1884

TO THE EDITOR OF THE ERA.
Sir, – Will you allow me through your paper to state my own experience of the riots at Lichfield, showing that the reports in the papers were not at all exaggerated? I am playing Lady Blanche in the *Princess Ida* company, which was at Lichfield last week.
  On Friday night the disturbances were so great, the remarks of the officers* respecting the persons on the stage were so offensive, that it was almost impossible to go on with the performance. I myself was kept waiting several minutes on the stage before I could make myself heard, so great was the noise.

After the performance the officers locked the manager in the pay office, and took away the key. He was only liberated by a gentleman bursting open the door.

On Saturday night, between the second and third acts, they took up the carpet in front of the stalls and threw it into the orchestra. After the performance they took possession of the hall, and, one of the officers sitting down at the piano, the others joined him in a disgustingly vulgar comic song. I was going to London by the midnight train, and the only way I was able to leave the hall was by being passed out through a house adjoining.

When the cab which I had ordered to take me to the station was drawn up at the door, it was immediately set upon, the cabman's hat was knocked off, and he was pulled off the box. They then rushed with the cab up the street, and I was obliged to procure another, and go by a circuitous way to the station in order to get clear of the riots. Yours faithfully, ADA DOREE. Banbury, June 19th, 1884
*Of the Royal Staffordshire Yeomanry, who were assembled in Lichfield for their annual drill.
21/6/1884

MISS KATE VAUGHAN was recently sitting writing in her dining-room, when suddenly there fell upon her head about five square feet of ceiling. She was rendered insensible for a time, but happily beyond a fright and a shock, sustained no personal injury. We heartily congratulate the bright and accomplished young actress upon her escape.

THERE was an amusing incident on Monday last at the Theatre Royal, Leeds. In the last act of *Proved True* there is a double scene, embracing interior and exterior. The villain of the play was seen eavesdropping, and the audience was breathless, when a voice from the front cried out to the characters in the interior "He's listening outside!" There was a roar of laughter not intended by the author.
5/7/1884

AMONG the annoyances the actor has to endure is one that comes from the industrious nut-cracker, who usually keeps up a running fire throughout the performance. Sometimes the annoyance is so great that the much-vexed Thespian ventures on a protest. At the Theatre Royal, West Hartlepool, the other evening, the villain of the piece – well played by Mr Stewart – having been brought to book, was being led from the stage by a couple of detectives, when, turning on his late victims, he observed, with appropriate dramatic gesture, "The greatest misery I wish upon you is that you may be cursed with an audience that cracks nuts throughout your performance." The nut-cracking ceased, and Mr Stewart went off amidst a storm of laughter and applause.
12/7/1884

CLARA JARDINE, a visitor from Denmark-street, Cloudesley-road, Islington, died suddenly in the ball-room at the Hall-by-the-Sea, Margate, on Tuesday night. The room was crowded with dancers at the time, and the occurrence caused great excitement. The deceased was twenty-six years of age.

WANTED, for Tour, a Through Practical PIANIST, to tour with Miss Millie Christine, the Two-Headed Nightingale*. Must be able to read music at sight, and dress well. Send full particulars to BOSCO, Acting-Manager, 22, Seymour-street, Liverpool.
*Millie and Christine McCoy (1851-1912) were conjoined twins who toured the world with their song and dance act.
16/8/1884

SUDDEN DEATH OF A MIDGET.
Lily Evans, alias the "Lilliputian Wonder," and the "Smallest Midget in the World," died suddenly in Birmingham on Tuesday. The child, who was two months old, was only nine inches in length, and weighed but ten ounces, her body being quite perfect. The parents, who had previously had several

healthy, full-grown children, let out the "Lilliputian" for 30s. a week to a showman of monstrosities, who has exhibited her in a hall at the corner of Albert-street, Birmingham. The levees commenced at nine o'clock a.m., and continued till midnight, the mite being shown to the audiences several times an hour by Madame Baker, the "celebrated phrenologist," and wife of the showman, who would "challenge the world to find so diminutive a midget and forfeit £100 if beaten." The child was born prematurely, and, according to the mother, the diminutiveness was owing to her having been frightened by a monkey which was capering on an organ shortly before the birth. On Saturday the midget, though apparently ill, went through her "performances" until twelve o'clock at night. The next morning the tiny creature became worse, and medical assistance, which proved of no avail, was resorted to. The coroner decided to hold an inquest on the little corpse on Thursday. [...]

Emma Evans, the wife of a mechanic living in Frances-street, and the mother of the diminutive infant, said that for the past two or three weeks she had let the child to Mr Baker, a showman, who exhibited it in a room at the corner of Albert-street and Dale-end, Birmingham, and for which she received 30s. a week.

The Deputy Coroner – Who issued this programme: "The Midget. Every person, from her Majesty down to the lowest subject, should pay a visit to this wonderful being?" Witness – Mr Baker did.

And then followed a challenge to the world to produce so small a child? – He did challenge the world.

Your baby has beaten them all? – Oh, yes.

Mrs Evans, continuing, said that many persons came to see the child, but she could not say how much the showman earned. The child was exhibited from dinner time to nine or ten at night, but not often longer. On Sunday morning the child was seized with a convulsive fit, and medical assistance was called in, but death took place the following day whilst being taken out for a drive, in order to get better, as it was to commence a tour at Nottingham with the showman next day.

Is it not a fact that you were drunk when the child was being exhibited last Thursday afternoon? – No. Some woman said that I was drunk. People have said all sorts of things about me, but I never get drunk.

In reply to further questions the woman admitted that the infant had been kept awake for exhibition purposes.

Mrs Whitfield, a woman who was engaged by the showman as dress-maker and attendant on "the Midget," said that she had to make a new dress of silk and satin every day for the child. The mother had been drinking very freely while the child was performing, as she received a lot of money from Mr Baker for letting him show it.

The Deputy Coroner – Was she drunk nearly the whole of the time? Witness – Yes, she was.

How did the child look? Like a regular show baby. It was exhibited every five minutes during the day, except when it had a rest at dinner and tea times, when it was suckled by the mother when sober. When the mother was drunk the child was fed on scalded biscuits.

But she was nearly always drunk? Yes. (Sensation.)

Mr Alfred Naylor Darlington, surgeon, testified to death ensuing from convulsions accelerated by exhibitions, and aggravated by the mother spasmodically giving it proper food. The child was not in a fit state to be exhibited when he saw it.

The mother, recalled, said, in answer to the deputy coroner, that she intended to bury the body, because she was now told it was "too far gone." She spoke to the showman about it, who said she could get £20 for the body. She would have sold it if she had thought she was allowed to do so, but did not understand the law.

The Deputy Coroner, in summing up, said the case was a most extraordinary one. The mother, not satisfied with killing the child, was anxious to make money out of the dead body. The child being kept awake for exhibition purposes during lengthened hours and the mother's drunken habits had undoubtedly accelerated death. Owing, however, to the evidence of the surgeon that he could not say that death had been directly brought about by the mother, he did not think the jury would be justified in returning a verdict of manslaughter against her, though she might deserve it. The child being so weakly, it was not likely that any doctor could say that it would have lived, although there was no doubt that the treatment it had received had accelerated death. The woman's conduct had been most brutal, but the coroner's officers would see that the body was not made a market of for her profit; that it was in no way tampered with; but that, on the other hand, it had a proper burial.

The jury found that the "Midget" died from convulsions brought about by the neglect of the mother, and accelerated by being exhibited, and that she deserved censure for her cruel conduct.

The mother being recalled, received a severe censure, the deputy-coroner stating that she had narrowly escaped being committed for trial for manslaughter, and added that she might yet be proceeded against by the police.

THE latest novelty in the "show" business is an exhibition of noses, which has recently been held in Austria. Eighty persons competed for the prize offered for the most extraordinary nasal protuberance in form, size, and colour. It was awarded to a competitor from Vienna, who is possessed of what is said to be a gigantic nose of deep violet blue.
23/8/1884

FUNERAL OF THE BIRMINGHAM MIDGET.

Some extraordinary scenes were witnessed at Birmingham on Sunday in connection with the funeral of the "Midget." After the death the mother was anxious to dispose of the body to a showman, but, in order to defeat this object, the deputy-coroner, Mr Weekes, ordered the corpse to be under police surveillance until after the burial. The coffin of the mite was 13½ in. long, 6in. wide, and 4½ in. deep, and bore the following inscription: – "Lily Evans, the Midget, died August 18th, 1884, aged six weeks and four days." Crowds of persons besieged the house since the inquest on Thursday to get a sight of the curiosity, which was, or the coffin of which has been, on exhibition since that time, and has drawn far greater audiences than when the "Midget" was in the hands of the showman.

Early in the afternoon a mourning coach drove up to the house to convey the remains to the Birmingham Cemetery, a distance of two miles. For nearly half an hour the funeral cortege could not be got away, owing to the pressure of the enormous crowd, which filled the street and adjoining thoroughfares. The desire to see the coffin was intense, and it was even thought that there would be some serious disturbance. The mother of the Lilliputian, who was censured by the deputy-coroner for "performing to death her child," was hissed and yelled at, and would probably have been lynched but for the efficient staff of police, who kept guard and prevented any serious disturbance during the funeral march, a distance of nearly three miles. Upon the arrival at the cemetery the undertaker, Mr Edwards, took the Lilliputian coffin in his hand to the church, to the irresistible laughter of the assembled crowd, not even excepting the number who were present in the sad position of mourners or relatives of persons being buried.

Throughout the day the house of the "Midget" was surrounded with persons, and notwithstanding the assertions that the corpse had been abstracted for embalming and exhibition purposes, it is a fact that the body was actually buried, the coroner's chief officer opening the lid of the coffin just before the funeral took place to see that there had been no "kidnapping."

TO THE EDITOR OF THE ERA.

Sir, – I am now on tour with my concert company, and on the 23rd inst. I made application for the Argyle Hall, Cambuslang. I enclose reply from hall-keeper of the above, which I have no doubt will prove amusing to your readers. I am, faithfully yours, HARRY LINN. Cambuslang, Aug. 25th, 1884.

"Dear Sir, I love you Tonight, and Begs to Let you Know that the Hall is not now being let for Concerts, and Dear Sir I would take this opertunity of warning you to flee from the wrath to Come. Do you ever think of the judgement Day it is certain to Come, and you cannot escape it. The Trumpet will Sound, the Dead will rise from their graves and stand before Christ to receive their Sentience and you will be their – if not Saved. How Shale we escape if we neglect a Great Salvation. – D.S."

NOTICE TO PROPRIETORS. – It has been said that MINNIE GOUGH depends upon nothing but vulgarity for her success. She has just concluded a most successful Engagement at my hall without the slightest taint of the above, and re-engaged for her refinement. – Yours, Signor DURLAND, Star Music Hall, Sunderland.
30/8/1884

WANTED, a DOORSMAN, that speaks the French language, for England's Champion Stout Barmaid Exhibition, now travelling the Continent; good salary given. Address, JOHN BLAND, Poste Restante, Lille, France. Would like to hear from Mrs Skinner.
13/9/1884

MR GEORGE GROSSMITH and Mr Rutland Barrington have been poisoned by oysters. They partook of a few "natives" for luncheon after rehearsal last Thursday week (September 18), and the next morning both were seized with cholerine. Mr Grossmith, who was at Datchet at the time, was so seriously indisposed that he could not play at the Savoy Theatre either Friday or Saturday. This is all the more unfortunate, for he has only just returned from an autumn holiday in North Wales, the first that he has had for seven years.

THE humble playgoers of Lancashire occasionally give vent to their feelings in a very rough-and-ready fashion. At the Theatre Royal, Oldham, on Monday evening, during the initial performance of *The Two Orphans*, a couple of amusing incidents took place. The first occurred in the second act, outside the church of St Martin, where Louise, the blind girl, is asking alms of the worshippers as they ascend the steps of the sacred edifice. At this point the vagabond Jacques very roughly handles the poor girl, and, amid breathless silence, some occupant of the pit, a female – unable, no doubt, to control her feelings – shouted out in right good earnest, "Thou art a bad 'un!" Incident No. 2 was reserved for the last act, the interior of Frochard's garret, where the old hag gives Louise a kick as she is reclining on her pallet of straw. The act was no sooner committed than another excited female in the pit called out – "Thou bad bitch!" It is needless to say that both these incidents caused much amusement.

A RECENT application at a police-court established the fact that daubing advertisements on the footpath by a stealthy application of a perforated tin plate and a paintbrush dipped in paint or pitch is a decidedly illegal proceeding. "I never knew an advertisement of this kind afford satisfaction but in one instance," says Mr E.L. Blanchard. "When Mr George Rignold occupied Drury-lane Theatre for a short season about five years since he had the announcement of his appearance in a Shakespearian play stencilled in this manner along the flagstones of the Embankment. I once had the good fortune, about this time, to encounter in my progress along that thoroughfare a proud father leading by the hand his little boy furnished with an armful of birthday presents. Stopping at a flagstone inscribed "*Henry V.* To-night," the little fellow, with his features beaming with pride and amazement, pointed to the mysterious record, and exclaimed – 'Look here, papa, the gentlemen of the pavement know my age exactly; but how did they learn that I was going to celebrate my fifth birthday this evening?' I fancy the parent, who was manifestly not well versed in contemporary theatrical history, was as much astonished as his little son Henry, for he applied to me, an absolute stranger, to obtain an elucidation of the mystery."
27/9/1884

WILLIAM LOOKER ROACH, a man attired in a red waistcoat and knee-breeches, tied with green ribbon, was charged on remand at the Westminster Police-court, on Monday, with assaulting Mr William Woodward, landlord of a public house, in Regency-street, Westminster. Mr T.D. Dutton prosecuted, on

behalf of the Westminster and Pimlico Licensed Victuallers' Association. Prisoner went into Mr Woodward's house shortly before closing time on Saturday night week. He was refused permission to sing character songs, and thereupon used very bad language. Mr Woodward endeavoured to quiet him, and received a violent probe in the stomach with the end of a thick stick, used by the prisoner as a shillelagh. Prisoner, who described himself as an "Irish delineator," said no serious assault was intended. Mr Partridge sentenced him to two months' hard labour.
11/10/1884

LATE on Friday night, the 24th ult., an indignant crowd completely wrecked a travelling show located in Stratford fair, in which, it was alleged, indecent performances were being given. The exhibition had just been cleared preparatory to another performance, when the crowd demolished it, or serious consequences might have ensued. As it was, a female performer narrowly escaped injury from the falling timber.
1/11/1884

AN ingeniously funny gentleman recently paid a visit to our office, and when he had gone we found that he had been amusing himself by writing upon one of our blotting pads the following lines: –
   Five and twenty years ago
   I swore that I would be a pro.,
   And now I work in travelling shows.
   How I live Lord only knows.
We print this as an awful example not to be imitated.
8/11/1884

ON Wednesday last in the final scene of *Romeo and Juliet* at the Lyceum, where Juliet slowly awakens while Romeo drinks the fatal draught, some little amusement was caused by an excited female in the pit, who called aloud, "Don't drink, don't drink! She's alive, she's alive!"

MR EDITOR. – Sir, would you kindly correct an error of your Leeds correspondent, who describes me as a one-legged dancer. I am thankful to say I have always possessed two of these members, and it should have been, yours respectfully, WILL WHITE, variety comedian and dancer, Victoria Music Hall, Bolton, November 13th, 1884.
15/11/1884

JAMES TURNER, the man in custody charged with raising an alarm of fire at the Star Theatre, Glasgow, and so causing a panic by which fourteen persons were killed and as many injured, was on Saturday liberated by order of Crown counsel in respect of insufficient evidence to establish a charge of culpable homicide on which he had been committed for trial. The statements of witnesses as to the locality in the theatre in which the cry of "Fire!" was first raised were most conflicting.

PROFESSOR BLACKIE delivered a lecture on the love-songs of Scotland last Sunday to four thousand persons in St Andrew's Hall, Glasgow. He said some people thought it profane to deliver such a lecture on Sunday, but what was said on weekdays should be said on Sunday. Ministers opposed his speaking on love-songs and beautiful women, but clergymen usually sought for beautiful wives, especially with big purses. He liked to see a woman's beautiful face but never looked at her ankles. Professor Blackie sang a Scotch ballad, "Will ye gang to Kelvin Grove, bonnie lassie, O."
13/12/1884

6
1885
SWEET SOUNDS FROM GAS

WANTED, the NAME and ADDRESS of the Unprincipled Person who is going about the Country representing himself as the Patentee of A. Slocombe's Automaton Birds for Shooting Saloons, &c. N.B. – The Patentee or his Authorised Agents are the only persons who can supply this latest Novelty. Apply, BAKER and Co., 9, High-street, Bull Ring, Birmingham.
3/1/1885

THERE was a bit of unrehearsed pantomime at the Theatre Royal, Oldham, on Saturday night last. A jolly sailor was figuring on the stage, rolling the goggle eyes of his huge mask, and doing his level best to please the crowded audience, but had not calculated how many paces he might with safety take to the front. There was a thrill of expectant excitement when he was seen to advance to the footlights; there was a still greater thrill when he was seen to tumble over them; and there was a burst of applause when he pitched over into the orchestra on top of the leader and the first flute player, breaking one of the music stands in his unlucky descent. He eventually recovered his equilibrium, and the performance then proceeded as quietly as if nothing had occurred.

THE NOSE MACHINE quickly Shapes the Cartilage of the Nose by judicious pressure. 10s. 6d.; free by post; of ALEX. ROSS, 21, LAMB'S CONDUIT-STREET, LONDON W.C.
10/1/1885

A LUDICROUS, but somewhat dangerous, incident occurred on Saturday night at the Foresters' Hall, Canterbury. An entertainment was proceeding, which consisted of dissolving views of Egypt and the Soudan War. The gas was lowered. There was a crowded audience of members of the Canterbury Mutual Improvement Society. In the middle of a passage of thrilling interest a crash was heard, and a man's leg made its appearance through the ceiling, simultaneously with a fall of laths and plaster upon those sitting underneath. In the semi-darkness a large proportion of the audience were unable to see the cause of the noise, and considerable alarm prevailed for a few moments. This was, however, allayed by the explanation that the son of the hall custodian had gone up to attend to the ventilators, and had accidentally fallen upon the false ceiling, with the result described, and with a narrow escape of falling through into the hall. A panic was thus prevented, and merriment took the place of alarm.
24/1/1885

MADAME NINA CASTELLI, who has been appearing as the Fairy Queen in the pantomime of *Aladdin* at the New Prince of Wales' Theatre, Greenwich, made application to Mr Marsham, the sitting magistrate, at the Greenwich Police-court on Saturday under circumstances she detailed. She said that on Monday evening she was insulted in the theatre, and refused to go on on Tuesday unless an apology were given.

Some persons in a box had a number of small bouquets, which they threw at every lady on the stage but herself, her good songs being passed over and flowers thrown to the ballet girls. In the last scene they threw flowers over her head to the chorus girls, and the last four, which were very wet, they threw on her bare arms. Mr Lloyd Clarance, who had charge of the pantomime, picked them up and offered them to her; but she refused them, saying she did not accept flowers after the ballet girls. Subsequently Mr Lloyd Clarance came to her dressing-room and abused her for refusing the flowers. He said "---- you, madam," which she would not put up with from her own husband, let alone from him. She sent a message that unless he apologised she would not appear on Tuesday, and she had not appeared since.

On Tuesday one of the chorus was put on in her place and under her name, and she was going to take proceedings for damage to her artistic reputation. She wanted to know if she could compel Mr Lloyd Clarance to pay her for the six weeks' engagement and "the run." Mr Marsham said her remedy could only be in a civil action. He thought she was justified in refusing to appear if she was insulted, but but advised her to explain that she would carry out her engagement if an apology were given. The applicant thanked his worship and retired.

31/1/1885

ON Monday and Tuesday evenings last Mr Carl Rosa's opera company appeared in Messrs Bass and Co's (the great brewers) branding room, at Burton-on-Trent, the pieces presented being *Il Trovatore* and *Maritana*. The large room, which is situated in the heart of the brewery, was tastefully decorated, and contained a first-class stage, built specially for the occasion; while every convenience was accorded the company in this novel situation, their railway carriage, containing luggage, &c., being taken by the firm's own engine to within a few yards of the stage door. A large and fashionable audience was present each evening

WE regret to announce the death of Captain A.P. Hobson, for many years manager of the Westminster Aquarium. It appears that a few days since Captain Hobson, in stepping from the stage of the Aquarium to the ground, placed his foot upon a cane-bottomed chair, which gave way, resulting in a fall, in which he received some slight abrasions on one of his legs. Evidences of blood-poisoning soon showed themselves, and he died at his residence at Ealing on Wednesday night. A meeting of the directors was held yesterday to appoint his successor, but the matter has not yet been finally decided.

HORSEWHIPPING AN ACTRESS.
AT the Ramsgate Petty Sessions on Monday last, before Mr H. Curling and a full bench of magistrates, Miss Sophie Miles, manageress of Sanger's Amphitheatre, was charged with assaulting Annie Ricketts, an actress at the same theatre, on the 6th instant; and Annie Ricketts was charged with assaulting Sophie Miles by horsewhipping her in Hardres-street, Ramsgate, on the 9th instant. The court was densely crowded. Mr G.W. Churchley, solicitor, of 15, Broad-court, Bow-street, W.C., and Ramsgate, appeared for Miss Sophie Miles.

It appeared that the 6th instant, the date of the first alleged assault, was Miss Sophie Miles's benefit, and the performance was under the patronage of the Mayor and Corporation of Ramsgate, and the officers of the local volunteer corps. The play announced was *Hamlet*, the beneficiare playing the title role, and Miss Ricketts being cast for Osric, but at the morning's rehearsal Miss Ricketts was so imperfect in her words that the character was taken from her and given to another lady. After rehearsal Miss Miles and Miss Ricketts went to an oyster shop, and while eating oysters the latter lady seized a knife and stabbed at Miss Miles, cutting her jacket, saying "If I don't play Osric you shall not play Hamlet. I will have your life." Miss Miles got away, and, while taking her rest in the afternoon, found Miss Ricketts in her apartment, and, according to the latter lady, Miss Miles violently assaulted her, nearly strangling her, and accusing her of impropriety with Mr Sam Storey (Miss Sophie Miles's husband). Miss Ricketts had to be turned out of the house, but obtained admission behind the scenes of the theatre, and had to be ejected thence, screaming violently, and causing considerable alarm amongst the audience. Miss Sophie Miles was so agitated that she fainted upon the stage and the performance had to be suspended. On Monday, the 9th inst., as Miss Sophie Miles was proceeding to the theatre accompanied by her husband and two other members of her company, Miss Ricketts was waiting armed with a whip, and struck at Miss Miles, but the whip was wrested from her and produced in court.

Miss Ricketts pleaded guilty, and was recommended to mercy by Miss Miles. The bench considered the justice of the case would be met by ordering each party to be bound over in her own recognisances in £10 to keep the peace for six months. An altercation afterwards ensued as to the possession of the whip, which was eventually borne off by Miss Miles's party as a trophy.
21/2/1885

AT a garden party given by the Governor of New Zealand in Christchurch, Miss Genevieve Ward was among the guests, and the wife of an archdeacon, noted for her dislike to the theatrical profession, was also present. The latter dame was not acquainted with Lady Jervois, the governor's wife, but, struck by the appearance of Miss Ward, jumped at the conclusion that she saw her hostess in the striking-looking lady who bore herself so regally. Without waiting for an introduction, she hastened to present herself, and a brief but pleasant conversation ensued; and the archdeaconess, turning to a friend who had watched the interview in surprise, exclaimed, "What a charming woman Lady Jervois is!" "What!" said her friend. "Why, that's Miss Genevieve Ward, the actress!" Paralysed with horror, Mrs Archdeacon gasped, staggered, and fled, and the incident will be a popular story in Christchurch for many a day.
28/2/1885

SPANISH FLY (Cantharides) quickly restores Hair and produces Whiskers. Marvellous for hair growth. 3s. 6d.; sent free for Fifty-four Stamps. Complexion pills, 2s. 9d. Harmless.
7/3/1885

ON Friday, the 6th inst., the Coroner for Central Middlesex, Dr George Danford Thomas, held an inquest at the Royal Free Hospital, Gray's Inn-road, respecting the death of Annie Jones, otherwise Mabel McKenzie, aged twenty, an actress.

Evidence was given showing that the deceased was upon Wednesday afternoon, the 23rd of last month, in the drawing-room of No. 5, Millman-street, Bedford-row, with a gentleman. She played at first the piano, after which she went and sat down on the same chair with Mr Shepherd. She then stood up by the mantelshelf with her back to the fireplace, and after being there a few minutes, owing to her having on a large dress improver*, the dress, which was of a light muslin material, caught fire, and she was soon enveloped in a mass of flames. The gentleman tried to get up the hearthrug with which to put out the flames, but before he could do so the deceased rushed out of the room downstairs into the street. Some gentlemen who were passing at once took off their coats, and wrapping them round her were thus enabled to put out the flames, after which they placed the deceased in a cab and conveyed her to the hospital. Upon her being asked by Dr Spicer how the fire occurred, she stated that her dress improver projected so far out her dress caught the fire and was set in flames. The occurrence was quite accidental, and no one was to blame.

The deceased gradually sank and died on Wednesday morning from the effects of the shock and exhaustion consequent upon the extensive burns that she had received. The jury returned a verdict of "accidental death."
A pad or flexible metal frame worn at the rear of a dress to exaggerate its fullness and make the waist look smaller.
14/3/1885

AT the Theatre Royal, Manchester, on Tuesday night, there was an accident which might have proved very serious. *Claudian* was the piece performed. The arch in Claudian's palace, which forms part of the

"earthquake scene," instead of falling forward towards the audience, fell backwards on Mr Leonard Boyne, who was compelled to bear its entire weight for nearly two minutes, until rescued by stage-men. He received a most severe muscular strain, and was carried to his dressing-room. After a delay of not more than fifteen minutes, however, he gamely struggled through the last act, but even the next day was suffering greatly from the shock.
21/3/1885

TO THE EDITOR OF THE ERA.
Sir, – When visiting Derby last autumn a gold watch and chain, enclosed in a silk purse or bag, were thrown to me on my last entrance in *Les Cloches de Corneville* by a Mr James Gentles sitting in the stalls. This gentleman was a perfect stranger to me, and I have never seen or heard of him since, till I received a letter last week from him, asking me to return the watch and chain and name a sum of money for parting with it. I returned him the articles in question, with a letter stating that unless there were very grave reasons for his conduct I should deem it an insult, and in any case should not dream of accepting any compensation. I received from him a letter stating that "at the time he threw it he was a minor, and consequently not responsible for his actions; that he considered the watch and chain to be *his* property, and that he had *lost* it – for he had *lost* it, as, if he had been in his right mind, he should never have parted with it, and was therefore entitled to have it returned to him." As the incident of the watch found its way into your paper at the time, I venture to hope you will kindly insert this letter as a warning to any lady visiting Derby, and becoming, in her professional capacity, the recipient of gifts publicly presented by Mr James Gentles, of that town. I am, yours faithfully, ANNIE HOWARD, Prince's Theatre, Bristol., March 24th, 1885.
28/3/1885

NOTICE. A Fortune to a good Showman. THE Greatest Monstrosity of the Age, the ELEPHANT MAN, is out of an Engagement. Would only show on the Continent. Has shown with great success in England. For photos and terms, apply to Agent, Mr SAM TORR, Gaiety Palace, Leicester.
25/4/1885

ON Tuesday Charles Henry Hodson, an actor, was indicted at the Liverpool Assizes for having thrown a quantity of vitriol over his wife, Louisa Hodson, with intent to maim her. It appeared that the prisoner and his wife were living apart, and the prosecutrix had fulfilled various theatrical engagements, part of the proceeds of which she had been in the habit of sending to her husband. In March last she was engaged at the Prince of Wales's Theatre, Liverpool, and the prisoner followed her to that city, intercepted her as she was leaving the theatre one evening, and threw a cupful of vitriol over her face. The result of this was that the sight of the right eye was destroyed, and the face permanently disfigured. The defence was that the prisoner, who was in a very weak state of health at the time, was exasperated by having got possession of letters which tended to show that his wife had been unfaithful to him. The jury found the prisoner guilty, but strongly recommended him to mercy. He was sentenced to five years' penal servitude.*
Hodson died in prison a few weeks later.
2/5/1885

ELOPEMENT WITH A SHOWMAN.
A remarkable case of elopement from Sunderland has just transpired. A moulder named Cook a few weeks ago allowed his wife to go to Hartlepool to visit her parents. He heard nothing of her until the 3rd inst., when she called at this house for some articles belonging to her, being accompanied by a man who carried a formidable stick. Cook then learned that his wife was sharing the fortunes of Momus de Faulke, "the great exposer of the shams of modern spiritualism," sword swallower, and itinerant showman. On Saturday Momus pitched his tent in Sunderland Market, Mrs Cook acting as money-taker.

The outraged husband entered the show, and told the story of his wrongs to the spectators with such eloquence that the personal safety of his wife was threatened. The indignation of those inside the show was communicated to the crowd outside, and the assistace of the police and the officers of the market was necessary to remove the woman. Mr Cook stated that his wife threatened him with the vengeance of "dear Fred de Faulke" if he dared to interfere with her choice. She is about thirty-three years of age and the mother of two children.
16/5/1885

BALLOON ACCIDENT AT DUDLEY. – At the Dudley Castle fête last Tuesday evening Captain Morton was ascending from the courtyard in his new balloon when the car caught in the ruins, dislodging four cornice stones, which fell on a stage below. Several acrobats had a narrow escape, and the aeronauts were crushed and bruised.
30/5/1885

AN impudent rascal named Rubinstein recently obtained from Mr H.R. Sharman, the secretary of the Albert Palace, Battersea-park, a season ticket, by describing himself as a representative of *The Era*. As it is possible this impostor will attempt a similar dodge at other places of entertainment, we put managers on their guard against him, and would suggest that, if opportunity occurs, they should hard him over to the tender mercies of the nearest policeman.

MR JULIAN CUNNINGHAM, M.A., on the evening of Monday last had a terrible experience, and one that we should say will lead him in the future to fight shy of historical dramas by the Poet Laureate. He had undertaken to recite Lord Tennyson's *Becket*, and so great was the public anxiety to hear him and it that there was a rush of exactly thirteen persons, of whom three or four were representatives of the press. One of the auditors went to sleep very soon after the commencement, and another quietly made his exit when he found that *Becket* was very dry and uninteresting. A policeman, however, made up for this desertion, and manfully stood out the first act, while the attendants now and then put in their heads with a grin on their faces, as though to say, "Well, this 'ere *is* a rum go." Mr Cunningham has a splendid memory, for he attacked his herculean task without the aid of book or notes, and seldom, if ever, faltered or stumbled right up the end of the long first act. How he got on after that, and whether he finished to an empty hall we are not in a position to state, for we confess that one act of *Becket* was enough, and more than enough, for us and our patience. In addition to a splendid memory, Mr Cunningham must be possessed of splendid courage. It is just possible though, that he was not aware what a beggarly array of empty benches he talked to, for he never so much as glanced at the few who listened, but, remembering that walls have ears, addressed himself to them. Mr Cunningham showed great want of judgement in selecting such a work as *Becket* for recital, and for his error, we suppose, will have to pay pretty smartly. Thirteen people, including press representatives, do not contribute much, we should say, towards the expense of hiring an establishment like Prince's Hall.
6/6/1885

AT the Westminster Police-court, on Saturday, Charles John Mansell, aged forty-three, music teacher and dealer in music instruments, in business in St John's-hill, New Wandsworth, was charged with being a lunatic at large, and not under proper control. Spooner, 281 B, gave evidence that at seven o'clock on Friday evening the prisoner behaved in a most extraordinary manner in Montpelier-street, Brompton. He ran about the roadway gesticulating wildly, and presented his card to witness, saying that he must take his number. He then said that he had been tuning an organ at a chemist's shop, where there was a lady in love with him. He jumped in and out of two hansom cabs, and was then taken in custody as a lunatic.

The defendant, in the course of a long address to the magistrate, said that he was an exhibitor at the Albert Palace, and had two stalls there. The other day, whilst playing the organ there, two ladies came up, and one of them looked at him in a very fascinating way. She gave him her card, and spoke to him in such a loving manner that that he had pleasure in acceding to her request to visit her, so that he might tune her piano. Afterwards he telegraphed to her, and on the previous day he went to tune the instrument, the house he visited being in Montpelier-street. Whilst he was tuning he was so overcome by the fascination of the young lady, who looked like Mrs Weldon*, and he felt so funny that he could not stop any longer, so he hurriedly put the piano together, packed up his traps, and got into the street.

Dr Ridger, of 321, Brompton-road, said the defendant told him the same story, and he considered that he was insane.

Defendant remarked that his experience might seem strange, but he was rational enough, and almost a teetotaller. In fact, he never drank spirits.

Mr Alfred William Mansell, builder and decorator, of Creek-street, Battersea, said the defendant, his brother, was a tuner by profession, and an exhibitor at the Albert Palace. He had been very strange in his manner during the past week, and his wife had left him, fearing his violence. He was certainly under the delusion that ladies were in love with him, and had the most extravagant notions on that point. A brother had committed suicide though insanity.

Mr D'Eyncourt remanded the defendant, so that arrangements could be made with the district relieving officer to remove him to a place of safe custody.

*Georgina Weldon, a notoriously litigious amateur soprano, spiritualist and campaigner against the Lunacy Laws.
27/6/1885

ON Thursday night considerable excitement was manifested in Deptford and neighbourhood, owing to the descent of the *Eclipse* balloon in a cabbage-field in Trunley-lane, Deptford. Two balloons were observed in the neighbourhood about a quarter-past six, one of which began to descend rapidly. It then remained stationary for a short time, to the great curiosity of several thousand people, who had been attracted to the spot by the unusual sight. The balloon, which proved to be the *Eclipse*, soon came down, however, and, with assistance, Mr T. Wright, the aeronaut, secured it. It appears that one of the valves had met with an accident. The other balloon sailed away in the direction of Woolwich. Both of them ascended at the Crystal Palace, where the Metropolitan and City Police Orphanage Festival was being celebrated.

To Hotel Proprietors and Managers. MR LOUIEN, Jun., the Celebrated Female Impersonator, the Original Male Barmaid, thanks all Proprietors for their past offers, and to state that he is not dead or blind, as reported, but alive and well, and now fulfilling a most successful Third Year's Engagement at MONARCH, LANDPORT, PORTSMOUTH.
4/7/1885

THE *Morning Post* is responsible for the following funny story: – Madame Sarah Bernhardt is staying at the Star and Garter Hotel, Richmond, whither she repairs by train after the performance* at the Gaiety. On Saturday night, however, when she made her début, the close of the theatre was so late that she missed her train, and, with a maid, took a hansom. "Richmond," said the fair one. "Which way?" said the driver. "Your way, any way, Richmond!" The cabman drove off, and wandered, till after some time it dawned upon Madame Bernhardt that they were not making much way to their goal. "Oú sommes-nous? Where we?" was now shouted through the trap. "Dunno, lost," was the unsatisfactory response. "Mais je ne veux pas être lostée," said Theodora, in her firmest tones. An explanation which ensued resulted in the cabman, in spite of offers of money, declining to go a step further, his "hoss was beat," he couldn't do it, and made some proof of sincerity by declining to take any fare.

It was now very late, and the belated Empress and her attendant wandered about until a light revealed to them the shelter of a police-station. They found they were at Putney, and a policeman volunteered to

show them the Richmond road, along which they walked a long way with him till by extraordinary chance they met a fire-engine returning from its duties at a small fire in the neighbourhood. This was hailed, and for a consideration drove them to the Star and Garter, where Theodora arrived on this extraordinary conveyance at four o'clock in the morning. The hotel was shut up, but in the early dawn a group soon collected, attracted by the appearance of the fire-engine, and imagining that it had been summoned to the great hotel. Shouts of fire soon brought the inmates to the windows, and the doors were thrown open to welcome their guest after her strange adventure.
In the title role of the Byzantine empress in Sardou's Theodora.
18/7/1885

A RESPECTABLE-LOOKING female came before Mr Biron at the Lambeth Police-court on Tuesday and asked his assistance. She stated that her daughter, at the age of ten years, went with a troupe of performers. The troupe visited Mexico and other places. She would now be seventeen, and applicant had not seen her for two years. She had been to the agent, who would not see her, but a little boy there told her the girl was dead, and that she had been shot by accident in Mexico. He added that a doctor saw her, but that she was buried without any coffin. She asked his worship to assist her in the matter. Mr Biron did not see how he could do anything for her. The story told to her might not be true. Applicant said she wanted to have the matter explained by the agent. Mr Biron said he would do what he could to help the applicant, and gave directions to Sergeant Underwood to make enquiries about the matter. The applicant thanked his worship.
It later emerged that the girl was shot dead whilst at dinner in a hotel in Zamora, Mexico.
25/7/1885

A HEALTH BATH FOR DOGS is obtained by using NALDIRE'S MEDICATED SOAP (free from poison). Fleas destroyed, skin cleansed, all doggy smell removed from the coat, and the animal soothed and refreshed. Sold by Chemists, Perfumers, and Stores. N.B. – See that you obtain Naldire's Soap (Prize Medal) – (ADVT)
1/8/1885

PIANOFORTE players have always complained of the difficulty of making the ring-finger work as freely as the others, and according to the *British Medical Journal* Mr Noble Smith, of Queen Anne-street, has by a delicate operation succeeded in enlarging the powers of the pianist. He says: – "I have just succeeded in freeing the ring-finger of the right hand of an accomplished lady pianist, without causing her much more pain than is felt from the prick of a needle. Before operation she was able to raise the finger only five-eighths of an inch beyond the others. Directly after operation she could raise the finger easily to one and a half inches, without the least loss of control over its action. The division was, of course, made subcutaneously, so that only a minute wound was left in the skin, one-eighth of an inch in length."
8/8/1885

Extraordinary Freak of Nature. FOR SALE, THREE-LEGGED LAMB, born February, 1885. No deformity in place of fourth limb, runs with flock, and is perfectly healthy and active. Very fine Lamb, and the first £10 has it. J. HOULT, Newbold Manor Farm, Barton-under-Needwood, Burton-on-Trent.
15/8/1885

DURING the performance of the comedy of *Muddles* on Tuesday evening last, at the theatre in the Winter Gardens, Southport, it was noticed that, no matter how hearty was the laughter, some one individual was persistently hissing. Mr F.W. Sidney, who was playing the part of Mr Paul Plowter in this amusing piece, sent his acting-manager, Mr Kennedy Miller, to find out the person who was hissing, and request him to leave the theatre, offering to return him his admission money. Mr Miller soon discovered that the noise proceeded from an old gentleman who appeared to be highly delighted with the comedy, and after the second act Mr Miller induced him to come out into the hall, where the gentleman explained that he had greatly enjoyed the piece, but having undergone an operation in his throat, in the course of which a silver tube had been introduced into his windpipe, every time he laughed heartily a sibilant sound was the result of his cacchination.

A TRIO of youthful adventurers are now on a visit to Canterbury, and attract a considerable amount of interest by their artistic vocal performances. Their turnout, for street vocalists, is elaborate. On a small car, drawn by a prettily harnessed and well-groomed donkey, they have a pianette, which is skilfully manipulated by one of the party, while popular songs and classical duets are sung in good style. It is believed that the three young men occupy good positions, and that they have conceived this idea of spending a "pleasant holiday". The tourists, who are each disguised past recognition, wearing wigs, false moustaches, coloured glass spectacles, and sombrero-shaped hats, have already visited Margate, Ramsgate, and the other principal watering-places on the Kentish coast.

OLD ARTIFICIAL TEETH BOUGHT. – Persons wishing to receive full value should apply to the Manufacturing Dentists, Messrs BROWNING. If forwarded by post value per return. Chief Office, 133, Oxford-street (opposite Berners-street), London. Established 100 years.
29/8/1885

THE effect of music is curiously illustrated by the keeper of the restaurant at Theodore Thomas's Concerts at Chicago. He says, "On the nights when they play Wagner's music I sell five times as much Lager beer as usual. On Mendelssohn nights nobody wants any ham sandwiches, and, as I get eighty-five per cent. out of them, I guess I don't think much of Mr Mendelssohn. Strauss is the composer to make the wine go off. A man feels well off while he listens to a waltz of Strauss, and he orders his bottle of champagne freely."

TO THE EDITOR OF THE ERA.
Sir, – From published reports of the result of the summons heard at Marlborough-street on Saturday last respecting the electric lighted balloon advertisement of the Prince's Theatre, it might be thought that my men had carried through the streets a number of powerful arc lights to advertise *The Great Pink Pearl*. I am unwilling that it should be thought that I am capable of announcing my entertainments at a risk to the public safety. May I therefore ask you to kindly state the following facts regarding the balloons which have apparently so offended the police?

They are constructed of a light wire framework covered in silk, bearing the words, "Prince's Theatre. *Great Pink Pearl*, every evening, at nine." They measure forty-five inches in circumference, and the light inside is equal only to five-candle power, and this is considerably reduced by the colour of the silk, an ordinary pink. The balloons were carried, by the aid of canes, at the height of ten feet above the pavement, and yet the witnessing constable objected to these dim and elevated lights, his reason being that they frightened horses. My men, when cautioned by the police, were walking quietly along Piccadilly pavement on their way to Kensington with a two-fold object in view, to advertise my theatre, and to add – in a small way, truly – to the street lighting, which is but indifferent in the neighbourhood of the Inventions Exhibition.

By the magistrate's decision it is evident that the police have power to forbid or allow these balloons to be carried in the streets. I am therefore petitioning the Commissioners for the necessary permission, which, I am convinced, will be granted me when the harmless nature of the instrument is shown to them. Meanwhile I am utilizing my balloons as a stationary after-dark advertisement outside my theatre only.
I am, yours truly, EDGAR BRUCE. Prince's Theatre, September 7th.

WANTED, by FRANKS the Mouldy, Mildewed, Motheaten Clown, a Situation. Offers invited. Address, 19, Clarendon-street, Hull.
12/9/1885

AT Bow-street, on Thursday, George Williams was charged with being drunk and assaulting the police in Craven-buildings, Drury-lane. In reply to Mr Vaughan, he expressed his regret, and said he had been drinking heavily. – Mr Vaughan: But why did you get so drunk? – Defendant: I had been to see *Human Nature*, at Drury-lane, and had taken a "drop too much afterwards." – Mr Vaughan did not consider this a sufficient justification for the assault, and defendant 12s.
26/9/1885

MUSIC from gas is the latest invention. A novel musical instrument called the "Pyrophone" will shortly be introduced to the public. Its compass is three octaves, with a keyboard, and it will be played in the same manner as an organ. It has thirty-seven glass tubes, in which a number of gas-jets burn. These jets, placed in circles, contract and expand like the fingers of a hand. When the small burners separate the sound is produced, when they close together the sound ceases. The tone depends upon the number of the burners and the size of the pipes in which they burn, so that by a careful arrangement and selection all the notes of the musical scale may be produced in several octaves. Some of the glass tubes in which the jets burn are nearly eleven feet high. When the "Pyrophone" is played upon with the keyboard it gives out a rich, full tone of remarkable delicacy, and to a great extent resembling the human voice. The inventor of the "Pyrophone" was the late Frederick Kastner. We have had music from stones, from wood, and from metals of all kinds, but only a scientific German would would ever have thought of producing sweet sounds from gas. Here is comfort for the gas companies in the event of electricity becoming the chief illuminating power. It will be odd to supply long or short meter from the gas meter.

FLYING FOXES. Great attraction for Public-house Bars. A pair sent, with suitable Cage, to any address on receipt of P.O. for 30s. J. WARNCKEN, 60, Jamaica-street, London, E.
3/10/1885

"THEIR whistling noise made the birds aghast." Shelley's line naturally occurred to us when we received a letter from a correspondent at Milan announcing the arrival in the city of the Scala a company of concert performers whose talents are decidedly peculiar. The troupe, which numbers some twenty-five members, are simply whistlers! They are stated to have mastered from one end to the other the full score of *Norma*, which they execute – that must for once be the right word – with the most conscientious fidelity. Shade of Bellini, may you be spared the ordeal of hearing them! One virtuoso whistles the rôle of the Druid priestess, another that of Pollione and so on; the choruses, not one of which is omitted, are rendered by a formidable group of sixteen strong-lunged gentlemen and ladies. The fair sex appear to supply the most accomplished members to this singular band, for no gentleman could be found competent to whistle the part of Orovoso, so the venerable grey-bearded high priest is personified by a girl of fifteen, who is said to acquit herself of her arduous task to perfection.

AN exciting incident occurred on Friday, the 24th inst., at the South London Music Hall. During the performance of sleight-of-hand by Professor Hermann the conjuror descended into the body of the hall in order to "find" a rabbit on the person of one of the audience. He selected a tall and bulky individual; but this gentleman, when Hermann touched his coat, rose and struck furiously at the performer, and a struggle ensued for a few seconds amidst a scene of great excitement. The conjurer, however, persisted, and drew a rabbit from the man's coat, and amid loud shouts the individual withdrew. Later in the proceedings, however, he returned, and and such a storm arose among the audience that he had to make a hurried escape.

FOR SALE, a DONKEY that comes in Two Halves, with Working Mouth, Ears, and Eyes, Protruding Tongue, and Tail which works in all directions. Price, £6 10s. A first-class Clowning Property. My old address, WALTER TAYLOR, 20, Oxford-street; or, Pavilion Theatre, Whitechapel.

Notice to Champion Dancers. I, CHARLES SEEL, am at Liberty to Dance any man in the World, Phil Raymond included, for thousands. Twenty Yorkshire Relish Steps off the Toe and a Pea Soup Breakdown. Competitors must find their own Basins, Spoons, Salt, and Pepper. Address for next Four Weeks, PEOPLE'S MUSIC HALL, MANCHESTER. Please bring your own bibs.
10/10/1885

MRS LANGTRY has been appearing during the week with brilliant success at the Theatre Royal, Nottingham, and had created no little admiration by her remarkably clever performance as Lady Ormond in *Feril*. It has been generally remarked, though, that an actress of so much ability and of such well-won popularity should not descend to such meretricious aids as may come of advertising one's dressmaker, and the remark has had its source in the following extraordinary lines which are to be found in the "bill of the play:" – "Mrs Langtry's dresses in *Peril* are so extraordinary that a brief description may not be uninteresting. In act first Mrs Langtry wears a brown plush tea gown, with front and sleeves of cream lace; the waist encircled by a gold girdle. Act second – A grey ottoman silk costume, simply made, showing white muslin kerchief and cuffs. Act third – Pale green satin ball gown, embroidered in gold, the skirt cut in panels, opening over a skirt of pale pink mousseline de joie, studded with roses. Act fourth – A striped grey Pekin tea gown, with a front of grey mousseline de joie, embroidered in steel, and gracefully draped over pale blue. They were all supplied by Mr Worth, of Paris."

A Leicester butcher named Hubbard is lying seriously ill at Leicester Infirmary from the effects of a desperate encounter in a show at the fair. Hubbard was witnessing a Zulu perform mimic warfare, and, being suspicious that the man was painted, wetted his forefinger and touched the Zulu on the back. The Zulu at once sprang upon Hubbard, and inflicted a very serious wound with an assegai on Hubbard's face. It is feared that the man will lose his eyesight. The spectators fled, but the Zulu was secured, and Hubbard was removed to the Infirmary.
24/10/1885

OUR Belgian neighbours have invented an ingenious instrument for emitting "the dismal hiss, sound of public scorn." It is a tiny bellows, with a whistle for mouthpiece, which the spectator places under his foot, and can thus defy the most lynx-eyed policeman. At the Ghent Theatre, where this innovation is on trial, the results are highly satisfactory, uninterrupted disorder prevailing during each performance. The expulsion every night of several innocent persons, mistaken for the delinquents, heightens the enjoyment of the entertainment.

SIGNOR FOLI was recently singing at St Helen's Signor Pinsuti's capital song "The Raft." When he had just ended the first verse an infant with tremendous lungs began to chime in. Signor Foli was just beginning the line "Hark! What sound is that which breaks upon mine ear?" The coincidence was too laughable, and the singer, unable to control his mirth, was compelled to quit the platform for a brief period until his infantine rival had been quieted.

ENGLISH GIRLS AND CONTINENTAL MUSIC HALLS.
TO THE EDITOR OF THE ERA.
Sir, – I wish to call the attention of ballet ladies and amateur serio-comics to an advertisement, "Wanted, young and pretty serio-comics and dancers for the Continent." These advertisements mostly crop up in

the summer, when things are at their worst in London, and young girls are only too anxious to snap at anything to earn a livelihood. To these I say, Beware, and I issue this warning to those mad enough to come abroad knowing nothing of the country or language. I mean girls who, not having sufficient talent or experience to earn a living in England on the boards of music-hall or theatre, rush to Rotterdam, Amsterdam, or Antwerp – a fifteen-shilling journey – to certain ruin and disgrace.

Abroad, as in England, at first-class music-halls talent is the only passport to success, but, unlike England, first-class halls are few and far between, and for every one such there are twenty dens of vice and iniquity called Tingle Tangles, where talent is wholly unnecessary, and all that is required is a pretty face and an aptitude for drinking large quantities of wine and grog. Previous training is nothing, and a decent-looking servant girl is quite as eligible as a ballet lady or a milliner. Some of these dens, as a blind, are (save the mark!) called theatres; so we have Alhambra Theatres, Walhalla Theatres, Thalia Theatres, &c. The duty of the so-called artists (generally a mixture of English, French, German, and Swedes, to attract sailors of different nationalities) is to sit on a platform in Eve-like costumes, sing (or howl) a song each in rotation, talk from the stage to the young and old mashers, have wine or grog sent to them, hob and nob with the audience, listen to such language as would make the cheek of a man of the world tingle with shame, receive notes, make assignations, and bargain for the price of sin, or to go into the wine-room (generally a den behind the stage), where only men able to spend money on champagne are admitted.

Many a decent modest girl have I seen come on the Continent alone, but never one so return. Some, in fact, never get back to England at all. In nine cases out of ten it is almost impossible for a girl to remain unstained in these places. In the first place, the girl is sure to be poor, her fare is paid, and she receives probably an advance of money; she comes in debt, and in debt she remains. She cannot, dare not, leave. In nine cases out of ten she is compelled to live in the house under surveillance. Although apparently free, she is as much a prisoner as a Dartmoor convict. She then, driven to despair, escapes for a moment, and flies to Her Britannic Majesty's Consul. These Consuls are delusions and snares. They will have none of her. She is only an artist, which name abroad is only another for prostitute. In England some people imagine a British Consul is obliged to help and assist all English subjects in distress. Don't believe it; nothing of the sort. Yes, the representative of Her Majesty will see into the wrongs of a sailor, a soldier, a mechanic – but an artist, no. They come at their own risk, and may be trampled on, ruined, disgraced, starved; but from the Consul they get nothing but the cold shoulder. Some girls apply to the police. Then a nice little farce is enacted. The chief inspector listens, but does not understand one word of every twenty, although he is supposed to understand English well. He will then send an inspector with the girl to inquire into the case. The proprietor of the den tips him, of course, and he reports that the girl is quite wrong and a bad character. So, driven to despair, the girl generally gives up the unequal fight, and goes in for the short and merry life.

I am not writing this letter for the fast and brazen class who will, despite this or a thousand warnings, come and seek their fate. There are young women found in every class of society whom neither warning, example nor an engine of fifty thousand horse-power could ever keep straight. To these I have nothing to say. Let them go their way. I am equally indifferent whether they go to the bad here or in England. I pen these lines to those who are yet modest and virtuous, and who, in the innocence of their hearts, are often lured into Continental engagements by men calling themselves agents, who knowingly send these girls unprotected to these dens of iniquity, so they may get a paltry commission – men for whom the whipping-post is too good. I cast no insinuations on respectable agents, and I am sure that none but those whom the cap fits will feel aggrieved. It is to such girls as I have last alluded to, that I say live at home on a crust, go to service, better starve or go to the workhouse than come to those plague spots to join a band already too large, who are a disgrace to their country and their sex. One thing I say, in conclusion, to those men who call themselves agents, whose sole business is a traffic in English girls – Beware! The law is often evaded, but not always; and if anyone dare to dispute this state of things, I will, from my diary, publish a list of the names of the majority of wretched girls whose cases have come under my personal knowledge within the last nine years, and the names of the dens "where they have been engaged." I am, Sir, yours, &c., EDWARD J. TOWERS. October 15th, 1885.

AN APPEAL.
TO THE EDITOR OF THE ERA.
Sir, – A terrible fire occurred last week at Mr W. Miller's Birley Arms Hotel, Preston, completely gutting the building, and destroying the whole of the contents. The landlord and his wife and family have now no home, no furniture, no clothing, and no money, and, worse than the pecuniary loss, is the loss of his little daughter Jane, aged eleven years, burnt to death. I am giving Mr Miller a benefit at the Gaiety Theatre, but I wish to ask my brother and sister professionals to assist Macolla, the left-handed Paganini. This young man was living at Miller's house, and, to save his life, he dropped from the third storey window, and, alighting on his heels, unfortunately smashed the bones of both ankles. I went to see him yesterday at the infirmary. I am afraid he will henceforth be a cripple (let us hope not). All his clothing, music, and travelling basket were destroyed, leaving him entirely destitute. If ever there was a truly deserving case for immediate relief, this is one. Subscriptions may be sent to, and duly acknowledged by, Yours faithfully, HARRY YORKE. Gaiety Theatre, Preston.
7/11/1885

AN incident sadly illustrative of Australian life in the "up-country" towns took place during Miss Genevieve Ward's two nights' visit to Ararat, a town of 2,000 inhabitants. During the performance a bell was heard to ring out, and some excitement was manifested among the audience. The bell was a summons for a search party to be formed to find a child that had strayed into the bush. On returning to her hotel, a sad and silent procession of torch bearers passed up the street, and inquiry elicited that the little one, a boy of five years, had been found drowned in one of the numberless holes left by the gold seekers in the days when Ararat and its neighbourhood had 40,000 men at work to find the root of all evil.
5/12/1885

SUICIDE IN A LONDON MUSIC HALL.
Late on Friday night, 4th inst., a shocking occurrence happened at the Metropolitan Music Hall, Edgeware-road. It seems that on the previous night a young man, about twenty-one years of age, was taken to the Molyneux-street Police-station by a man well known, who stated that he thought it best to bring the young man there for the police to look after, as he seemed to be incapable of taking care of himself, and, owing to the company he had been seen with, was in danger of losing his property. It was ascertained that the young man had a purse in his possession, and it contained several sovereigns. Suddenly he disappeared out of the station, and as he was drunk the inspector sent after him, had him brought back, and charged him with being drunk. He gave the name of Thomas Stokes. About seven o'clock on Friday morning he was liberated on his own recognisances to appear and answer the charge at the Marylebone Police-court at ten o'clock the same morning.

He did not, however, surrender to his recognisances, and nothing more was heard of him until late on Friday night. Shortly after ten o'clock on that night great alarm was caused in the pit of the Metropolitan Music Hall by the discharge of firearms near the orchestra. Someone near the spot saw a young man draw a revolver from his coat pocket, place it to his left breast, discharge it, and fall down immediately. Constable Smith, 88, happened to be in the hall at the time, and seeing what had occurred immediately had the man conveyed to the St Mary's Hospital in a cab. On being examined by the house surgeon it was found that life was extinct, the bullet having, it is believed, passed through the heart. Near to where the deceased fell was found a six-chambered revolver, five chambers of which were loaded. Detective-sergeant Record afterwards saw the body at the hospital, and recognised it as the man who had been charged with drunkenness. Inquiries had been made, and it turns out the deceased name is Thomas

Arrend, and that he was footman in the family of Sir George Burrows, M.D., residing at Cavendish-square and at St Leonards.

At the inquest held by Dr Danford Thomas on Tuesday, Inspector Giles informed the court that, from inquiries made, the police had been informed that something had occurred which caused Arrend to leave St Leonards-on-sea, but that Sir George Burrows was aged eighty-five years, and declined coming up to London during such weather. The Coroner read a letter from the son of Sir George Burrows, stating that Arrend had only been in their service six weeks.

Mr William Fisher, a chemist, 32, Frankfort-terrace, said he was a visitor at the Metropolitan Music Hall on Friday night. He saw Arrend, who sat on his left hand side. During the performance the lights are lowered, and suddenly witness saw a peculiar flash, which went upwards, and witness thought that the man had shot himself in the forehead, because there was a blood mark there.

Mr E. Percival Cocksey, house surgeon at St Mary's Hospital, deposed that the cause of death was a shot wound in the upper region of the left chest.

The coroner, remarking on the case, said the man had committed some act at his employer's, was seized with remorse, got drunk in London, and in this condition committed suicide.

The jury found that the act was that of a suicide while in a state of unsound mind, brought on by excitement and excessive use of alcohol.

WANTED, Well-behaved Dwarf for a Nobleman's Costume Party in London, January, to amuse them. Send photos; shall be returned. Also Conjurers, Ventriloquists, and other Drawing-room Entertainers. MANAGER, London Entertainment Company, 31, Oxford-street, W.

WANTED, Artistes in all lines to read this. Beaver, coma, knock, ravage, recess, inject, compact, flamingo, knife, ravenous, commerce, engineer. Swivel, fleece, lottery, fleshly. Budge, paint, lottery, bucolic. – Woods's Code.
12/12/1885

ANOTHER "Peeping Tom" has been discovered at Birmingham at the Prince of Wales's Theatre. On the last night of her engagement Mrs Langtry noticed a man's face against the glass of a little window of the ventilator in her dressing-room. An alarm was raised, and it was found that an assistant in an adjoining shop had made a platform connecting the back premises with the theatre, and had by this means obtained access to the window. Mrs Langry's maid, who was with her in the dressing-room, declared that she had seen something like a man's face at the window on two or three occasions. The culprit although not discovered at the time, was unable to deny the evidence against him, and has been dismissed by his employer.

BOTH amusement and excitement resulted last week from a wager, which was made with Mr J.H. Stringer, business manager of Mr Wilson Barrett's *Hoodman Blind* company, by a musical gentleman of Hull, that he would, in fourteen days, teach a camel to dance to music. Mr Hawtrey, of the *Private Secretary* company, as well as Mr Stringer, made a bet of £50 with this individual on the disputed point, and a telegram was received from Mr Cross, of Liverpool, saying that the camel had been dispatched to Hull to take his dancing lessons. A widely-spread report soon after stated that the animal had got as far as Hessle, where it had escaped from the stables in which it was placed, and was then roaming over the adjoining country. Letters and leading articles appeared in the local papers on the subject; but eventually it came out the affair, so far as the alleged forwarding of the camel by Mr Cross was concerned, was a hoax of an elaborate nature. Whether the bet still holds good, and whether the "musical gentleman" maintains his ability to teach a "ship of the desert" to "tread a measure", is not stated in the communication which has reached us.
19/12/1885

7
1886
HE IS EATING MY BRAIN

WANTED, by the Manager, London Entertainment Company, 31, Oxford-street, W., Ventriloquists and Dissolving Views. We only advertise for what we do require. I beg to state what I have often mentioned in letters, so-called Second-Sight is not a success in the Nobility's Drawing-rooms. Their intelligence enables them to detect the manipulation of words (or code). Such rudeness as the flannel petticoat, flat-iron, and pawnticket dodge would not be tolerated. Moreover, I am writing a most complete work on the subject, notes by eminent writers, giving Heller's, Anderson's, and Keller's Ten-word Code, and the system of other small fry, entitled "The Fakes, Life, and Adventures of Dr Duck Blinker and his Second-Sight Marvel."
2/1/1886

WANTED, Little Alice, Second Sight Marvel, requests that any miserably Jealous Imbecile, pitifully struggling to damage my reputation, will not resort to the cowardly, mean, and contemptible subterfuge of Manager. Any malicious impostor ashamed of his name attacking me under such disguise, though only a child, I will find means to crucify such a despicable coward on the odium of public opinion, or with what he richly deserves, a thorough good horse-whipping. The idea of an insignificant fifth-rate would-be conjurer, that has neither talent nor brains enough to feed a nobleman's pigs or clean out his dog-kennel, talking of what is suitable for his drawing room is more than enough to make angels weep.
N.B. – There is a Home for Lost Dogs who have no name. I am proud of mine, and can be seen at ST JAMES'S THEATRE, MANCHESTER. 18th, my Fifth starring Engagement at Talbot, Nottingham.
9/1/1886

Throw Physic to the Dogs. WANTED, Professionals to Know the Manager, London Entertainment Company, 31, Oxford-street, will publish his wonderful work on Played out Second Sight (this does not apply to the Marvellous Kaspers) with a most realistic picture on second page of a quack doctor, who has been bitten by a mastiff crouching behind a child, firing off quotations from Irving Bishop's Truth. Eighteen Stamps.
16/1/1886

PISTOLS that won't go off when wanted are very aggravating properties, and have spoiled many a good "situation." There was one at the Adelphi on Tuesday. It had been borrowed to take the place of that one – under repairs – with which Mark Helstone in the second act of *The Harbour Lights* shoots Frank Moreland. Mark Helstone pulled the trigger once, he pulled the trigger twice, he pulled it thrice, but there was neither a good nor a bad report, and as the spectators were beginning to titter, he had to come from his hiding place and despatch his enemy with a blow from his fist.

VICTOR HUGO'S *Les Misérables* had been produced at the Brussels Nouveautés. On Tuesday last, in the second act of *Les Misérables*, there was a long stage wait, and the two ladies on the stage, after gagging and doing as much extraneous business as they conveniently could, folded their arms with a resigned air as much to say that it was not their fault. At length the curtain was dropped, and speedily raised, when the stage-manager announced that the play could not proceed owing to the refusal to go on of certain actors, whom he named. *O! Les misérables!*

ON Thursday, the 14th inst., Mrs Scott-Siddons was the heroine of an adventure in Cheshire, which, though happily concluded, she is not likely soon to forget. The talented artiste was specially engaged to give a dramatic reading in connection with a series of lectures organised by a literary society at the Concert Hall, Liscard, near Birkenhead. The capacious hall was crowded with an eager assembly long before the time announced for the commencement of the entertainment, fixed for eight o'clock. Half-past eight came, and still no Mrs Scott-Siddons, whose non-appearance was as great a puzzle to the committee as the audience, for it was announced that the lady had arrived in the district during the afternoon, and the indulgence of the people was asked for a little while longer. At last, shortly before nine o'clock, Mrs Scott-Siddons entered the hall, greatly to the relief of the audience.

It appeared that the unfortunate delay had arisen in this wise. Through some strange oversight, the lady had been left to find her own way from the hotel to the concert hall, and she, having forgotten the name of the place, could only tell the cabman that she was engaged to deliver a reading in connection with a series of lectures in the locality, and he must find the place. What out-of-the-way places cabby got to nobody knows, but he managed to take over an hour in a journey which should have occupied only about ten minutes, eventually, however, reaching the right destination. Mrs Scott-Siddons was greatly agitated when she arrived, and will doubtless long remember her enforced journey through the parish of Walasey in search of an audience, as well as the sympathetic way in which her graphic recital of the facts was received. The weary waiting was soon forgotten in admiration of the talents of the charming entertainer, who exerted herself to the utmost to give a happy ending to the night's adventures, in which, of course, she was completely successful.

TILLY, will you write to me? I am in awful suspense. All will be forgiven. DICK.
23/1/1886

AMERICAN bachelors ought to be grateful to Mr D'Oyly Carte for the number of attractive and marriageable young ladies whom he exports in the choruses of his American companies. No less than five of these damsels have been wedded since the *Mikado* company went out last August. One, a Miss Findlay, married a physician in a very good position; another, Miss Ina Weddle, was quite recently led to the altar by a wealthy gentleman of Newhaven, U.S.; and a third lady, Miss Pollard, has lately entered into the bond of wedlock with the principal of a flourishing business in New York. Mr Carte has frequently to ship off fresh consignments of choristers to fill up the blanks caused by the marriageable qualities of his young ladies.

A FALL FROM THE GALLERY.
An accident of an extraordinary character, which was fortunately unattended with any serious results, occurred last Saturday evening at the Theatre Royal, Birmingham. A man named Alfred Manning, aged thirty-two, employed as a packer by Mr Davis, of Macdonald-street, and who resides at four house, nine court, Wrentham-street, went to the gallery of the theatre to witness the performance of the pantomime *Robinson Crusoe*. Apparently with the intention of securing a front seat, he made a leap from the third row of seats, towards the front. Miscalculating his distance, however, he fell on to the iron rails, and for a moment held on with his hands. He was unable to sustain himself for more than a few seconds, and then fell into the pit below. The fall was fortunately broken by some brasswork which surmounts the

front of the upper circle, and in his descent he came into contact with a chandelier projecting from the upper circle. He fell lengthways with considerable force upon the benches in the pit, slightly hurting two or three of the audience, but escaping himself in a miraculous manner, with a severe shaking and a few cuts about the head. A number of people quickly ran to the injured man, who lay in an unconscious condition. A cab was procured, and he was conveyed to the Queen's Hospital, where upon examination he was found to be suffering from no further injuries than a few cuts about the face. He was detained during the night, but on Sunday afternoon he was allowed to go home. The accident occurred a few minutes before seven, and the theatre was nearly full. A five-barred iron railing some time ago was erected above the woodwork in front of the gallery with the object of preventing such an accident.
30/1/1886

ASSAULTING A PANTOMIME CHILD.

At the Birmingham Police-court on the 6th inst., before Mr Kynnersley (stipendiary), James Norris, 48, photographer carrying on business in Berkeley-street, was charged on a warrant, taken out at the instance of Inspector Noon, with assaulting a girl named Alice Vaughan. Prosecutrix said she was eleven years of age, and lived in Tyndal-street. She went to the prisoner's studio, in company with a companion named Annie Rann, on Sunday last to have her photograph taken whilst wearing the costume in which she appears at the Prince of Wales's pantomime. Before leaving she asked him if she could join a club, and he replied "You can hold one yourself if you like." He then asked her to see him on the following Monday, and he would make arrangements. Witness went alone to the prisoner's studio at half-past five on Monday, and on entering the room he immediately locked the door, and then assaulted her. He cautioned her about telling anyone about the occurrence, and then let her go.

In consequence of what witness said, her mother on the following day went to Norris's place of business, and there charged him with the offence. He said, "I am very sorry, but what do you want? Is it money?" Mrs Vaughan replied that she required an explanation of the affair, and he then said, "If money will satisfy you, I will give you any reasonable amount when I get my pension." Police-constable Robbins deposed that he was present when the prosecutrix's mother accused the prisoner with the assault, and he answered, "My wife would go mad if she knew, and I would not have it made known for the world." There was no real defence to the case, and the prisoner was sentenced to six months' imprisonment with hard labour.
13/2/1886

MR CHARLES HERMANN has just had a serious loss in the death of one of his beautiful dogs used in *Uncle Tom's Cabin*. It was poisoned through the stupidity of a veterinary surgeon's assistant at Pembroke. At the theatres visited by Mr Hermann poor old "Tiger" was well known and welcomed.

IN *Waiting for the Verdict*, which was recently played at the Worcester Theatre, the hero, Jasper Roseblade, is convicted of a murder of which he is innocent; and one of the most excruciating scenes occurs in the prison cell, where the unhappy convict takes a pathetic farewell of wife and child. When the parting words have been spoken a fresh scene should descend, hiding the condemned man from sight as he kneels in prayer. On Saturday, Feb. 6th, the scene shifters, instead of dropping a curtain in front of the cell, withdrew the "flats" forming the prison walls, and exposed a woodland scene which should not have been shown till later on. Mr W.R. Glenny, the impersonator of Jasper Roseblade, was, fortunately, equal to the emergency. Arising from his kneeling position, and looking like one awaking from a dream, he gazed around for a few seconds as though wondering how he came to be in such a place. Then he said he remembered all. He had taken advantage of a favourable opportunity to scale the prison walls and escape; and there he was. To explain the condemned man's reappearance in the prison in the last scene some further dialogue was improvised. All this was done by Mr Glenny with so much readiness and neatness that with few exceptions the audience was unaware of the *contretemps* which had occurred.

WANTED. – Young Man, Grotesque Leg Performer, wishes to join Ballet Troupe. Address, J. WILSON, 48, South Coburg-street, Glasgow.

WANTED, £5 for Model of the Latest Illusion, viz., the Submerged Lady in Crystal Aquarium surrounded by Fish. Can remain submerged for a week. No information will be given without the P.O. MERMAID, 267, Kennington-road, S.E.
20/2/1886

AN unrehearsed scene was enacted the other evening at a cafe-concert in the Boulevard du Nord, Brussels. Two swells, who had been dining not wisely but too well, interrupted a Nigger dwarf, Tom Lucette, in one of his songs, with cries of "Va au Congo" ("Go to Congo"), "Va te laver" ("Go and wash yourself"), &c. The dwarf stood it as long as he could, and then asked his tormentors to be quiet, but without the desired result; so at the end of his song he quietly walked up to the principal disturber and gave him a blow on the nose, amid the applause of the audience.
27/2/1886

A SINGULAR competition was witnessed in the streets of Dublin on Thursday evening. A member of Ginnett's circus called Rossini undertook to run a race on stilts against a tramcar from the College of Surgeons, Stephen's-green, to the Harcourt-street terminus. The start was made a little after six o'clock, Rossini, who was mounted on stilts said to be 20ft. high, having opposed to him a Rathmines tram drawn by two powerful horses. For a few minutes all went well, and the stilt-walker looked like winning, but then a car crossed his path suddenly, and as he swerved to avoid it some of the crowd jostled him and he fell. He was not seriously hurt, however, and offered to continue the race, but his friends would not permit it.
27/3/1886

CERTAINLY the portrayal of the Rev Robert Spalding is productive of strange results. Mr Arthur Helmore has again been honoured with a most remarkable present. This time the form taken was that of a bouquet, handed to him from "the front" during the performance of *The Private Secretary* at Southport on Saturday last. It was composed entirely of Bath buns, arranged symmetrically on wires, and graduating in size as they reached the apex; while from out the centre of this queer nosegay grew a soda-water bottle of milk, the rev. one's favourite beverage. It is needless to say that the presentation was the cause of roars of laughter.

DONKEYS AT A THEATRE.
Mr Chirgwin, the white-eyed musical Kaffir, on the occasion of his benefit at the Britannia on Ash Wednesday, offered to give as a prize his "highly-trained donkey, Edward," to the owner of the prettiest donkey in harness to be then and there shown. The competition was declared to be "free to all donkey owners." It was near midnight before the competition commenced, it being the last item on the programme. The conditions provided that the donkeys should be led in a circle upon the stage, and that as each arrival came to the footlights the audience should, by show of hands, express their votes. This arrangement was found to be impractical, owing to the large number of donkeys and owners who crowded the stage in almost inextricable confusion. Partisan feeling, too, evidently ran high; and the braying of the donkeys, the shouts of their owners, the whistling, hooting, and screaming, and other popular manifestations of feeling, prevented an orderly execution of the original plan.

By dint of great exertion the animals were at last got into something like order, and were led in turn to the front of the stage, when votes were taken by a show of the hands. It was soon seen that the real contest would be between Tweed's Jim and Kingsland Neddy. The latter eventually took the prize. Kingsland Neddy was a light-coloured little donkey, newly-clipped and singed; he wore a handsome set

of silver-mounted harness, decorated with a brow-band of scarlet leather, and a bunch of scarlet ribbon fastened upon each side of his head-dress. All the animals shown were in excellent condition. The Baroness Burdett-Coutts gave her patronage.
10/4/1886

AN unexpected tribute was paid to Mr Osmond Tearle's rendering of Othello recently at Birmingham. During the progress of the "smothering scene" a lady in the gallery was so carried away by her feelings that when Othello, exclaiming "Thou shalt not linger in thy pain!" raises his dagger and stabs the luckless Desdemona, the excited "goddess" broke the stillness of the house by yelling at the top of her voice, "*Oh, you pig!*" This, says the local chronicler, had the undesired effect of turning the tragedy into comedy for the time being.
17/4/1886

ALTHOUGH Her Majesty the Queen will not be able to visit any of the Liverpool theatres in the course of her visit to the city next week, it is interesting to know that, by the aid of modern science, an operatic performance will be brought within the Royal hearing. The management of the Court Theatre, Liverpool, have had the satisfaction of seeing the telephone apparatus affixed to the stage of the theatre placed in communication with Newsham House, which will be the Queen's temporary residence during her visit. Her Majesty, who very rarely ventures out after nightfall, will thus be enable to hear the opera of *Les Cloches de Corneville* on Tuesday and *La Mascotte* on Wednesday (performed by Messrs Barry and Hogarth's company) as she sits in one of the Royal private apartments. The telephone instruments have been tested during the past week with perfect success by members of the *Erminie* company, now located at the Court.
8/5/1886

MR EDITOR. – Sir, – Will you kindly mention that we saved our scene and a basket of costumes and music only forty minutes before the terrible fire at Derby*, and that we gave up for lost a basket containing a mechanical donkey, which, however, was found intact? Yours respectfully, GEORGE LUPINO, Jun., Theatre Royal, Nottingham, May 11th, 1886.
The Grand Theatre, which had opened only six weeks earlier, was badly damaged by a fire in which two people died.
15/5/1886

TO THE EDITOR OF THE ERA.
Sir, – At a time when many of the English actors and actresses are making praiseworthy efforts to attain to a high standard of acting, it would be as well that English audiences should cease to discourage these efforts. How is it possible for an actor to play to people who neither understand what he is driving at nor have the slightest comprehension of the meaning of a situation? A week or so ago I went to see Mrs Langtry in *The Lady of Lyons*. Next to me sat a splendid specimen of the genus "masher," accompanied by a very pretty, but very silly-looking, young lady. In the garden scene, where Claude tells of the glories of his palace, Mrs Langtry first gazes into his face with an air of rapt attention, and then, as he breathes forth words of ardent love, closes her eyes that she may the better drink in the sweet sentences undisturbed by any outward surroundings. Gradually she lets drop her flowers one by one, then her hat. The idea was an admirable one admirably carried out. But as the hat fell from her unconscious hand my precious pair burst into a loud laugh, with the exclamation, "Why, she is going to sleep!" I am afraid I made use of some very bad language, but I trust that, having regard to the extreme provocation, the recording angel has not entered it up against me.

A few nights afterwards I dropped in at the St James's. Everyone who has seen *Antoinette Rigaud* must remember the striking scene where the husband, while supping, recounts to the terrified and conscience-stricken Antoinette the tale of the man who shot his wife. More admirable acting has been

seldom seen on the stage than Mrs Kendal's in this scene, and nothing can be more effective than the way in which the light and almost playful remarks of the husband add to the tragic intensity of the situation. But the terror and despair in Mrs Kendal's face, in the tones of her voice, in the convulsive movements of her hands, were utterly lost upon her audience. It was enough for them that Rigaud's manner was light and playful, that he talked while eating, and that he proposed to smoke a cigar. The whole thing was, of course, a farcical comedy, and the house resounded with peals of laughter. English actors are now educating themselves. Would that someone would educate English audiences! Yours faithfully, R.K.H., Arundel Club, May 17th.
22/5/1886

IN the American burlesque *Adonis*, produced at the Gaiety Theatre on Monday evening, appeared no fewer than four Robinson Crusoes. They wore white wool coats extending only to the hips, they wore tights without trunks, and they carried umbrellas which we hope were intended to hide their blushes. Probably the costumier, in his desire for realism, wanted to show us how Robinson Crusoe looked after losing all his clothes by shipwreck; but this nude departure will hardly recommend itself to those who prefer something like decency even in burlesque. *Adonis* may or may not prove successful, but at least its producers will be able to boast that in the matter of indecent dressing they have gone a very long way ahead of anything previously seen on the London stage.

WANTED, Barmaid, at once. Male personator preferred. One not been out before not objected to. PORDAGE, The Limes, Faversham.
5/6/1886

A FEW nights ago the audience at a certain theatre was unusually small, and the manager was standing at the door disconsolately watching the crowds rush by. His unpleasant meditations were interrupted by a boy who had come down from the gallery. "Say, mister," said the god, "can I please have a seat downstairs?" "What's the matter?" asked the manager, "isn't upstairs good enough for you?" "Yes, sir; but I'm afraid to stay up there all alone," was the timid response.

OUR New Zealand correspondent says that the genial Liddy (now with Rignold) tells a story which is too good to be lost. When piloting a comic opera company through the gold-fields towns he employed a bellman to herald the performance of *Les Cloches de Corneville*, and that functionary solemnly announced that the company would appear in *The Cockroaches of Cornwall*!
12/6/1886

A STORY of Miss Mary Anderson comes from America. While she was rehearsing the part of Juliet an eminent physician, an intimate friend, was present. The performance delighted him till towards the conclusion of the play, when his countenance wore a troubled expression. When it was over he went up to the actress. "My dear young lady," he said, "you are wrong in one of your effects. Don't you know that a corpse doesn't stiffen for at least six hours after death?" "My dear doctor," responded Mary slowly, speaking in deep, rich tones, and adopting a strong American twang, "do you think I'm going to keep my audience *waiting for six hours while I stiffen?*"

TO THE EDITOR OF THE ERA.
Sir, – You would do a great service to the theatre-going world if, by inserting this letter, you could draw the attention of ladies to the fact that their bonnets, however elegant, are not transparent, and that, if they cannot be dispensed with altogether during the performance of a piece (which would be the most satisfactory solution of the difficulty), they should, at least, be worn as low as possible.
   I was present last week at an afternoon performance in St George' Hall, and occupied a seat in the second row of the dress-circle. In front of me, totally excluding all possible view of the stage and the

players, was an enormous bonnet, perpetually in motion, bobbing first to one side and then to the other, round the corners of which bonnet, by craning my neck and inclining my body at an angle of forty-five degrees, I was occasionally able to catch a glimpse of what was going on, though not at all in a connected form. This was not the worse of it, however, for on my right sat a lady, with whose arm my own came in contact when the position of the bonnet made a movement in that direction necessary, and, though this lady sat out the first piece, I found, when returning after the ten minutes' interval, that she had either been incommoded by my movements, or, worse still, had imputed to me intentional rudeness, for she and her two friends had exchanged places with some gentlemen, who had been seated a little further down in the same row. The mere thought of the committal of an intentional insult being possibly attributed to me of course spoilt my pleasure for the afternoon, and the lady herself and her friends must have been equally indignant with me.

Now, I would ask, Sir, whether ladies cannot remove their bonnets at the theatre, as men do their hats? The bonnet, which, including trimmings, is frequently taller and much more intrusive than the modest hat, is, at the theatre, the pest of society, the cause of much bad language, and sufficient to incite the most sober-minded of us to revolutionary ideas, to acts of violence, and, by a necessary consequence, to the destruction of Church, Theatre, and State. I enclose my card, and have the honour to be, Sir, Yours obediently, FAIR PLAY. June 15th, 1886.
19/6/1886

WHILE the "Two Macs" were staying at an hotel in Berlin recently an amusing though somewhat painful incident occurred. The waiters, seeing their performance one night, seemed much puzzled as to how one of the pair stuck the hatchet into the head of the other, and tried to induce the brothers to divulge the secret. They refused. On the day after, returning from a drive, they were met at the door of the hotel by the host, excitedly exclaiming, "Oh, Mr Twomacs, Mr Twomacs! My waiter, we shall lose him, come on!" It turned out that the waiters had got possession of the props of the Two Macs, and had been trying to do the hatchet trick. Instead of wearing the artfully padded scalp which the brothers use the waiter had put an ordinary old man's scalp on. The consequence was that his colleague gave him a crushing blow on top of his cranium, and down he went. He was not, however, very seriously injured.
26/6/1886

AN American paper says that on the first night of *Jack* a strange man forced himself upon the authoress in her box, and denounced the piece as a plagiarism of one he had written three years before. Mrs Beckett received the intimation quite calmly, and informed him that her play was half a dozen years old. The indignant claimant, somewhat abashed by this, said – "I suppose you know the story has been in book form here. I took my plot from it." "Well," replied the authoress, "I wrote the book." The claimant retired.

A TELEGRAM from Calais states that a man named Bijou, who used to perform as a man-monkey, has been devoured by a lion in a menagerie.

WANTED, Doorsman, able to Box with Female Boxer. Good Salary. Sobriety indespensible. Address, F. D'GREY, Post Office, Burnley, Lancashire.

WANTED, Proprietors to know that Professor Potter's Speciality, Retza, the Human Fly, Antipodean Wonder, and only Lady Ceiling Walker on Looking Glass, performs Feats never attempted by any other Artist. Gatti's Westminster, immense success. Permanent address, 57, Latchmere-grove, Battersea.
3/7/188

DURING the performance of *The Bells* at the Lyceum Theatre on Saturday night an opera-glass from a box over that occupied by the visitors fell on the head of Mr Horatio Chipp, the well know violoncellist, who was playing in the orchestra at the time, causing a serious wound on the side of his head, which bled profusely. Mr Chipp had his wound dressed and was conveyed home.
31/7/1886

MERMAID. – New Striking Novelty, suitable for Pantomimes, Circus, Side Show, &c. A beautiful Woman representing a Living Mermaid, Tail, Scales, in motion by electricity, Fins and Tail end of coloured fire. Performs many very difficult Feats under deep water. Crystal Tank on wheels. Twenty Minutes' Show. Private Rehearsals to responsible person, few days, by Miss JULIA VICTOR in ALBERT PALACE. Notice. – This is no Mythological Soap-bubble Invention.
21/8/1886

THE effect sometimes produced by the songs of Mr Henry Russell (who, by the way, is alive and may be seen in excellent health on any day at the Boulogne Casino) is well exemplified by the following little anecdote. On one occasion, after the singing of "The Newfoundland Dog," a piece in which a dog is described as saving a child's life, a north countryman exclaimed, "Was the child saved, mon?" On being answered in the affirmative, the man asked earnestly, "Could ye get me a pup?"

THE COMEDIAN AND HIS DOG.
AT Warrington, on the 20th inst., Mr Rass Challis, a comedian who has been playing at the Theatre Royal in *The Curate*, was charged with shooting a dog belonging to Mr Buckley Mellor. Mr Percy Davies, who appeared to prosecute, said the defendant was a writer of plays, an actor, and a very clever man. He owned a dog which was also clever, and, like other dogs, it was very fond of bones. It was a very little one, and it was in front of some houses playing with the prosecutor's dog, when another came up, and all three began to play with a bone. Mr Challis's and Mr Mellor's dogs began to argue about the bone, and ultimately resorted fighting as a mode of settling the dispute. The defendant then came out of the house, but went back, and returned with a loaded revolver, took deliberate aim, and shot the prosecutor's dog. Strange to say, the animal was alive, although the bullet which he produced passed through its body to the left side, where it was extracted.

Captain Reynolds – The charge is against a comedian but this is a tragedy.

The Mayor – But comedians can be tragic.

Mr Davies then called Sarah Jane Monks, who said she was endeavouring to separate the animals when the defendant came out and fired the revolver without making any attempt to stop the fighting. She said to him, "You'll catch it for this."

Prosecutor spoke as to the value of the dog, and said that a Mr Tinsley, of Gorton, had offered him £7 10s. for it, which he had refused. It was a great racing dog, and out of four matches it had won two. Mr Tinsley had won £150 with him. Its grandmother was a famous Manchester dog.

Defendant said he was told that his dog was being killed, and going out he saw it was in great danger. He went back into the house, took his stage pistol, put in a bullet, went out and shot the dog in order to save his own, as all other means to separate the animals had failed.

The Mayor remarked that he had acted very rashly.

Defendant – Suppose your worship had a dog which was being worried, what would you do? The Mayor – I don't think I should take firearms.

Captain Reynolds – The Mayor would have taken a rope. Defendant – Well, we don't think of these things at the time.

The prosecutor's dog was exhibited in court, and the Mayor remarked that its injury did not seem to have interfered with its locomotion.

Defendant added that his dog was a pet of his wife's.

Mr Davies – And you are your wife's pet? Defendant – Yes, aren't you?

The Mayor said the defendant would be fined 10s. and costs, making £2 0s. 6d. in all. They would not go into the question of damage to the dog.

28/8/1886

AT Worship-street Police-court, on Monday, Timothy Scanlan, aged nineteen, described as a blacksmith, of Young's-place, Old-street, St Luke's, was charged with creating a disturbance at the Britannia Theatre, Hoxton, and further with assaulting one of the attendants there. Mr Ogle prosecuted.

The evidence of Mr Alfred Lane Crawford, acting manager for Mrs Sarah Lane, proprietress of the theatre, showed that at about half-past nine on Saturday night the prisoner, who had patronised the theatre at half price, created a disturbance in the gallery by shouting, singing, and whistling. When requested by the ticket-taker to desist and keep quiet, he was very abusive and continued his shouting. Assistance was sent for; but meanwhile the prisoner made his way to the front row of the gallery at the side and there defied the officers, including two constables, to remove him. He fixed his legs under the seat and clung to the iron railings and one of the small chandeliers projecting from from the front over the pit, and was with the greatest trouble removed by the combined efforts of six men. During the struggle the performance had to be stopped, and the whole house was greatly excited. A fortnight ago there was a similar disturbance, and the prisoner was said to have been recognised as a leader upon that occasion. Mr Bushby passed a sentence of fourteen days' hard labour.

IN addition to the tame hedgehog which Mrs Weldon has been accustomed to fondle at the tea-table in *Not Alone*, she has now introduced two little monkeys, "Joseph and Annie," which she caresses with equal tenderness. Mrs Weldon has evidently a natural tendency towards the "zoological drama."

ON Saturday morning, at Longton, Staffordshire, Mr Harry King, proprietor of Dr Correy's panoramic entertainment, committed suicide by shooting himself. He had been in a depressed state of mind, and it is supposed that insanity had developed itself. About nine o'clock, after breakfasting with his wife, he went into the yard, and deliberately placed a pistol to his head and blew the top of his skull off. A quantity of buckshot was found in his pocket. A letter, which was found in the pocket of the deceased after the terrible tragedy, was as follows: – "Longton, Friday night. Dear mother and father, – I am happy to say that I am doing first-class. I do feel so happy, only my head is rather queer. I don't know what is the matter with it; but I know that someone is inside it. If you can come and bring a screwdriver, and open it and let him out I shall be all right. Don't fail to come by first train, and bring your tool-box with you. I will help you to get him out. With God's blessing on you both, and everybody else, I remain, your affectionate son, HARRY KING. Don't fail to come by first train, as he is eating my brain. Come at once, or I am gone." Sergeant Spendlove added that the deceased purchased a pistol shortly before his death, stated that he wanted it for stage purposes. The coroner, in directing the jury, observed that it was one of the clearest cases of insanity which had ever come under his notice. The jury returned a verdict of suicide whilst in a state of temporary insanity.

GINNETT'S circus paid a one day's visit to Willenhall, Staffordshire, on Saturday last, and during the evening's entertainment, which was well attended, a cry was raised that the lions were escaping. Numbers of people rushed pell-mell into the open air, losing hats and caps in their hasty flight, and many falling into the brook which crosses the grounds where the circus was located. After order was obtained it was found that one of the horses had kicked down a number of seats, thus giving rise to the scare. It was some time before the public anxiety was relieved and the performers were enabled to proceed.

4/9/1886

WANTED, a Dozen Second-hand Burlesque Hobby Horses in best condition, and dressed. BUCKNILL, 14, Scarsdale-terrace, Kensington.
11/9/1886

"CLINGO," the monster bloodhound used by Mr Charles Hermann in *Uncle Tom's Cabin*, died a few days since at Accrington, through paralysis of the hind legs. This is the third dog Mr Hermann has lost since Christmas. "Clingo" was know throughout the provinces as the stage-carpenter's terror, and cost his owner, in bites, lawsuits, &c., over £300.
18/9/1886

Beauty may be added,
If your face looks faded;
Don't give way to gloom,
Use BRIDAL BOUQUET BLOOM.
EVER YOUNG. – The fresh and health-like tinge which it develops on the neck, hands, and arms seems to give them a more graceful contour, softening down the angles, if any, or lending a new charm to rounded outlines, where these elements of fascination already exist. Sold by Chemists and Perfumers at 3s. 6d. (ADVT)
25/9/1886

OUR Wolverhampton correspondent writes: – Quite a novel interpolation was witnessed in the representation of *Jim the Penman* at the Theatre Royal, Wolverhampton, on Monday evening. The performance had reached the point where Mrs Ralson is engaged in earnest conversation with her whilom lover Louis Percival, when a large dark object was observed to fall at the feet of Miss Fanny Enson. A moment's reflection revealed the fact that the object was a huge rat that had probably secured a point of vantage in the flies, and that in its anxiety to see and hear had lost its balance and toppled over. It showed signs of a desire to join the ranks of the pittites, but in passing near the footlights it evidently realised the fact that the place was getting too "hot" for him, and he beat a retreat in another direction. It should be added that, although momentarily surprised by the appearance of so unusual a visitor, Miss Enson continued the performance in a thoroughly calm and collected manner, and was loudly cheered.

A RATHER good thing was overheard in the Strand the other day. Two ladies were looking at some photographs of professional celebrities when one, recognising a favourite actress, exclaimed delightedly, "Oh, isn't she pretty, and isn't she clever. I do like her because *she's always the same*." The tone implied intense admiration, but the compliment, to say the least, was rather equivocal.

WANTED, by a Lady Professor of the Piano, to give lessons to Ladies who have neglected their Music. PROFESSOR, 112, Turnpike-lane, Hornsey.

Tricycles. WANTED, Two made for a Pair of Small Elephants. Send prices and when could be delivered to WM. CROSS, Liverpool.
2/10/1886

AN amusing occurrence took place at the Town Hall, Longton, on Monday. Mr Dexter, the conjurer, was engaged to appear, under the patronage of the mayor and the committee of the Liberal Club. The "vanishing lady" was advertised for ten o'clock. At 9.45 Mr Dexter was crossing the stage when suddenly he disappeared. By mistake he had stood on the trap prepared for the "vanishing lady." When ten o'clock came the spectators had ceased to wonder "how it's done."

ONE of our well-known tragedians, whilst starring in the provinces, played an engagement at Cheltenham. He opened in *Othello*, and after the play, being in a hurry to join some old friends, he raised a loud outcry because there was no hot water to take the colour off. When the man whose duty it was to look after such matters arrived, he was met with a torrent of such reproach as fairly startled him. Some time after another star arriving also played Othello, and when he had finished his performance, he sought his room gasping and out of breath. Scarcely had he done so when the old attendant burst into the room, and planting a huge can of boiling water on the floor exclaimed, "There! All right this time; you can take your confounded black off as soon as you like!" But again he was startled with a burst of indignation, for the Othello on that occasion was poor Morgan Smith*, the coloured tragedian!

Samuel Morgan Smith (1832-1882) was born in Philadelphia but lived and performed in England for many years, mostly in the provinces.

DISGRACEFUL CONDUCT AT A CONCERT.
On Tuesday evening a grand concert was given at the Philharmonic Hall, Liverpool, by Mr Sims Reeves, assisted by Miss Antoinette Sterling, Miss H. Nunn, Miss P. Siedel, Signor Foli, Mr Nicholson (flautist), and Mr Maunder (accompanist). There was a very large audience, and the veteran tenor sang several favourite numbers with considerable success, responding to an encore in one instance with "Tom Bowling." Towards the close of the second part he gave "The Bay of Biscay," which elicited enthusiastic applause from all parts of the hall. Mr Reeves repeatedly appeared on the platform and bowed his acknowledgments, but refused to comply with another encore. Thereupon the exacting portions of the audience became more furious.

Finally Mr Sims Reeves appeared on the platform, leading Miss Henrietta Nunn. Again bowing to the audience, he withdrew. Mr Maunder sat down at the piano, and showed signs of his willingness to begin, he unseemly row entirely prevented a note being heard. Miss Nunn remained several minutes, the audience in the gallery at the time being for the most part on their feet. Wild shouting and stamping on the floor in the galleries continued. Mr H. Nicholson came round one side of the platform at this moment, and within full view of the audience stood looking upon the disorderly scene with blank astonishment written on his face. Miss Nunn ultimately retired, and was conducted from the platform by Mr Nicholson. The celebrated flautist reappeared immediately with his instrument and a piece of music in his hand. Placing a sheet before Mr Maunder, who had remained seated at the piano, he raised the flute to his lips, but had no sooner done so than the confusion, which had just slightly subsided, was recommenced with redoubled ardour. Nothing daunted, Mr Nicholson manfully kept to his post, and, giving Mr Maunder a sharp tap on the shoulder to start, the musicians proceeded with the piece. The deafening noise from the galleries and the back part of the hall rendered it perfectly impossible that either Mr Nicholson or Mr Maunder could hear their instruments. They played for quite three or four minutes, and then the flautist gave up, and he and Mr Maunder quickly withdrew in the midst of loud jeering. The concert was thus brought to a sudden termination.

This exhibition of rowdyism was most disreputable to a section of an audience supposed to be composed of respectable and intelligent people.

WANTED, Engagements for Performing Fleas. Best on the Road. Address, HARRY DICKS, Albert Palace, Battersea, S.W.
16/10/1886

A SERIO-COMIC'S JEWELLERY.
At the Westminster Police-court, on Tuesday, Dennis Halpin, aged eighteen, porter, of 38, Lamont-road, Chelsea, was charged before Mr d'Eyncourt with stealing a £5 note, a diamond ring value £20, and a gold bangle, the property of his sister, Catherine Halpin, of the same address. The prosecutrix, a stylishly-dressed young woman, who stated that she was a music-hall singer, deposed that on Monday

fore-noon she missed a jewel box containing the ring and bangle and the bank note from a table in her room. She suspected her brother, as he left the house suddenly, just before the property and money were missed. Constable Walshe, 434 B, said that he found the prisoner on Chelsea Embankment, after looking about for him for three hours. The young man had the note and jewellery in his possession. His account of the matter was that he was taking care of it, as his sister had been drinking. Prosecutrix recalled denied this, but admitted drinking overnight. Prisoner was remanded for a week.
23/10/1886

MR EDITOR. – Sir, – will you kindly correct a statement that appeared in your issue of last Saturday concerning a vicious "singing" donkey. My singing donkey is not vicious, and did not bite the groom. He was bitten by another animal I am training. I am pleased to say that the man progresses favourably. Yours faithfully, WHIMSICAL WALKER, Hengler's Grand Cirque, Argyll-street, W.

MR T.H. CROWTHER, skater, swordsman, and bicyclist, arrived per. S.S. Germanic on Saturday from Mexico. En route through America, he says, he performed the daring feat of riding his mammoth eight-feet bicycle over Niagara Falls on a plank, nine inches broad, fixed from the suspension-bridge.

MR JULIAN CROSS, the representative at the Standard Theatre of Jonas Norton in Messrs Willing and Douglass' new drama *A Dark Secret*, poisoned his feet last week with some scarlet tights, but, nevertheless, went through his part on Thursday, the first night of the piece, with great success.

A JEALOUS ACTRESS.
At Westminster Police-court, on Monday, Lottie Jackson, aged twenty-eight, described as an actress*, of Albany-street, Portland-road, was charged before Mr D'Eyncourt of assaulting Amy Dumas, at the Victoria Station of the District Railway. She was further charged with being dressed in male attire for a supposed unlawful purpose. The defendant, who had been admitted to bail, now appeared before the magistrate dressed in a fashionable costume of blue velvet. Mr Bernard Abrahams defended, and Mr J. Hix Osborne appeared on behalf of the District Railway Company.

Constable Orchard, 220 B, said the prosecutrix was not in attendance. About midnight on Saturday he was called to the District Railway Station at Victoria, and found the prisoner, who was dressed as a young man in a dark tweed suit and black felt hat, detained by the station inspector. Two young ladies complained of being assaulted by the prisoner in a railway carriage, and they went to the station, where one of them preferred a charge and signed the sheet. One complainant said her bonnet had been pulled off, and the other said that she was struck in the breast.

Mr D'Eyncourt – You took the prisoner to the station dressed as a boy? The constable – Yes, Sir, and these were the clothes she was wearing (the officer produced a pair of trousers and a coat).

Mr Abrahams said that the defendant had got herself into the scrape through jealousy. She suspected the fidelity of the gentleman to whom she was engaged, and with the intention of following him without detection she assumed the garb of a male. She was so far successful that she discovered that her suspicions were well founded. She found the gentleman paying attention to two other young ladies, and on following them to the railway carriage the fracas occurred. No great damage had been done, and the defendant hoped that the magistrate would think she had sustained enough punishment by the ignominy attaching to being charged and having to stand in front of the dock.

The station inspector got into the witness box, but in answer to the magistrate he said that personally he had no charge to prefer against the accused.

Mr Abrahams remarked that the lady's disguise was so complete that the gentleman did not recognise her himself in the first instance.

Mr D'Eyncourt allowed her to be discharged.

It was later revealed that Miss Jackson's theatrical experience consisted of a brief appearance "in the second row of the ballet".

TO THE EDITOR OF THE ERA.

Sir, – The profession has waited with breathless interest to hear what Mr Ernest Montefiore had to say on the subject of long runs, and now that he has spoken all no doubt are satisfied. During a run of three weeks I played "shouts outside," and my friends noticed that at the end of the run that I was given to shouting at them. Again, for a run of six consecutive nights, I carried a banner, and my friends all noticed at the end of the run that I had got into the habit of carrying my walking stick over my shoulder. This, I presume, is the consequence of attempting to identify oneself too completely, or merging one's personality to too great an extent with the character one assumes.

I enclose my card, not for publication as I have no wish for a gratuitous advertisement. Oct. 6th, 1886. I am, Sir, yours, &c., A.G.S.

AT the Whitby Police-court, on Tuesday, Steven Kingstone, a jet ornament manufacturer, was charged with being drunk and disorderly, and also with doing wilful damage to the trousers of John Readman.

The complainant stated that he was one of the check-takers at the Waterloo Theatre, and that on Monday night defendant ran past him and into the theatre. Defendant was very drunk, and commenced to cause a disturbance. Witness endeavoured to keep him quiet, but he continued his rowdyism, and he (witness) was obliged to seize him and put him out. Defendant resisted very much, and struck witness a blow on the face. In the struggle defendant tore his (witness's) trousers to pieces. Eventually defendant was ejected from the theatre.

By the Bench – Do you admit drunken people to the theatre? Witness – No, not even if they pay.

In reply to the magistrates defendant admitted that he was drunk, but had no recollection of tearing witness's trousers. "He did not know it was the check-taker – he thought it was a policeman."

The magistrates fined defendant for being drunk and disorderly, and ordered him to pay the cost of a pair of new trousers.

30/10/1886

WANTED, Everybody to Know that the Victoria, Darlington, closes Nov. 20th, as I find it impossible to make it pay, owing to the Salvation Army singing in the entrance every Night and in the Hall every Sunday. Only two Engagements cancelled. Thanks to Bros Webster and George Fairley for cancelling same. Signed, HARRY WALLEY.

13/11/1886

AN ASININE ACTOR.

THE patrons of Mr Fynes's popular place of amusement, the Theatre Royal, Blyth, have had placed before them a bill of fare of a most attractive description, Mr T.J. West's comedy company appearing nightly in the screaming absurdity *Muldoon's Picnic*. On Wednesday evening, the 24th ult., an amusing incident took place, fortunately not attended with any serious results. The donkey, which is a Blyth genius, and used in the third act to drive Mr and Mrs Muldoon to the picnic, made an unexpected advent to the stage from the wings in the drawing room scene. Mr Mulchay just at this time was singing his song, and on turning round beheld the animal close upon him with ears back and mouth open, and the unexpected sight evidently disturbed the singer's nerves, as he made a very precipitate retreat behind the piano on the stage. The audience commenced to alternately scream and laugh, which possibly alarmed the donkey, as, instead of retreating, it advanced to the footlights, walked on to the piano, and finally fell into the orchestra, causing a general stampede of the orchestra performers with their instruments. The incident caused a severe nervous shock to Miss Fynes, who officiated at the piano, and who had a

narrow escape from being crushed. She was unable to return to her duties for the succeeding acts, and Mr Battersby, the manager of the company, kindly officiated for her.
4/12/1886

WANTED, Purchaser, Shark, 17ft. Long, 10ft. Round. Cured and Stuffed. Price, £20. Apply, MR BERRY, Malt-cross, Nottingham.
11/12/1886

FLETCHER'S, PORTH, SOUTH WALES. Wanted, to see the Faces on Monday of all who are Engaged, under a penalty of being shot.
18/12/1886

8
1887
WE CALLS 'EM PIKELETS IN PRESTON

DINNER TO SANDWICH MEN.

On Christmas Day between seventy and eighty "sandwich," or boardmen, were entertained at a substantial dinner of good old English roast beef, with vegetables and bread, plum pudding, and a liberal supply of beer, by Mr Archibald Nagle, the well-known advertising contractor. The dinner took place in Ham-yard, Great Windmill-street, and its kind donor and his wife presided at the tables, and saw that each of the poor fellows – men having no regular homes and being for the most part unmarried and friendless – were amply provided for.

IN the Drury-lane pantomime *The Forty Thieves* there is introduced an exceedingly pretty ballet by the little pupils of Madame Katti Lanner. The stage is filled with well-dressed juveniles, who suddenly receive the order to prepare for bed. On the instant they commence to unrobe, and presently are found attired only in their night-dresses. They have danced as they undressed, and now they dance again even while they take their pillows and indulge in that pastime dear to boarding-school pupils, and known as a pillow fight.

Now it happened that one of the prettiest and one of the smallest of the youngsters was in difficulties directly the order to undress was given. There was an awkward fastening that refused to give way, and so when all her companions were in their night-dresses she was found still as she first came on. She danced all through her difficulties, but these were so evident that sympathy went out towards her from the whole house. This sympathy was increased tenfold when, breaking down at last, the poor little mite began to cry. Her troubles, however, were now speedily brought to an end by friendly hands at the wings, and when she came skipping on again to join in the revels of her companions there was a great roar of applause to give her welcome. That little child's distress had touched a chord of sympathy, and it gave forth no uncertain sound. It was but a small incident, but we venture to say it will be talked of and long remembered by all who were present on Boxing Night.
1/1/1887

A COMMENCEMENT was made on Tuesday in clearing the site for a new theatre which Mr Charles Flower proposes to build in close proximity to the Shakespeare Memorial at Stratford-on-Avon. Workmen are engaged demolishing the cottages that stand upon the site, and it is understood that as soon as cleared building operations will be commenced. The decoration of the inside of the memorial theatre, the last stage of the work connected with the project, has also just been undertaken by the contractor.

AN unfortunate accident recently occurred to Captain T.B. Transfield, late proprietor of Middlesborough Circus. His daughter is engaged as principal rider at Mr Tayleure's circus, Cardiff. While he was in the dressing room one of the clowns loaded a pistol for his performing pig. The pistol exploded, and the Captain had the full charge in his face, slightly injuring his left eye, and tattooing his face on one side with gunpowder. He is compelled to keep to his room, but will be able to resume business in a few days.

MR ARTHUR CORNEY, whilst proceeding to his engagement at Collins's Music Hall on Monday last, met with a rather serious accident. The hansom cab in which he was being driven was overturned in attempting to scale a heap of snow, and Mr Corney's hand was sent through the window, and was severely cut. He was conveyed to the Royal Free Hospital, where his injuries received prompt attention. *8/1/1887*

MR W.J. HILL seriously endangered the success of *The Lodgers* at the Globe Theatre on Tuesday by not knowing the words of his part of Maggridge, the railway porter. We deeply regret that one of our leading comedians should thus set an example of unfairness to his authors and disrespect to his audience.

AT Edinburgh Police-court on Thursday, John Dodd, market gardener, was charged with having created a disturbance at the Theatre Royal on Wednesday evening. Dodd, who was in the gallery, became disorderly, and on being challenged got over the railing and slid down the supporting pillars into the dress circle, to the great alarm and disturbance of the audience. The magistrate ordered an enquiry into the prisoner's state of mind.

THE Two Macs, who have been appearing at the Theatre Royal, Birmingham, recently received information that their house in London had been burglariously entered on Saturday night last, and that a considerable amount of property had been removed. Hurrying up to town they discovered that almost a clean sweep had been made of all the portables in their residence, which had been locked up unoccupied pending their Birmingham engagement. Pictures, jewellery, presentation plate, ornaments, and curios collected in Europe and America, and other valuables to the amount of some £200 had disappeared. Amongst the remaining effects was an imitation "trick" safe made so exactly like the real article that the thieves had used a crowbar to open the wooden property, which is used by the nimble pantomimists in one of their entertainments. The thieves, it seems, had occupied the whole of Saturday night and Sunday morning in removing the goods, and when the policeman on the beat, thinking the proceedings unusual, made inquiries, two individuals who represented themselves as the Two Macs met him, and gave good reasons for the sudden flit. Up to the present no trace of the thieves has been discovered.

A sad disaster took place on Tuesday evening at the Hebrew Club, 3, Prince's-street, Spitalfields, a place of recreation and amusement in use among the German and Russian Jews, who mainly reside in the vicinity of Commercial-street and Spitalfields. A benefit performance was organised by a dramatic society in connection with the club for the purpose of affording help and assistance to a sick member of the club, and a special notice having been circulated of this performance there was a very large attendance, estimated at from 400 to 500 persons, a large proportion of them being women. The piece selected for representation was *The Spanish Gypsy Girl*, a favourite melodrama with the frequenters of the club, and it was given in the Hebrew tongue. The audience was augmented as the performance went on, until both the floor of the hall and a gallery above were well filled. The galleries ran along two sides of the hall, and were approached by a flight of steps from the entrance-hall of the building, sufficiently wide to admit of four people passing up and down at one time. The gallery on the right-hand side of the hall was approached by stone steps on an angle, so that those at the top could not see what was going on at the bottom.

When the performance was in full swing, at about half-past eleven, some youths in the gallery, who wished to gain a better view of the stage, climbed up a gaspipe which was affixed to the wall, and in doing so broke it in half. Henry Gilberg, who, with his wife and family, was sitting near, at once ran to the spot and tried with his handkerchief to stop the gas from escaping, and was successful in doing so, but some person shouted out, "Turn off the meter," and the hall was thrown into partial darkness. A cry was immediately raised of "Fire!" either by some person at the back of the hall, as stated by some, or by someone in the gallery, as declared by others, while a third version is to the effect that one of the characters in the play made an exclamation in one of his lines just at that moment in which the word "fire" occurred. It threw nearly the whole of the assembly into a state of fright and panic, and they all rose in eager haste and rushed for the doors. A collision was the result, in which seventeen persons were killed, and many seriously injured.

22/1/1887

LIBEL ON AN ACTRESS.

AT the Mansion House Police-court on Monday, Mr John Corlett, proprietor of the *Sporting Times*, appeared upon a summons, before Alderman Sir Andrew Lusk, for publishing a false and defamatory libel of and concerning Miss Violet Davis, otherwise Dashwood. Mr Poland appeared for the prosecution.

Mr George Lewis said he represented the defendant, who had been summoned for libel by a young lady, Miss Violet Dashwood, who was in the chorus at the Avenue Theatre. The paragraph in question referred to the young ladies in the chorus at the Avenue, and spoke of them as "tarts." It was suggested on the part of the prosecution that the word "tart" really meant a person of immoral character. Whether this was so or not he would not stop to inquire. […] But he might say that in one of Captain Marryat's books – "The Pacha of Many Tales" – he found "the beauteous Babe-bi-boba, for such was the name of the princess, and which in the language of the country implied the cream tart of delight." So that the word tart had evidently been applied in quite a different sense to that which the prosecutrix seemed to have imputed to it. […]

The *Sporting Times* was in no way a malicious paper, but was devoted to sport, the theatre, and fun, and in this case commenced by referring to the young ladies as "real jam," and then the paragraph proceeded to speak of them as "tarts". That probably led this young lady to suppose that there was some bad meaning attributed to the phrase, and Mr Corlett was extremely sorry that the words should have been used. Defendant denied altogether that the word was used in the sense imputed; but as the prosecutrix seemed to have considered that that was the sense in which in which it might have been applied – and possibly from the previous numbers of the paper which had been shown to him it might fairly have been supposed by the young lady to have a meaning other than the refreshment used at dinner or as the cream tart of delight, Mr Corlett wished, through him, to express his great regret to the prosecutrix that her name should have been mentioned in such a connection to have caused her pain. […] Under these circumstances, he hoped that Mr Poland would be satisfied with the apology he had made, together with the offer to pay the costs of the case, and that, with the permission of the Court, he would now allow this very serious libel charge to be withdrawn.

Mr Poland said he appeared for the prosecutrix, a young lady of irreproachable character. She was not in the chorus alone, but had also a part in a play now performing at the Avenue Theatre, and her name appeared in the bills. She lived at home with her father, mother, and brothers and sisters, and was maintaining herself by her industry as an actress. She hoped, also, to make by her study and industry a good position in her profession. Mr Lewis was quite right, therefore, in stating that this paragraph caused very great pain indeed. […] After what had been said, the prosecutrix had no desire to proceed further in this matter, and was willing that the summons should be withdrawn. […]

Alderman Sir A. Lusk said the case had been placed very clearly by Mr Lewis, who with the best motives had endeavoured to bring about the arrangement, while Mr Poland had met the offer as a gentleman, as he always did. [...] The press was a very powerful instrument, but its gigantic power ought not to be used so as to cause pain, or to provoke laughter at the expense of others. It was undoubtedly a very serious thing to provoke, as was often done, fun in this way, particularly when those who indulged in it forgot altogether the suffering they caused. He sympathised very much with the young lady, although he did not know the exact meaning of "tart."

Mr Lewis – You do not read the *Sporting Times*, Sir Andrew.

The Alderman – No, I do not; it is not in my way at all.

Mr Poland – It is a very good thing you do not, Sir Andrew.

Mr Lewis – Mr Poland is anxious to protect your morals.

The Alderman said the defendant had apologised for the libel, and, the prosecutrix being willing to accept it, he had no objection to the summons being withdrawn.

The parties then left the court.

WHILST an exhibition of Poole's Panorama was being held at the Colston Hall, Birmingham, last Thursday afternoon, in the presence of a large number of school children, some alarm was caused by a shutter falling in the gallery, and in the excitement a boy fell from the gallery to the body of the hall, fracturing his skull. His brother, a lad aged twelve, was so shocked at witnessing the accident that he died suddenly from fright.
29/1/1887

THE members of a Baptist chapel in Lincolnshire recently passed the resolution, "That all theatre-going is detrimental to the best interests of the Christian Church, an impediment to the advancement of Christianity, and out of harmony with the entire teaching of Christ." No amendment was moved, and the resolution was carried by 32 to 1. Doubtless this enlightened resolution will prove a death-blow to all theatres.

TO THE EDITOR OF THE ERA.
Sir, – I address you on a subject that is nearest my heart – the right to call a lady "my own." During the past four days I have been troubled by incessant and untimely visits from the local postman, who has almost hourly presented me with congratulatory letters – and other things – from my numerous friends in the profession. The cause of all this annoying ebullition of congratulations and imprecations combined is the announcement in last week's provincial notices of *The Era*, under the heading "Redditch:" – "Pat and Louise are in the hands of Mr and Mrs Mark Leonard, in Mr Mulholland's *Unknown* company." The lady who has lately been playing Louise is, by a coincidence, Miss Constance Leonard, and on that account your reporter has evidently drawn his own conclusions. *Hinc illae lachrymae!** I beg to assure the ladies who have written reviling me for my apparent perfidy that I still invite good offers, and remain,
Yours unplightedly, MARK LEONARD. Theatre Royal, Cheltenham, Feb. 2nd, 1887.
**Hence these tears.*

TO THE EDITOR OF THE ERA.
Sir, – On Saturday night, while our luggage was being taken from the Theatre Royal, Castleford, to the railway station, a small portmanteau belonging to Miss Clara Santley, and containing her pantomime dresses, was missed. On Sunday morning the portmanteau had been brought to the station by one of the stage men just as we were leaving. On Monday, when preparing our dresses, Miss Santley found hers stripped of all the gold bullion and other trimmings. We suspect the bag had been purposely taken away, the trimmings stolen, then brought back. If you will kindly insert this it may save another artist from being so victimised. Yours sincerely, MURIEL SANTLEY. Miss Lillie Sephton's Pantomime Company, Masonic Theatre, Lincoln.   *5/2/1887*

THEATRICAL TROUBLES.

At the Preston County Court, on Tuesday, before his Honour Judge Coventry, Mr Howell-Pool, author of the drama *Wronged*, brought an action against Ann Clifton, of Garden-street, to recover the sum of £3 4s. 1d., being the value of certain articles detained by the defendant.

The evidence for the plaintiff was that in August last he took three rooms from the defendant for himself and three other members of the company, which was at that time performing at the Theatre Royal, Preston. The price agreed upon was 22s. for the week. The defendant proved inattentive to the wants of her lodgers, and on the evening of the third day on which they were in the house she started playing a musical box in the room below the one in which they were sitting. She wound it up at least twenty times. To avoid the annoyance, the following day the plaintiff and his fellow lodgers went out for a drive, and when they returned they found that a quantity of furniture had been removed from the sitting-room. Defendant declined to return it, and she said that four chairs were sufficient for them to sit on.

At night it was some time before they could get into the house, and at midnight Mrs Clifton burst into the sitting-room intoxicated. Miss Raynor, who was in the room, became hysterical in consequence of her conduct, and when her brother, Mr Raynor, went into the lobby to remonstrate with the defendant, she threw her arms round his neck, and shouted out, "Oh, if my father could see me now." He repulsed her, and said that her father would be very much ashamed if he could see her. Mr Blackhurst, who appeared for the defendant, said it was something new for Preston ladies to squeeze gentlemen. As a rule, it was the other way about. The plaintiff alleged that a number of his socks and collars were detained by defendant, and on Friday he had to leave the place and take apartments at the North-Western Hotel. Mr Poole, Mr Raynor and Miss Raynor gave evidence of the annoyance they experienced owing to the defendant's conduct.

The defence was a total denial of the charges, and Mr Blackhurst stated that it was simply an attempt to get money from a poor woman and to damage her character. In her evidence Mrs Clifton said that on one occasion Mr Poole and Miss Raynor sat up until three o'clock in the morning, and they amused themselves by throwing soda-water bottles at one another.

His Honour said that the whole of the case ought to have been set up as a defence to an action in which Mrs Clifton had obtained judgement against Poole for the lodgings. It appeared to him that Mrs Clifton did lose her temper and was abusive, and the plaintiff not being able to stop at the place was entitled to some compensation. As, however, he ought to have defended the other case, he only gave a verdict for 10s., without costs.
12/2/1887

IT is well known that for months past the old theatre in Northampton has been used as the barracks of the Church Army. On Sunday night the Army was holding its devotional services there, when the news was brought that the building was to be used for dramatic purposed during the week, and the captain offered up a prayer that this might be averted.

A DISTRESSING calamity, it is said, has fallen upon Mr George Maxwell, one of the brightest and most efficient young members of Mr Wilson Barratt's company. During the recent engagement of the company in Cincinnati, Mr Maxwell, who was playing the part of Guildenstern, in *Hamlet*, exhibited some signs of mental disquietude, and in the scene with "the recorders" faltered in the words of a speech addressed to the Prince, and was unable to deliver the lines. He was very much distressed at this mischance, and apologised to Mr Barratt, who kindly made light of the matter, and told him not to feel vexed about it. The incident naturally created remark within the company, but no particular weight was attached to it until the next day, when Mr Maxwell developed unmistakable symptoms of derangement of intellect. He was seized with peculiar hallucinations, and finally became so violent that it was

necessary to restrain him by force. His condition when the company quitted Cincinnati was so grave that he was obliged to be left behind in care of a medical attendant*.
*Mr Maxwell had "overtaxed his brain by the endeavour to combine acting and journalism", and soon made a full recovery.

POOR PICKLES!

A correspondent writes: – On Monday morning a mournful procession, headed by the fireman of the theatre, crossed the stage of "Old Drury." The fireman was closely followed by four stalwart men, who bore on their shoulders a miniature coffin. Behind them came the mourners. The members of a country company who were using the stage for the purpose of rehearsal were astounded. In reply to their inquiries, they learned that poor old "Pickles" was about to be buried in the adjoining yard. "Pickles" was a very favourite cat in the theatre, and everyone at once recognised the propriety of the ceremony, for "Pickles" and Drury-lane Theatre have for years been inseparable.

"Pickles" was at one time induced to become a public performer, being brought on in a pie by Mr Harry Payne, the clown, but, as Mr. Payne now says, nobody, after the first two nights, was able to catch that cat in time for the performance, although it habitually turned up at the wings to see what its understudy made of the part. Another amusing reminiscence of the deceased cat is that during the run of a nautical melodrama it calmly walked across the raging waves as though they had merely been painted on canvas.

"Pickles" is supposed to have come by his death by tackling a poisoned rat. However that may be, "Pickles" is greatly regretted by all who ever performed at Drury-lane as a cat who could pick out a success from a failure, an actor from an amateur; and who would show his appreciation of those pieces and performers he approved of by attending their rehearsals, and studiously avoiding those of people he had found wanting.

The following epitaph is over his grave:

Sacred to the Memory
of
"PICKLES,"
the Drury Lane Cat.
Born Oct., 1880,
Died Feb., 1887.
Here lies the body of poor old Pickle,
He was always true, and never fickle.
Tho' his grave is humble and his coffin plain,
He was always a pet with the men at the Lane.

OLYMPIA. – On Tuesday last some 300 children of the Foundling Hospital attended the afternoon performance of the Hippodrome, on the kind invitation of Mrs Batley, of Elvaston-place, South Kensington. The chaplain, secretary, masters, and mistresses, and many of the nurses were also present, and with the children filled one section of the grand circle. It was a sight not soon to be forgotten to see them in their snowy white linen caps, tippets, and aprons, a costume well known to those who frequent the church attached to the Foundling Hospital. It was as though snow had fallen heavily on just one portion of the vast building. The children took the liveliest interest in the whole performance, and broke into peals of merry laughter at the comical bull fight and the funny doll in the stag hunt, and clapped their little black-gloved hands vigorously at the chariot races.
19/2/1887

ON the last night of the pantomime at the Queen's Theatre, Dublin, a sealed packet was sent to Miss Pollie Randall, and was found to contain a very valuable pearl and sapphire brooch and a complimentary note for Robin Hood.　26/2/1887

THE GERMAN BAND NUISANCE.

At the Marylebone Police-court on Friday, last week, Jacob Young, aged thirty-nine, a German musician, of Plummer's-row, Whitechapel, was charged with playing a musical instrument to the annoyance of Henry George Taylor, a private secretary occupying a flat at Manor-mansions, Belsize-park-gardens, Hampstead.

The prosecutor said he was at home on Thursday night about a quarter to eight, when a German band commenced playing. He went out and requested the men to go away, but they simply laughed and jeered at him. Prosecutor went to find the porter of the Mansions, and while so engaged the band commenced playing again. The band was standing in front of a house about two doors away. A policeman was fetched, and the prisoner was given into custody, as there had been some difficulty about getting the name of the prisoner, who appeared to be the spokesman for the rest. The playing of these bands had seriously interfered with his wife's health, and it had made him so nervous that he could not get on with his literary work, which at present was of an important nature. Between two and eight o'clock on Thursday there were two bands and an organ. He could not say whether anyone in the Mansions had given the prisoner and his colleagues encouragement, but some people a few doors away did encourage them, and when other people objected those people got the men to enter the garden and play. These bands frequented the locality every day. The prisoner said he did not play after the gentleman objected to their doing so. Another band had played there about twenty minutes previously. They had been in the habit of playing in the same road regularly for fourteen years.

Mr Cooke told the prisoner that he was silly to have refused his name and address, because that had resulted in him being placed in the dock. No street musician had the right to play when a person objected on the ground of illness, or of its being an interference with him in his business pursuits. Some people liked the music, but others did not, and when the latter objected and the band did not leave, each member was liable to a fine of 40s. The prisoner would have to pay a fine of 10s., and he had better take warning as to the future.

FOR SALE, a Wonderful FREAK OF NATURE. To Collectors of Animals, Novelties, Showmen, and Others, a Hybrid Dog, being Half Dog and Half Cat, perfect, and in good health, &c. Photos of the same can be had by sending a stamped envelope with six stamps for all particulars to the owner, Mr GEO. CHEW, 37, Back-lane, Blackburn, Lancashire.
5/3/1887

MADAME MARIE ROZE has been in Birmingham for the past three weeks, and stayed at the Great Western Hotel. Last week the room adjoining the prima donna's sitting-room was let for a large meeting of creditors, and whilst the business was progressing Madame Roze opened the piano in her room and began practicing her part in the night's opera. One might have thought her sweet notes would have been welcomed as a pleasant relief to the tedium of a dry creditors' meeting. But no. Business men, immersed in commercial matters, are an unartistic race, and a message was sent down to the manager of the hotel informing him that there was a lady making a noise in the next room, and requesting him to ask her if she would mind removing to a more distant apartment. The idea of Madame Roze singing the operatic airs which have made her name famous throughout the world being described as "a lady making a noise" is really funny.

AT the Southampton Police-court, on the 14th inst., Frederick Albini was summoned for assaulting Jessie Phillips, at the Royal York Music Hall, on the 2nd inst. Mr A.C. Hallett appeared for complainant, a serio-comic and burlesque actress, and Mr Tayler for the defendant, a conjurer.

Complainant said that she was standing by the side of the stage on Tuesday evening, before the final performance, when defendant was on the stage. The curtain was down at the time. He said to her "Clear down there," and, after he had repeated this, she went down into the green-room, or dressing-room. At the close she heard loud talking upstairs, and went up. She asked him why he wanted to insult her, and he said "You dirty old thing, if you were a man I would pull the nose out of your face." She made reply, satirically, "I have been told you are a perfect gentleman," adding, "You are a low cad." He dared her to repeat the expression. She did so, and he struck her a violent blow in the face, which blackened her eye. She believed it was done with the open hand. She went to Dr Cheesman almost immediately. She had a perfect right to be on the stage, and was not connected with the defendant.

Mr Tayler cross-examined at length, from which it appeared that her performance was over by eight o'clock; but complainant was at that time – about ten – helping another lady professional She had not previously noticed the defendant preparing his tricks in regard to the vanishing lady. Defendant called Mr Edmonds, who requested her to leave the stage, and this she at once did. She did not strike the defendant on the ear with a hand bag.

William Elgar, stage-manager, whose professional name is "Bogie," said he was a lady's man, and sometimes helped them to change; but on this occasion complainant was helping a sister artiste in dressing, and, having a perfect right to be there, did not like to be ordered off by the defendant. He corroborated the striking of the blow.

Dr Cheesman deposed that the centre of the blow was at the exterior angle of the left orbit.

The Magistrate's Clerk (Mr Eldridge) – In English, that means a black eye. Dr Cheesman – Yes. The young woman was perfectly sober, and behaved in a most decorous manner.

This closed the case for the prosecution, and a cross summons against Miss Phillips was then taken, the previous defendant, Albini, giving evidence. He said that he was a society conjurer, having been in business sixteen years. He was "last turn," and defendant first. His performance was a speciality to retain the audience, and it took him about half-an-hour to prepare it, and he found Miss Phillips in his way. He requested her to leave – he was very polite to ladies at all times. She refused to go. He sent for the proprietor, who told her to go, and eventually she did, saying, "Your trick's done – it's played out, and I'll tell the audience." She did speak about it in the bar. She also called him a cad, accompanied with other words, which he refused to utter, and the whole matter culminated by her striking him a violent blow on the ear, which bled considerably. He then struck her with his flat hand.

Mr Edmonds, the proprietor, stated that Miss Phillips had no right to be in the wing of the stage, after her performance, although the rule was not rigidly enforced.

The bench here stopped the case, considering that there were faults on both sides. Both summonses were dismissed, both parties to pay their own costs.
12/3/1887

A rather amusing incident occurred while Mr Barry Sullivan was playing in *The Gamester*, at the Grand Theatre, Glasgow, last Saturday evening. It was the last act. Mr Sullivan – that is, Beverley – had swallowed the poison, and while groaning over his rash act, was asking the forgiveness of Miss Beadnell – otherwise Mrs Beverley – for "dying meanly." In the left corner of the orchestral stalls a voice was heard to say, in a very audible whisper, "Why don't they fetch him a stomach-pump?" A titter arose amongst those around who heard the words, amid suppressed murmurings of "Order" and "Hush!" Then, in a still more audible whisper, came an answer from another wag, "Oh, they won't have any amongst their properties." That settled it, and the sentiment of the scene was completely spoiled for those who sat on the prompt side of the stalls. The players, however, could know nothing of what was going on below them, nor would Mr Sullivan know of the joke that was being perpetrated at his expense.

ON Sunday evening, as Mr Auguste Creamer's *Robinson Crusoe* pantomime company were on route from Preston to Burnley, a pig, one of the features of the "comic" scenes, finding the door of the covered truck insecure, jumped out on to the line. His loss was discovered on the arrival of the truck at Burnley.

By telegraph means, the railway officials were sent in pursuit of the porker, who was found running along the line unhurt.

SEVERAL lady members of the choir of a U.P.* Church in the East-end of Dundee have been put under ban for having taken part in the recent performance of *The Bohemian Girl* by the Amateur Opera Company in Her Majesty's Theatre. The ladies have been interdicted from taking their places in the choir in future, and they have likewise been notified that their services will not be required in a forthcoming recital in which they were to have taken part.
United Presbyterian.
19/3/1887

ON March 13th, at West Cornforth, Durham, Herr A. Blitz, illusionist (one of the members of Harry Clifford's concert party), while on his way home from the entertainment, met with a severe accident by falling down a cellar of a house unoccupied, there being no grating over it, the night dark, and no gas in the street. He severely cut his head in two places, and injured the left eye. He was picked up insensible and carried to Dr Walker's, who immediately dressed the wounds, and pronounced them not dangerous.

RUPTURES CURED. – A NEW TRUSS. – Mr C.B. HARNESS, the renowned inventor of Electropathic Belts and other Curative Electrical Appliances, has lately introduced a new XYLONITE TRUSS, which is highly approved of and adopted by the medical profession. It gives the wearer complete comfort and support without irritation. It has a perfectly smooth, flesh-coloured, washable surface. Is cheap, and will last a lifetime. Advice free. Call or send for particulars. Note address, the MEDICAL BATTERY COMPANY (Limited), 52, OXFORD-STREET, LONDON, W. (corner of Rathbone-place). (ADVT)
26/3/1887

MR EDITOR. – Sir, – Your Leeds correspondent in your last issue announces me as a dog and monkey performer. My entertainment consists of birds of all nations, over sixty in number. Kindly rectify this mistake, as it may mislead proprietors and managers. Yours, &c., LEONI CLARKE, the Bird King.

WANTED, for Easter, a Duff Painting of a Fat Donah. Must look young and must be worth the money. Apply, FRED. CARROLL, 42, Chappell-street, Salford, Manchester.
2/4/1887

THE wife of the popular and generally esteemed Mr Bram Stoker*, with their only child, a bright little boy of seven years of age, was among the sufferers, but happily not among the lost, in the sad disaster which befell the Newhaven and Dieppe steamer *Victoria* on Wednesday morning. With seventeen other persons, none of whom seemed to know anything about the proper handling of an oar, Mrs Stoker and her child were placed in the third boat that was sent off from the steamer. For twelve hours, cold and wet, they drifted about in the rough sea, expecting every instant to be swamped, until fortunately they were sighted by a steam tug, picked up, and carried in a state of exhaustion to Fècamp, where they were received by the mayor, the doctor, and the curé of the place, who speedily attended to their wants. Mr Bram Stoker's anxiety on hearing of the disaster was naturally very distressing. He had the warmest sympathy of many friends, but it was not until after long and weary waiting that the welcome news arrived that his wife and child were safe.
Stoker, best remembered as the author of Dracula, *was for many years the acting and later business manager of the Lyceum Theatre.*

A "FAT WOMAN" ON SHOW.
At the Norwich Guildhall, before W.J.U. Browne (chairman) and J.D. Smith, Esqs., John Hastings and Arthur Crompton, showmen, were summoned recently by Inspector Scarff, "for unlawfully keeping a

booth for the purpose of exhibiting an indecent, disgusting, and loathsome performance". The Town Clerk prosecuted, and Mr Linay defended.

Inspector Scarff, in company with Detective Rushmer, visited the booth kept by the defendants at a fair. He found that Hastings was the proprietor, and was outside inviting people to enter, as also was Crompton. Hanging to public view were two large paintings, representing a nearly naked fat female dancing with a man, with the superscription "How she took them down to the ball." The other picture was of a similar creature reclining on a couch smoking a cigarette. The charge for admission was twopence each, and Scarff and Rushmer having paid their entrance fee were admitted to the show. Inside was hung a curtain at the back part of the booth, dividing it into two portions. There were about fifty people inside, all men.

Presently, after an introduction from Hastings, the curtain was withdrawn, and a person – presumably a female – was seen standing on a platform naked, with the exception of a small pair of green knickerbockers. Crompton then gave a description of the "lady," and said she weighed thirty-five stone. The individual in question had long hair hanging down the back. One of the audience was asked to feel the fat one's legs, which he did. When the audience had gone out Scarff spoke to the defendants, and got their names. Turning his attention to the "lady," she, after some hesitation, gave the name "Stainton." Being pressed for her Christian name she said "William."

In answer to Mr Linay, Inspector Scarff said the "woman" had a pair of shoes and socks on. He had seen persons bathing, and thought that the "object" had less on than they. The man in the court was the "Parisian beauty," exhibited as a female. The picture outside did not represent a female in "tights." Detective Rushmer corroborated the statement made by Inspector Scarff. Defendants pleaded not guilty in answer to the charge, and made their defence through Mr Linay, who held that the exhibition of a fat naked man to men was not so indecent. Mr. Browne said what was seen was supposed by the audience to be a female. Mr Linay admitted that, and said the audience pretty well knew what they were going to see. It was probably a proper case for investigation, but he contended that there was not sufficient evidence to justify the defendants being sent for trial at the assizes. The Bench then retired. On their return defendants were committed for trial, bail being allowed in £10 each and two sureties for £5 each.
16/4/1887

A TWICKENHAM correspondent says: – Prince Alexander*, son of the Duke and Duchess of Teck, was one of the performers at a concert given at Petersham, near Richmond, on Thursday night, his contribution being the comic song entitled "The Speaker's Eye." The Prince acquitted himself to the entire satisfaction and amusement of the audience, the whistling passages in the song, which were faithfully interpreted, being much appreciated. The Duchess of Teck was present.
*Prince Alexander was the thirteen-year-old brother of the future Queen Mary.
23/4/1887

COLLAPSE OF A CIRCUS.
The Olympia Hippodrome and Circus – not of Paris – visited Yeovil on Tuesday and met with a sad misfortune. The day was boisterous, and the procession through the streets was shorn of much of its anticipated splendour. The large marquee was fixed in a field, and in the afternoon there was a good attendance of children and others. The heavy rain made it very uncomfortable, and suddenly a tremendous gust of wind lifted the tent and poles from the ground and then the whole collapsed. Fortunately the marquee had been lashed to heavy caravans, and was not at once brought bodily to the ground. However, great consternation prevailed, and the attendants, in order to allow the occupants to escape quickly, cut holes in the canvas, and many of the visitors crawled out. It was reported that two children were injured, but if so they soon made their way home. None of the animals, performers, or attendants were hurt. The performance had not commenced when the accident happened, and the circus was not full, or more serious results might have occurred. The damage was estimated at £130.

BETWEEN Saturday night and Monday morning last there passed through Derby station of the Midland Railway Company no fewer than sixteen companies, comprising about four hundred members of the profession.
30/4/1887

THE Dumfries Theatre was the scene of a ludicrous incident on Saturday night. The curtain did not rise till nearly an hour after the time, and then the acting-manager appeared and intimated that one of the members of the company had got "overwhelmed in strong waters," and consequently they could not perform the pieces in the programme, and those who wished their money returned would receive it at the door; but for those who chose to remain the company would provide a variety entertainment. The majority of the audience kept their seats. Those who retired got out in time to witness the conclusion of a free fight in the street between the inebriated member of the company and a captain of the Salvation Army.

YORK. – From EDWIN to FRED. Come Home at once. Will get you a free passage if you will let me know correct address. That little affair is settled. Mother is upset, but will be better when you return. A loving welcome awaits you.
7/5/1887

AT the Prince of Wales's Theatre, on Tuesday evening, during the performance of the farce *A Happy Day*, one of the bags of gas used in producing the lime light exploded in the wings, on the O.P. side of the stage. The limelight man was lifted off his feet and very much shaken, some of the boards were blown out of place, and part of the scenery fell down. Fortunately, the house not being full at that early part of the entertainment, a panic which might easily have occurred was avoided.
14/5/1887

OUR Chester correspondent writes: – "We regret to announce that on Saturday afternoon a serious accident happened to one of Mr Lindo Courtenay's indefatigable servants, John Kendrick, at the New Royalty Theatre. When in the act of posting bills, between one and two o'clock, on the high boards in Grosvenor Park-road, his ladder was swept from beneath him by the gale, and he was hurled on to some spiked railings, one of which pierced the lower part of his back about four inches. He was rescued from this terrible position by some passers by with considerable difficulty, the blood flowing copiously from the wound, and taken to the infirmary, where he remains under the treatment of Dr Lees. On the same morning the substantial transparency erected by Mr Chas. Cawdery over the dress-circle entrance received such damage from the high wind as to necessitate its entire removal."

A PIKELET TEA.
Landladies are divided into two classes. The landlady born and bred, and the landlady who becomes one from circumstances. The former one is not popular. […]
    It was on a Monday afternoon, some nine years since, that I knocked on the door of a house in Preston. I had wandered half over the town, with the object of securing apartments, the cheapness of which would allow some little margin for food. My labours were rewarded with success, for, although my landlady belonged to the hated class, the characteristics of which I by this time knew only too well, the rooms were so cheap that I engaged them at once, and my spirits rose when I found she did not require a deposit. I had one shilling and twopence in my pocket, which, although insufficient as a deposit, is very useful when prudently expended on food. Dinner was out of the question. Nothing less than three-quarters of a pound of steak would have satisfied my wants for dinner, so I concentrated all my faculties on tea.

My landlady proposed a number of dishes, all excellent in themselves, but, under the circumstances, not to be thought of. When one's money is limited to the sum of one shilling and twopence, the choice of edibles is not extensive. I was beginning to despair when my landlady said "Pikelets are very nice." Pikelets – little dried fish, I thought. "Um, not bad; not much stay in them, though." Pikelets do not appeal powerfully to the imagination of a hungry man, but as it was absolutely necessary to observe a rigid economy I decided to try them. "How many?" said my landlady. Little dried sprats, I thought, one penny a bundle, about twelve in a bundle. "Well, madam, I'll have two dozen." "Two dozen, sir," she said, seeming surprised. "Yes," said I, indifferently. "I am very partial to pikelets, and I'll have two dozen, and be sure to have tea ready by five o'clock."

When one is poor it is hard to practice the virtues; I practiced one that afternoon – punctuality. As the clock struck five I entered the sitting-room, and awaited with the keenest expectation the arrival of the tea-pot. The tea-pot came first, and a tolerably long wait acquainted me with the fact that the tea never came from China. […] Again the door opened, and the landlady entered, followed by her daughter, who placed at my side what appeared to be a bill. I didn't notice it, for my attention was riveted upon the dish my landlady was carrying. A greasy circular edifice of livid muffins somewhere about eighteen inches high. "What are these?" I gasped. "These are not pikelets." "Yes, sir," replied the landlady, "we calls 'em pikelets in Preston. They are the same, I believe, as muffins and crumpets in London. If you want the teapot filling please ring the bell."

"Two dozen," I murmured, as I gazed at the pile. I felt depressed. It requires a man of high stamp to bear up against a pikelet tea, and after I had consumed a dozen my spirits began to droop and I stopped, but a glance at the paper at my side, which proved to be the bill, was sufficient to arouse me to a fresh onslaught. I drank enormous quantities of tea; the tea-pot was twice watered. I strove, perspired, and swelled – in fact, assumed colossal proportions, and still there were some left. There seemed no end to them. What a loss of time; what a waste of power! The dish was empty, but I was undone.

"You don't seem pleased with your tea," said my landlady as she cleared away the tea things. I was breathing heavily, but I managed to inquire whether she expected me to display rapture over two dozen pikelets. "I don't know about rapture," snapped the born and bred one, "but I shall be pleased if you'll settle this 'ere bill, as I hear you are all shamefully poor." "On Saturday," I responded in a deep voice. "Now, at once!" she shouted, "or out of the house you go with your rubbishing things." "Don't you think you are rather rude?" I remonstrated. "I never puts on my company manner with professionals," she replied, "and least of all with those who can't pay." "I shall pay," I gurgled, "if you'll wait till Saturday. Surely you can trust." "Trust!" shrieked the enemy, "oh, indeed! A likely thing. Not for Emma Wimpole – not if she knows it. Emma Wimpole would never have had as good a silk gown as any woman in Preston if she'd trust to lodgers. If you can't pay a trifle like this, what can you pay, I should like to know?" She called it a trifle.

	s.	d.
Two dozen pikelets	1	0
One pound of butter for same	1	4
Tea	0	4
One loaf bread	0	4 ½
¼ lb. of sugar		1 ½
½ lb. Butter	0	4
Milk	0	0 ½
½ lb. Cheese	0	5
	3	11 ½

And only one shilling and twopence to pay it with. She went to fetch her husband, and I waddled as quickly as I could to the street-door. I did not run. It was impossible. There are few people in a position to realise the amount of inconvenience the carrying of two dozen pikelets entails. Impelled by the

instincts of self-preservation, I reached the bottom of the street, and made for the theatre. Swollen but ruined, I walked sadly along. I did not feel well. The gracious influence of the evening breeze only increased my indisposition. I met with one of the company, and, after exerting all the eloquence at my command, managed to borrow twopence. I expended it on some medicine, which I took at once, and next day I breathed freely. Fleeting indeeds are the joys of the table.
ARTHUR GOODRICH.
28/5/1887

A CORRESPONDENT of an American paper makes an ingenious suggestion of a method whereby Mr Mansfield, the representative of the dual leading character in the recently produced drama *Dr Jekyll and Mr Hyde*, might imitate the celebrated transformation. He wrote: – "Mr Mansfield will wear a rubber suit. This suit will act as an air bag. When he wants to be Mr Jekyll it must be expanded. When he is Hyde it hangs loose upon him. The suit has a valve which can be opened or shut by the turning of a button. Let us imagine Mr Hyde entering his room. He goes to a sideboard for the wonderful liquid, or to any part of the stage where he can apply to the valve in the rubber suit a tube concealed in the scenery. The sudden growth to Mr Jekyll is thus a simple matter. But how does he manage the escape of air when he wishes to resume the form of Hyde? To open the tiny valve is to let the air escape, but the difficulty is to avoid the hissing sound that would attend the collapse of Jekyll. This is but a matter of another visit to that part of the stage where an invisible tube can be applied. This tube is a piece of hose an inch or more in diameter. The air is quickly drawn out by a powerful suction without noise. This particular bit of mechanism was invented by a rubber company especially for this scene, and that company has a patent on it. This will, for a time, give Mr Mansfield a monopoly of the novelty of dwindling perceptibly in size."
4/6/1887

THE danger of wearing a chemically-prepared or "everlasting" clean collar has recently been exemplified in a very painful manner. Mr William Allen, the musical director, while wearing one of these collars, had occasion to light the gas, and in doing so he held the flame of the match somewhat near to his neck. The collar immediately burst forth into flame. His wife, perceiving the danger, immediately threw a cloth on the flames, but not before he was burnt so severely as to render necessary his removal to St George's Hospital.

TO THE AFFLICTED. – The Advertiser will send, on receipt of Twenty-Eight Stamps, a sufficient supply of LADY ST JOHN'S SAMARITAN SALVE to cure any ordinary cases of Bad Legs, Bad Breasts, Tumours, Ulcers, Cancers, &c., however long standing; Erysipelas, Burns, Scalds, Piles, Blotches, and all Diseases of the Skin. Address, J.J. QUEMBY, of ST JOHN'S HOUSE, 324, WANDSWORTH-ROAD, LONDON. List of Cures and Trial Box sent to any part of the United Kingdom on receipt of nine stamps. To order of all Chemists. Trade Mark, 54, 620.

VICTOR ROSENBURGH, an effeminate-looking young fellow, with long, dishevelled hair, was charged the other day at the Liverpool Police-court with stealing a watch and chain belonging to Mr Ware, publican. He had been engaged to appear at a free-and-easy at Ware's in his great character of a male barmaid. After he left a watch was missed, and found pledged. He was arrested in female attire in a public-house in Derby, appearing as the Jersey Lily and the beautiful Duchess of Devonshire. He was committed to the sessions.
11/6/1887

AN exciting scene occurred on Thursday night at the Queen's Theatre, Manchester, during the progress of *A Mother's Sin.* Towards the close of the third act, when the hero seems to be in the power of the villain of the piece, a man in the gallery rose to his feet, shook his fist at the actor who was personating the villain, and then took a fearful leap from the gallery on to the stage, on which he fell with a sickening thud just beyond the footlights. Actors and audience were much excited, and shrieks were heard from all parts of the house. The man was at once carried off the stage, and removed to the Royal Infirmary, where it was found that his leg was broken. The distance from the gallery to the stage is 30ft. The man's name is Mandeville, as is that of the heroine of the piece.

EXTRAORDINARY MUSICAL FEAT.

An extraordinary feat in piano playing has been accomplished in Stockport by Mr N.* Bird, pianoforte teacher, St Marygate. It appears that a few days ago Mr Bird and a number of others were discussing a similar feat which had been accomplished in India by a gentleman who played for twenty-three and three-quarter successive hours. Mr Bird ventured to say he could exceed that performance, his saying so being justified by that fact that all his life he had been accustomed to piano playing, but his ability was questioned, and a challenge was thrown out to him and was accepted, the terms being that he should beat the record for playing for twenty-five successive hours, with the stipulation that, unlike the Indian performer, he should not be allowed to use one hand at meal times while he fed himself with the other. [...]

The Albert Hall was engaged, and nine o'clock on Tuesday night was fixed as the time for the commencement of the feat. Mr Bird procured an ordinary upright iron grand piano by Messrs Hardy and Sons, of Stockport, by whom he is employed as a tuner, and arranged that food should be given to him as he played, this consisting of chicken, toast, brandy, beer, &c. He mainly depended for refreshment, however, upon ice, which he sucked in small pieces. Two seats were provided for him, one an ordinary piano stool and the other a high stool with a low back. These could easily be exchanged while he continued playing, and were a means of affording him considerable relief. [...]

When Mr Bird took his seat to commence his task there was a very large audience in the room. When the signal to start was given Mr Bird, who had previously divested himself of his coat, struck up "God Save the Queen," amid loud cheering. This over, he dashed into a number of lively airs, gliding from one to the other without any apparent effort at selection, and the audience, or the large majority, finally left him thrumming away quite comfortably. Some of the judges and a number of enthusiasts remained all night. About his usual bedtime Mr Bird felt slightly sleepy, but soon overcame this feeling, and in the small hours of the morning was, we are assured, playing merrily away, as lively as a cricket. At five o'clock, to use his own words, he felt as though he was "only just beginning." His wife gave him food in small portions when he asked for it, and his seat was occasionally changed. As the day wore on Mr Bird showed no signs of exhaustion, and his repertoire of pieces seemed inexhaustible. He used no music. Occasionally he sang to his own accompaniment, and added a little more variety by means of a triangle, which he worked with his left foot.

The audience kept coming and going all day, and expressed surprise at what was being done with an evident probability of success. A visitor with a good voice, which he was willing to use, was an acquisition, and at intervals the hall rang with choruses. Solos were also contributed, Mr Bird being never at a loss for an accompaniment, although, as we have stated, he used no music. [...]

The performance was to finish at ten o'clock on Wednesday, and it was natural that the few hours preceding that time should be the most interesting and exciting. At about seven o'clock a large number of people collected outside the building, and two hours later they formed a dense crowd. Inside the building much excitement prevailed. The room was hot and crowded, but Mr Bird seemed by no means inconvenienced by that. On the contrary, he put greater energy into his task, and polka, waltz, schottische, chorus, glee, and song were dashed off with astonishing freedom. Sometimes pieces of widely different emotional effects were placed in juxtaposition, but when the opportunity occurred there were always some ready to join in the choruses, and a more than usually lively piece was was sure to call forth loud applause. The twenty-third hour was the most troublesome the pianist experienced, a stiffness then affecting the muscles at the back of his hands. This, however, wore off, and and when the completion of the twenty-fourth hour was announced, amid tremendous applause, Mr Bird's fingers were chasing each other over the keys as though they had never known stiffness.

In the last hour he played eighty-four different tunes. At ten minutes to ten he led the audience in "Christians awake," five minutes later he struck up "God Bless the Prince of Wales," at two minutes to ten he was making a lively attack on "Rule Britannia," and when the long hand pointed at the hour he played "God Save the Queen" amid loud and enthusiastic cheers. Rising then from his seat he came to the front – who can estimate the pleasure of the change? – and the cheering was renewed again and again. […] Mr Bird was then shaken heartily by the hand by numbers of people who pressed up to the platform, and as he left the building he was followed by ringing cheers. We understand that for twelve years Mr Bird travelled with Tannaker's Japanese as pianist, and that for the last six months he has been professionally engaged at the Dog and Partridge, Churchgate, Stockport. He is a young man of slight build, and lives in St Marygate.
Napoleon.

WANTED. – Mim. Mim, Mim. Who is Mim, and what is Mim*? Watch for Mim, and don't forget Mim. Mim, Mim, Mim. Mim, Mim, Mim.
Mim turned out to be an Australian ventriloquist and mimic.
18/6/1887

CHARLIE KEITH, the well-known and popular clown, put out an original bill for his benefit at Nottingham on Friday. He issued a proclamation announcing a Jubilee performance, and promised a Jubilee welcome to all his patrons. The bill concluded in this fashion: – "As a Jubilee treat to all Jubilites who desire to Jubilate on this festival of Jubularity, all persons who have been married fifty years, or who have fifty children of their own, all persons who have never told a lie in fifty years, or have never quarrelled in fifty years, all young ladies who will acknowledge their age to be fifty, all persons who have been drunk for fifty years, or any person who can prove they have been perfectly sober for fifty years, will on this night have admission free."

WANTED, Three Boys, from the age of Seven and Nine, to bring up as Musicians. Apply to WM. BRIERLEY, Star Music Hall, Wigan.

WANTED, to Know who says the Beautiful Witch is dead. Miss Daisy Cope is still concocting fresh Magical Spells. Watch.

WANTED, Suite of Rooms, West-end, for Exhibiting a Coloured Fat Baby; also for a New Registered Exhibition of Performing Frogs. First time ever shown on earth, Jubilee Day. Letter only, D. BAKER, Albert Palace, London.
25/6/1887

ONE of the vilest ways in which enmity and envy display themselves is anonymous letter-writing, and one of the cruelest things possible is to disconcert and dishearten during a dramatic performance an actress who is striving her hardest for the gratification of her audience. These two forms of evil were combined by the sender of the nameless missive* which was received by Miss Houlistan during the performance of Mr Richard Davey's translation of *Manon de Lorme* at the Princess's on Tuesday afternoon last. The warmest sympathy of every lady and gentleman is due to the young actress who suffered so severely from the infamous epistle.
In the same issue of The Era *we are told that the offending words were "she was playing vilely, and that everyone was laughing at her."*
2/7/1887

AT the Marlborough-street Police-court on Thursday Alfredo de Vartas, described in one of his show-bills as "Trumpeter in the Guards of the King of Belgium" and "the Tallest Soldier in the World," a man nearly seven feet high, was charged before Mr Mansfield with assaulting James Broach, Edward Mulally, and James Reed. Mr Bernard Abrahams, solicitor, conducted the defence.

Mulally, whose head was enveloped in surgical bandages, deposed that at half-past ten o'clock on Wednesday night, as he was walking along Little Newport-street, attempting to blow a toy paper horn, he accidentally knocked up against the prisoner, who struck him a blow with his fist, knocking him down. He got up and asked him what he did it for, when the accused struck him with a stick he had in his hand, and again knocked him down. A friend who was with the giant kicked him as he lay on the ground, and also struck him. Witness also saw the prisoner strike a man named Reed, and knock him down. Reed was so injured that he had to be taken to a hospital, and he was not well enough to attend court that day. The giant struck a third man. The companion of the accused ran away.

James Broach, a fishmonger, deposed that he saw a crowd in Little Newport-street on the previous evening. Suddenly the crowd appeared to open, and the prisoner rushed towards him and struck him on the head with the stick produced, knocking him down. For a time he was rendered insensible. When he recovered his senses he saw the accused knock a man down who had only one leg. He also assaulted two other gentlemen, one of whose ears was split open.

Cross-examined – He did not in any way interfere with the prisoner. Everyone seemed frightened of him because he was a giant. He could not say how the head of the accused became cut. The neighbourhood was a most dangerous one.

Detective Kitchen deposed that on the previous night, seeing a crowd in Little Newport-street and hearing cries of "Murder," he went to ascertain what was the matter, when he saw the prisoner surrounded by a crowd of persons. He saw him knock down the man Reed by hitting him with a stick on the head. The accused made a blow at Detective Cracket, who was in company with witness, and who had seized hold of the giant, saying, "We are police." Witness then made a blow with his stick at the prisoner in order to disarm him, and in doing so inflicted a wound on his (prisoner's) head. Broach then came up and managed to take the stick of the accused away from him. When he first saw the accused he was endeavouring to fight his way out of the crowd by freely using his stick. With great difficulty he was got to the station. Cross-examined – The mouth of the giant was bleeding when witness first saw him. About five or six hundred persons were present and it was with great difficulty the police succeeded in preventing the crowd from lynching the prisoner.

Edward Bower, house surgeon at Charing Cross Hospital, deposed that a man named James Reed was brought to that establishment on the previous night suffering from a severe wound on the head. Witness had also examined Mulally and Broach, both of whom were suffering from wounds on the head.

Mr Mansfield remanded the accused, and refused to allow bail until it was ascertained that Reed was out of danger.

A MUSICAL DRESS IMPROVER.

Mr Justice Kekewich was occupied in the Chancery Division on Tuesday with the hearing of an action relating to patents in dress improvers. The court was strewn with various specimens of these articles, and considerable amusement was caused by the spectacle of a judge and several leading counsel, including the Attorney-General, arguing gravely on the intricacies of the various designs for dress improvers. Mr Justice Kekewich, after looking at several designs, said – I hope you are going to produce another of these articles, Mr Aston, which I do not see here. It is called the Jubilee. Mr Aston – I have never heard of it, my lord. His Lordship – It is one which, when a lady sits down, plays the National Anthem. Later on, Mr Aston argued that a dress improver was virtually the same as a garter. His Lordship – Do you mean that seriously? Mr Aston – Yes, I do, my lord. They are the same, though not in size. His Lordship – Very well, Mr Aston. I can see I shall want a jury of matrons in this case before it is done.
*See note on page 57.   9/7/1887

DISGUISE is a stock expedient of the melodramatist for creating excitement and interest; but it is not often that we find personal transformations utilised in the affairs of daily life. A short time since a young lady who described herself as an "actress" dressed up in boy's clothes for the purpose of detecting the infidelities of a faithless swain; and now we have Mr Nathan, costumier, of Bear-street, Leicester-square, who is driven to conceal his identity for the purpose of serving a summons upon a creditor of quick movements. In order to prove service on Miss Maude Forrester, Mr Nathan, it appears, put on a fur cap and a long beard, and, thus transmogrified, approached the lady at Euston Station. The incident must have closely resembled that celebrated "point" in *The Ticket-of-Leave Man*, only that, instead of replying to the query as to his identity in the memorable words, "Hawkshaw, the detective!" Mr Nathan merely remarked "I am Mr Nathan; you know me." Mr Nathan is evidently a very persevering man, and is not to be deterred from demanding what is due to him, either by excuses from Miss Forrester or personal violence from her "gentleman friends." Miss Forrester is strangely unfortunate. She is often in receipt of a respectable salary, yet there is always some unlucky reason which prevents it reaching her creditors. On a former occasion, her brother was the recipient of her wages; now she has been obliged to "buy dresses" with her hardly-won earnings. We should have thought that the Godiva* costume, at all events, was not very expensive; but, doubtless, smallness of superficial area has little to do with cost of material in these cases.

Miss Forrester, who claimed not to recognise Mr Nathan until his beard fell off, had recently appeared as Lady Godiva in the historical pageant at Coventry.
16/7/1887

TO THE EDITOR OF THE ERA.
Sir. – It has been stated in a certain newspaper that I have lost my leg and substituted a wooden one. I read this with amazement and pain, and beg to inform the theatrical world through you that it is wholly untrue. It has been reprinted, and becomes serious. I have taken legal advice on the matter, and shall shortly take means to prove to the general public that there is neither any truth in, nor any pretence, for this cruel statement. I am, Sir, yours faithfully, EMILY KENNION. Lessee Grand Theatre, Nottingham, and Theatre Royal, Leicester.
30/7/1887

WANTED, to Sell, Suspension Apparatus for exhibiting Chloroformed Child sleeping in Mid Air. A show by itself. Also Costume for same. Splendid lot. No use for same. £4. NORMAN, 6, Charlton-place, Islington-green.
13/8/1887

ON Saturday evening last a young man, a student at the Dublin University, named Landon, belonging to Cork, and residing at the Grand Hotel, Douglas, Isle of Man, was killed whilst riding on a switchback railway at the Derby Castle grounds, Douglas. It appears that the deceased was attempting to accelerate the progress of the car in which he was travelling, when he fell off, and was precipitated with great force against one of the barriers, death being instantaneous.

WANTED. – King and Queen of the Feathered Tribe. Carles, the only acknowledged Champion Pigeon Charmers of the World, big success. McFarland's, Dundee. Evening Telegraph, Aug. 16th – The Carles, with their performing pigeons, met with an enthusiastic reception, and the extraordinary feats of the birds, trained and introduced by Madame Carle, were loudly applauded. One bird sat on a hoop whilst part of it was enveloped in flames. Another was placed on the muzzle of a gun, and remained there while a shot was fired; while a third flew from the hands of Madame Carle and alighted on a gun, immediately after the gun had been discharged.
20/8/1887

AN exciting incident took place last Saturday night at the Theatre Royal, West Bromwich, while Mr Claude Shaw's *Shoulder to Shoulder* company were giving their final performance to a house packed from floor to ceiling. At the end of the third act a steamer runs into a small boat. The scene had worked the audience up to such a pitch of excitement that a lad of about fourteen years of age, in his anxiety to get a good view, overbalanced himself and fell from the gallery on to the heads of the people below. Mr Shaw and the constable on duty elbowed their way with all haste through the crowd and got out the boy, who, to their astonishment, though bleeding from the mouth, has sustained no more serious injury than the loss of one of his teeth. When informed that there was no possibility of his regaining his former seat among the gods he began to cry and make such a fuss that Mr Shaw ordered him to be placed in the dress circle, there to witness the remainder of the show.

A STRANGE scene, which attracted many hundreds of spectators, was witnessed on Wednesday in West Derby-road, Liverpool, upon the occasion of the marriage at a Registrar's office of one of the cowboys in the troupe of "Mexican Joe," now performing at the Liverpool Exhibition. The bride was a Miss Mary Currie, an attendant at a stall at the Exhibition. The bridegroom was resplendent in the costume alleged to be characteristic of the Wild West, and was accompanied by the whole of the troupe similarly attired, while the "historical" Tombstone Coach was pressed into service as a wedding equipage. The bridegroom's name, which figures in the programmes as "Montana Bill," was given for matrimonial purposes as Oliver Frank Baxter. Together with his companions, Texas Jack, Lassoo Mack, Buckskin Bill, Mustang Jim, and Rocky Mountain Dick, he was the object of not less hearty reception than the bride and her attendants, and the party had some difficulty in finding a way through the crowd which gathered round the Registrar's office, and saluted the pair with the customary showers of rice.
27/8/1887

MR TOM WOOTTWELL, the loose-legged comedian, has had a series of misfortunes lately. On Thursday week last, when going from the Foresters' Music Hall to Harwood's, he was thrown out of his trap in Bethnal-green Road; on Saturday last, in Pitfield-street, he had a portmanteau stolen containing various items of costume; and the other night his house, 2, Riversdale-road, Highbury Park, was entered, every door, box, and drawer broken open, and the house completely ransacked from top to bottom.

WANTED. – Signor Trevori will Back his Singing Dog against any other in the World for Stakes, Beefsteaks and German Sausage.
10/9/1887

A MOST mysterious outrage, or otherwise accident, is reported from Leeds. Mr Hodgson, a young gentleman residing at 12, Burley-street, accompanied by a friend, went to a shooting saloon in New Briggate, known as "Walton's," to amuse themselves by a shooting competition. None of the ranges were at liberty, and a small crowd was standing near each range. Seeing that they could not be attended to, the young gentlemen turned towards the front door, and were apparently about to leave when Mr Hodgson suddenly cried, "Oh, I am shot." Blood was soon perceived to be streaming from his left shoulder, and an examination showed that a bullet had pierced him under the shoulder-blade. The police were called in, but the rush of people was so great that it was impossible to discover the person who was believed to have deliberately shot Mr Hodgson. The police are investigating the affair. The bullet is six inches deep in Mr Hodgson's shoulder, and only an inch from a vital part.

WORMS IN A FOX TERRIER. – "The Cottage, Sandhills, Walsall, March 3rd, 1887. Please send me one of Naldire's Worm Powders. I consider them splendid. I had a fox terrier almost dead last Sunday, and got one of your powders from a friend, and in fifteen minutes after the dog had it he passed a tapeworm almost 60ft. in length – FRANK J. BRAWN." – NALDIRE'S WORM POWDERS for Dogs are sold by all chemists in packets, 1s., 2s., 3s. 6d., and 5s., with full directions for use. (ADVT)

WANTED, Engagements for John Sanger and Son's Celebrated Performing Elephants: Two Groups of Six and Four in Number.

Group of Six Elephants, performing together in an entirely novel entertainment, forming a Grand Military Band, each animal playing on a different instrument, and the whole forming a complete orchestra. Also the only Boxing Elephant in Europe.

Group of Four Performing Elephants, the Largest in Europe. An entirely Original and Unique Entertainment.

Vide Press. – We have been accustomed to see elephants made to clamber on a tub and lift their feet and shake their heads, but when it comes to elephants being drilled as soldiers, taking part in a farce, and playing a set of musical instruments so as to form a complete band, it sounds like fairy tales, and yet this is what we saw at John Sanger and Son's Circus on Thursday.

The above to be let on very reasonable terms, for Short or Long Engagements. Apply, Sanger's Works, St Anne's-road, Stamford-hill, London.

17/9/1887

ON Sunday week a boating party started from Great Marlow, and included Mr Benjamin Terry (father of that popular and talented family of which Miss Ellen Terry is the chief), his two sons, Mr George Terry (of the Lyceum) and Mr Fred Terry, and Mr Henry Wright. In placing Mr George Terry's waistcoat in the stern of the boat Mr Wright let it fall overboard. The vest contained a gold chain, and attached to it were a watch, a guinea piece (a gift from his mother), and a sovereign purse containing several gold coins. On Monday the lock-keeper rose before the lark, and after dragging the river for several hours his patience was rewarded, for the articles were fished up none the worse for spending a night at the bottom of the Thames.

A SERIOUS accident occurred yesterday to "Mexican Joe" and his troupe, engaged in the "Wild West" show at the Liverpool Exhibition. They were driving full speed through the streets on the Tombstone coach*, when the coach overturned, and the bandsmen and two ladies were pitched into the street. Four were taken to the Infirmary severely injured. All the instruments belonging to the band were smashed.

Less than a month later the Tombstone coach had another accident in Willenhall, when one of its wheels came off during a procession.

1/10/1887

ON Tuesday, at the Barnet Police-court, Henry Broad, aged thirteen, described as an errand-boy, living at 13, Queen's-cottages, Essex-road, Islington, was charged with the unlawful possession of a Colt revolver. It appears that the prisoner had been employed by Mr Hutchinson, fruiterer, of Barnet, but had recently left that gentleman's service, and in consequence of complaints made to the police he was arrested on the above charge. A large silver-plated revolver, embossed "Colt's frontier six-shooter," and several cartridges were found on him. The lad states that he visited the "Wild West,"* having in his possession a fancy fan which had been given him by a second-hand furniture dealer. An Indian chief took a fancy to the fan, and intimated by signs that he wished to possess it and would be willing to give the revolver in exchange. The exchange was made, and the lad brought home the revolver. He says the "chief" told him the revolver was a present from Buffalo Bill. Prisoner was remanded in custody. The police are inclined to credit his story.

A show held at Earl's court.

WANTED, Miss Claire Eversleigh to Know that her father is dead, River Plate, South America. Send address. Money waiting. Admiralty.
8/10/1887

WANTED, Purchaser for real Russian Sable Carriage Cloak, with Hood. Lined throughout with Quilted Satin. Only worn twice. Front, 45 in. long, 96 in. round. Cost 45 guineas, will take £17. Worth double. Address, RUSSIA, Gilyard's Agency, Bradford.
15/10/1887

A FEW days ago a little group was observed standing outside the stage-door of the Alexandra Theatre, Liverpool. The members of it were all very merry, and evidently enjoying their pleasant reunion, when suddenly the mirth was hushed by one of the party, who, having donned his eyeglasses, had caught sight of a board exhibited immediately above their heads, and inscribed thus: – "Notice. – No loiterers allowed. By order." He pointed it out to his companions, who in turn put up their glasses to inspect the new regulation. The situation was too much for them, and, with a hearty laugh, which was taken up by the small crowd of admirers that had collected, they gracefully adjourned. The loiterers were Mr Henry Irving, Mr J.L. Toole, Mr Charles Dickens*, Mr H.J. Loveday, Mr Bram Stoker and Mr George Loveday.
**The son of the famous novelist.*

MR EDITOR. – Sir, – I read in *The Era* of the 8th an account of attempted suicide of an actress named Josephine Hubert. Having once met her in Dundee I called at 19, Brooksby-street, Barnsbury, where the unfortunate lady lived. I found her and her little girl, eleven years of age, in a small back room denuded of furniture, except a wretched bed, just large enough to hold a child of about five years. There was no fire, and they had neither of them broken their fast, although it was three o'clock in the day. The place was clean, also the mother and child, but almost bare of clothing. They have gladly accepted an offer to share my home until something can be done for them. Miss Hubert is refined, intelligent, an excellent pianist. She tells me she can teach music. If she only had clothes and an instrument she could do something to earn a living for herself and child, who has been educated by her in spite of her failing health. Mr George Canninge has been kind enough to send her some help, which has enabled her to pay her debt to her late landlady. It is owing to the kindness of Mr Hannay that she has a dress to wear. Now, sir, many can help one, and amongst the thousands of readers of *The Era* surely there are some who could afford to help this unfortunate lady and her little one either with money or employment. I am unable to do more than give her a temporary home. Yours faithfully, AMY FORREST. 53, Gloucester-crescent, Regent's-park, N.W., Oct. 21st.
29/10/1887

ALLEGED SHAM ENTERTAINMENT.
A curious case came under the notice of the Burnley police on Saturday afternoon. It seems that a man, who has given the name of William Henry McLaughlin, announced a children's entertainment at St James's Hall, and, as a further inducement to obtain a large audience, a number of prizes of a varied character were offered. As a result of the glowing statements on the handbills no less than 1,500 children put in an appearance on the afternoon in question. The children waited for a couple of hours for the entertainment to begin, at the end of which time McLaughlin produced two dolls from a tin box, sat down, and did, not something wonderful, but nothing. Inspector Rawsthorne, whose notice had been drawn to a large number of boys and girls who were looking through the hall windows, entered the building, and being convinced that the entertainment was a swindle, took the prisoner into custody.

He was brought up at the Burnley Borough Police-court on Monday, and charged with obtaining money by false pretences, on Saturday afternoon, at St James's Hall. Inspector Rawsthorne, in the course of his evidence, said after some of the children had complained to him that they had been waiting in the room nearly two hours, he asked the prisoner to begin the entertainment or return the children's money. This he refused to do, and said the reason why he was not going to give his entertainment was because the children refused to be quiet. The prisoner afterwards went to a box, got two dolls out of it, sat down on a chair with one on each knee, and did nothing. He did not proceed with the entertainment, and in his (witness's) opnion there was no preparation for such an entertainment as was announced on the bills. He afterwards got prisoner to return the money. The Chief Constable (Mr Harrop) asked for a remand until Wednesday. Mr Wilcock, who defended the prisoner, objected on the ground that there was no charge against his client. Prisoner was a conjurer and ventriloquist. The remand was granted, the prisoner being allowed out on bail in the sum of £20.

WANTED, by Bernard Sloman, the Great Man-Bird. At Liberty Christmas Pantomime. Novel feature for Bird Ballet. Parrot, in "Robinson Crusoe," or "Babes in the Wood." Now causing great sensation at the Winter Gardens, Berlin, where please address.

NOTICE. – In consequence of Serious Indisposition of J.L. Dixon, owing to being in a damp bed, he has been ordered by his medical advisor to take a rest. Address, 34, Belgrave-street, Leeds. Sambo Sutton is doing a good Single Turn.
5/11/1887

MISS HELEN BARRY had an unmistakable proof of how powerful a spell her acting exercises over her audience when performing in *The Esmondes of Virginia* the other day at Sheffield. In the second act, at the most thrilling part of the play, when the receipt of the fatal letter which changes the character of the wife takes place, a little dog belonging to one of the company came bounding upon the stage. Miss Barry, with remarkable presence of mind, seized the animal, and threw him to the prompter at the wings. Despite the ridiculous nature of the incident, so thoroughly engrossed was the interest of the audience that it did not even raise a smile.
12/11/1887

ON the 12th inst., Josephine Gladys Hubert, aged twenty-nine, an actress, St Clements-street, Barnsbury, was charged at the Marylebone Police-court, on remand, with stealing a blanket, worth 6s., on the 25th ult., the property of Amy Forest Roberts, an actress, residing at 53, Gloucester-Crescent, Regent's-park. The parties in the case came before the Court in the first instance when making complaints against each other. Miss Roberts asked for process against Hubert, who, she said, had bitten her own child's arm very badly, leaving teeth marks visible. Hubert, on the other hand, asked for process against Roberts for the detention of her child. Inspector Moon, S Division, attended the court, and made a communication to the magistrate, in consequence of which Mr Cook did not grant any process, and the matter was allowed to stand over. Then followed the charge against Hubert for stealing a blanket.

Miss Roberts said she missed the article from one of her back bedrooms, and spoke to the prisoner about it. She and the prisoner were actresses, and and they first met at Dundee, where they were playing in the same piece. A short time ago Hubert attempted suicide, for which she was arrested, and charged at Clerkenwell Police-court. Prosecutrix found that Hubert had been associated with a man named Walter Bentley, an actor. She also found that she was living with her child in a wretched home, and that she was driven to despair, so she took her and her child into her home. Cross-examined, the prosecutrix said it was not true that she had accused anyone else of stealing things in her house. She had found that the blanket was in pledge.

The prisoner – I accepted your home under a false impression.

An assistant to Mr Caresbie, pawnbroker, of Camden Town, produced the blanket, but could not say who had pawned it.

The prisoner – I declare I never pledged it.

Inspector Moon said he arrested the prisoner, who denied the charge. He had been informed that the ticket had been burnt.

Vivian Hubert, an intelligent and well-spoken little girl, aged eleven, said her mother took the blanket from the second floor back room; she saw her do it. The child was cross-examined by her mother, the prisoner, who spoke in a theatrical tone of voice.

Prisoner – Darling, don't be afraid to tell the truth, the whole truth, because Miss Forest is here. Child – I know the blanket was pawned, and that the ticket was torn up into four pieces, and you threw them into the fire.

Prisoner – Now, dear child, tell me have you been directed to say this? Have you been instructed to say this? Child – Certainly not. Miss Forest told me to tell the truth.

Prisoner – Now, darling, listen to me. Have you not been instructed to say this? You know I have brought you up religiously and properly. Now, my darling, since you have corruptly told lies, please say what sort of a house this is that you are in with Miss Forest. Child (promptly) – The house is a respectable house, highly respectable.

Several other questions were put, and the child, while admitting that prisoner had corrected her many times for telling lies, said she had now spoken the truth.

A person of ladylike appearance said she was the prisoner's sister. Her family had cut her (the prisoner) off; also the child, because if they had the latter the prisoner would be sure to follow her.

The prisoner absolutely denied the charge, and said she would rather be tried by a jury.

Mr Cooke then committed the prisoner for trial, he having previously remarked that the only evidence against her was that of the child.

The child, Vivian Hubert, was then charged by the police under the Industrial Schools Act as not being under proper guardianship. Inspector Moon, in giving evidence in support of the case, said he was informed that both the women were actresses, and that the child was the illegitimate child of an actor. Hubert's friends would not have the care of the child, so Miss Roberts took her. Mr Cooke remanded the child to the workhouse until the result of the trial of her mother shall have been ascertained.

A SOMEWHAT amusing, but at the same time touching, little incident took place in the Royal Princess's Theatre, Glasgow, during the visit of Mr Henry C. Arnold's company. A respectable-looking working man and his wife were seated in the pit, and both were watching with breathless interest the progress of *The Lights o' London*. The feelings of the pair were evidently much touched throughout the latter portion of the play, but the good lady's sympathies fairly overcame her in the pathetic scene between Harold Armytage and his wife in the Slips in Regent's-park, for, turning to her husband, with a deep sigh, she exclaimed, "Oh, Rubbert, why dinna' some o' the folk on the stage bring them somethin' tae eat! Puir bodies!" Her sterner half, who had by this time learned to control his emotion, said, "Tuts, woman; haud yer tongue. It a' comes richt in the end."
19/11/1887

WANTED, Second-hand Inflated Fat-Boy Dress, for Pantomime. Must be in good order. Address, HENRY BLAKE, 12, Parkville-road, Walham-green, London.

WANTED, to Sell, Two Live Sheep, One with Six Legs and one with Five. To be sold Cheap. Apply, H. ROYAL, 9, Leas-lane, Birmingham. And a Fine Shark Cheap.
26/11/1887

THE ACTOR AND HIS LITTLE DOG.
Mark Melford was recently summoned for allowing a dog to enter Victoria Park, Landport, on the 28th ult. Mr Melford was walking through the park followed by a small dog, when he was stopped by the head gardener (Mr Hatch). At first he declined to give his name and address, and declined to go back

with the dog. He gave the name of "Mr Jones, of Bluebottle-street." Defendant said that he was unaware that the dog, which was about the size of an Ostend rat, had followed him. He left the park by the nearest gate. He was ordered to pay 1s. and the costs.

TO THE EDITOR OF THE ERA.

Sir, – I have lately returned from Liverpool, after being on tour with a travelling company under the title of "Gordon's Varieties," and under the management of Mr Harry De Brenner (late of Moore and Burgess's Minstrels). The party consisted of Mr James Harlow, W. Spence, Mr Carter, Mr Last, Mr Graham, the manager, and myself. The lady talent were the Sisters Hammersley, Miss Kate Gurney, Miss Galbratnie, Mrs Graham, and others. We started on tour at Wrexham, Ruthin, Denbigh, Rhyl, and from thence to Skilmersdale and Bootle, where we were left without a single penny.

Some of the company were fortunate enough to get engagements; whilst Mr Carter, Mr Last, and myself had to dispose of our valuables to take us to London. Even by this means we had not sufficient to come back by train, but had to avail ourselves of the journey by boat. The fare was 15s. each, steerage. We could manage this, but what about food? The captain said he would do his best to assist us, and only charged the fare for two, allowing the other 15s. to provide for food. We left Liverpool on board the S.S. Faithful, Captain J. Smith. After being delayed by the weather, we called in at Falmouth, Plymouth, and Southampton, and then made for London. We reached the Thames, and were run into by the North German Lloyd S.S. Capillia, cutting our vessel almost in two, which quickly sank us, leaving only just time to save ourselves and what we stood upright in. The value of my lost property alone I estimate at quite £70. I am, Sir, yours faithfully, WALTER HOWARD Jr., Banjoist and Comedian. 28, Brighton-terrace, Brixton, S.W.

WANTED, to Sell Cheap, a Large Dragon's Head, also Three Boy's Monkey Dresses, new. W. MAY, 108, Drury-lane.
10/12/1887

THE BALLET DANCERS' PARTY.

At Bow-street Police-court, on Tuesday, Alice Philips, aged thirty, a ballet dancer, was charged before Mr Vaughan with assaulting Mrs Hogge, wife of the proprietor of the Kemble's Head public house. Mr Smyth in opening the case said several ladies, members of the ballet, were invited by a gentleman to supper at the house in question. Several bottles of wine were ordered and consumed, and no doubt the party was somewhat exhilarated. There were thirteen present, eleven ladies and two gentlemen. Mr Smyth then called the complainant and other witnesses in support of the charge.

Mrs Hogge deposed that her husband, Mr William Hogge, kept the Kemble's Head, Bow-street. On Monday night a gentleman gave a banquet to eleven ladies. Twelve were expected to be present, but only eleven attended, and Mr Hogge and the founder of the feast were the only gentlemen present. A quantity of wine was ordered, and witness prepared the supper. While looking in the room she saw Mr Hogge with his arm round the defendant's waist, while her head was resting on his shoulder. In order to acquaint them of her presence, witness threw a small tin box on to the table. She then went to the adjoining room. Defendant followed her, and asked for an explanation of witness's conduct in throwing the box on the table. Witness said, "I have seen quite sufficient of my husband's conduct with you." Witness then went upstairs. Defendant followed, and on the landing she struck witness in the eye. Two blows were struck.

The cook and housemaid in complainant's employ gave corroborative evidence.

Mr Smyth (to the housemaid) – Was defendant sober? Witness – I don't think she was.

Police-constable 148 E examined by Mr Smyth, said he was called at a quarter to ten to the Kemble's Head: – Mrs Kemble said – Mr Smyth: – Mrs Hogge said, you mean. Witness: – Yes; she complained of being assaulted, and blood was running from her nose.

Defendant was taken into custody. She now denied the charge, and averred that Mrs Hogge first attacked her. She could call no witnesses. They had all been dancing, and were jolly together.

Mr. Vaughan said there did not appear to have been the least provocation given by Mrs Hogge. On the contrary, every provocation had been given to her, and she had conducted herself very well under the circumstances. Defendant must pay a fine of 40s., or be imprisoned for twenty-one days.

WANTED, to Sell, the Remains of Mary Bateman*, the Yorkshire Witch, in a beautiful state of preservation. Lowest price, £100 cash. Address, F.D. GREY, Exhibition, Fort-street, South Shields.
*Bateman was executed for murder in 1809.
17/12/1887

A SIGN that public taste is turning in the direction of the opinions expressed by us in a recent issue, with reference to the employment of mere infants upon the stage, was given at the opening performance of the Empire last Thursday, when, on a mere baby, apparently between two and three years of age, being brought out and placed upon a bicycle, a chorus of hissing and hooting greeted the painful and disagreeable exhibition of infantile talent.

A YOUNG man named Cullings has recently attempted to commit suicide whilst imprisoned in York Castle. He was lately property master for the *Man to Man* company, having joined that combination in Oldham last October. In explanation of the attempt, he said that the committal of a murder preyed upon his mind. He and another young man were in Middleton-road, Chadderton (a suburb of Oldham), at midnight, on a certain date, when they waylaid a sailor, robbed him, shot him dead, and then buried his body behind a high wall. This startling revelation was telegraphed from the police authorities at York to Superintendent Tindall (in whose division the alleged crime is asserted to have been committed), and that officer at once gave instructions for a search. A number of places have been excavated, but up to Wednesday evening no confirmation of the statement has been forthcoming. The man whom the prisoner implicated has been arrested, and the affair has created no little excitement in Oldham and its vicinity.

MR JOHN B. LAWREEN, who, as his large red bill says, is the "author of over *four thousand* productions, consisting of theatrical dramas, comedies, comic operas, burlesques, and pantomimes; music hall, sensational, sentimental and comic entertainments; and songs of sense, sentiment, and humour," took a complimentary benefit on Wednesday last at the Middlesex Music Hall, numerous "lady and gentleman artists" appearing. We should have thought that the profits from so many and various sources as Mr Lawreen's compositions would have placed their voluminous author beyond the necessity of a benefit, or the assistance of "lady and gentleman" artists.
24/12/1887

AT the Star Theatre, Wolverhampton, on Boxing Night, a crowded audience has assembled to witness the pantomime *The House That Jack Built*. Miss Sappho as the hero Jack was doing a skipping-rope dance with a rope that had been saturated with inflammable material, and then ignited, when some sparks fell upon her bare arm, and very naturally she dropped the rope, which was at once covered by Mr H.C. Hazlewood with a blanket. This trifling incident has furnished some of the local reporters with the sensational head-line "An Actress on Fire."

THE harlequinade at Covent-garden was not presented on Boxing Night, and the stage-manager, Mr Cave, had to offer an apology to the disappointed audience. It seems that some of the principals among the pantomimists, tired, perhaps, of waiting to "go on," or under the influence of Christmas good feeling, forgot business and gave themselves up to pleasure, so that when the time for business came they were found wanting. There were fines next morning, and since then the fun has come along in its proper place, with clown and company.

31/12/1887

9
1888
A SLIGHT CASTIGATION WITH HIS TOE

A COMEDIAN COMMENDED.

At the Lambeth Police-court, on Tuesday, Henry White, aged thirty, was charged with burglariously breaking and entering the dwelling-house of Mark Nathan, Kennington-road, and stealing therefrom two beaver muffs. Early in the morning of Tuesday week Mr Robert Vokes, a comedian, was returning home with some friends, when he heard glass smashed, and saw the prisoner at the front of the prosecutor's shop. The prisoner had broken the window, and had taken out the property mentioned in the charge. Mr Vokes seized the prisoner, and declared he would give him into custody. Whilst he was holding the prisoner a constable, afterwards ascertained to belong to the A division, came up, and Mr Vokes called upon him to take the prisoner into custody. The constable, it was alleged by Mr Vokes, said "I'm not on duty, and this is not my district," and then walked off. Mr Biron, upon hearing this statement in court, said the conduct of the officer was most disgraceful, and he trusted that the fullest inquiry would be made.

On the remand, Mr Biron asked what had been ascertained with regard to the constable in question. An inspector stated that the fullest investigation had been made, and the constable mentioned had been identified and suspended from duty by the Commissioners.

Mr Biron said that Mr Vokes and those who were with him on the occasion in question deserved the utmost credit for the manner in which they had acted, and then committed the prisoner to take his trial at the Central Criminal Court.

EARLY on Monday morning a policeman on duty in Wolverhampton heard glass falling, and, in the belief that a burglary was being committed, he quietly proceeded in the direction whence the sound came. To his astonishment he found two elephants, which had escaped from a circus, battering in the back doors and windows of an ale and porter store. The keeper of the animals having being summoned, they were led back to their quarters.

WANTED, Known. My influence prodigious, energies inexhaustible, honesty proverbial, system inimitable; victories, consequently, phenomenal. Breathless after that. Edwin Drew, Agent, 124, Gower-street.
21/1/1888

AT Liverpool, on the night of the 10th inst., Madame Georgina Burns' jewels, which she wore in Meyerbeer's opera of *Robert the Devil*, at Carl Rosa's representation at the Court Theatre that evening, were stolen. During the performance of the opera great enthusiasm was manifested by a party of

Liverpool University College students, who were located in the gallery of the theatre. On the termination of the opera they insisted on drawing Madame Georgina Burns' carriage to her hotel, and on her objecting to this they determined to escort her thither, and afterwards serenaded her on her arrival at her residence at St James's-place. In the carriage was placed a handbag containing Madame Burns' jewels, which must either have been cleverly abstracted en route or after her arrival at her lodgings. The handbag, probably owing to excitement, was only missed some little time after her arrival home. The police so far have failed to obtain a clue to the missing property, which is valued at £500.

THE theatre at Burton-on-Trent on Saturday night was the scene of a very painful and startling accident. The piece produced was *Maria Marten*, and Mr Harry Lorraine, son of the tragedian of that name, was, under the assumed name of Ernest Bright, playing William Corder. The piece had proceeded to the barn scene in the first act, where a struggle takes place between Corder and Maria Marten. Lorraine raised his pistol and pulled the trigger. The cap snapped, but the pistol hung fire, and Lorraine lowered it to his left hand to raise the trigger again, when the charge exploded and shattered his hand, blowing his first finger across the stage. Great excitement ensued, and several persons fainted. The curtain was lowered, and a doctor sent for. The accident caused such sensation that it was impossible to proceed with the performance.
18/2/1888

WE may congratulate ourselves that at none of our London music halls would a performance be tolerated like that which is to be seen nightly at the Palais de Crystal, Marseilles, a place as large and as handsome as the Alhambra, London, where a *quadrille incohérent* is danced by two men and two women, the latter being attired in extremely thin tights, the suggestiveness of which is increased by the super-addition of drawers made of "open work." The effect of this disgusting spectacle when the acrobatic exercises of the can-can are gone through can be more easily imagined than described. For both ladies turn somersaults, hold their legs in an absolutely perpendicular position above their heads, and finish up in the "splits." Thank goodness, we have a censorship in London.

WANTED, Twelve Big Showy Girls to take part in Military Spectacle, commencing March 19th. Apply, J.P. CURLE, Albert Hall, Edinburgh.
25/2/1888

THERE was the usual "scene" at the Theatre Royal, Nottingham, on Saturday night, with the close of the run of the pantomime, "the boys" making matters exceedingly lively throughout the performance. Miss Violet Evelyn, the representative of Will Scarlet, met with some undeserved hostility, because, not quite grasping the situation, she seemed not to appreciate the compliment intended when to her were thrown the colours of the Notts and Forest Football Clubs; but explanations have ensued, and the lady and the footballers are now on the best of terms. Miss Evelyn says – "I did not know what the flag meant, being quite unacquainted with the colours of the local clubs; and, besides, the stage-manager, to prevent serious accidents, had told us not to pick up anything until the scene was over, as two of the children had been badly hurt with coppers, and one of the ladies stunned by a potato being thrown on the stage. Directly it was explained to me what the flag meant, I wore it on my dress; which, however, I am afraid the "boys" did not see, or they would never have hissed me."

"THE MYSTERY OF A HANSOM CAB".
At the City Summons Court, on Tuesday, Thomas Morris, in the service of Mr Kelly, the manager of the Princess's Theatre, was summoned by the police for unlawfully exhibiting advertisement bills upon a private hansom cab in Holborn.

Police-sergeant Coldrey, 61, deposed that on the morning of the previous Wednesday he saw the defendant driving a horse and hansom cab in Holborn. On either side of the cab was attached a bill announcing a performance at the Princess's Theatre. There was a third bill on the back of the cab, and another attached to the whip so as to give it the appearance of a flag. Inside the cab there was a dummy dressed as a gentleman. The witness stopped the driver and told him that it was an offence against the laws of the City to expose advertisements on vehicles. The facts were admitted. Mr Kelly, it was said, was an American, and was unacquainted with the laws of the city of London. Sir J. Whittaker Ellis thought the law had been vindicated, and dismissed the case with payment of costs; but he hoped and believed that that the consent of the Commissioner of Police would not be obtained to the continuance of such an advertisement.

HOME EDUCATION. – A Lady living about Thirty Miles from London would receive One or Two little Girls (Sisters), to Educate with her own Children. Thoroughly Comfortable and Happy Home. Best Alderney Milk, &c. apply, C. WELLBORNE and SON, 17, Duke-street, London-bridge.

I, JOSEPH DAVID HOOSON, the Husband of Madame Lennard Charles, do hereby Publicly Apologise to my said Wife for inserting in "The Era" of the 18th Feb. last a Notice to the effect that I would not be Responsible for my said Wife's Debts.

I now wish to Withdraw the Same, and express my very deep regret that I was induced, through malicious advice, to insert such a notice, more especially as my wife has incurred no debts whatsoever. J.D. HOOSON. Dated this 1st day of March, 1888. witness, ALBERT H. SPINK, Solicitor, 101, Dale-street, Liverpool.
3/3/1888

"TINY," the small elephant, which was so well-known at Sanger's as the "boxing elephant," is dead, and is being mounted by Rowland Ward, of Piccadilly, as a hall porter's chair, the inside forming the seat. It presents a very humorous and novel appearance.
10/3/1888

AS our readers will see by report on another page, we have this week been the defendants in an action brought against us by a Miss Vivienne Dallas. The cause of action arose from our desire to do away with the practice of employing infants upon the stage. Miss Dallas stated in her evidence that she kept a Bible class for her company of children, and took them to church on Sunday; but in spite of the religious instruction thus afforded, we think that children only *two-and-a-half years old* are better off the boards.

MARIONETTES IN COURT.
In the Court of Appeal, on Monday, (before Lords Justices Cotton, Lindley, and Bowen), their lordships had before them an appeal from a refusal of Mr Justice Kay to grant an injunction to restrain an alleged infringement of a patent to produce dancing figures. The arguments were of a technical kind, but amusement was caused by the dancing contest that took place between the rival dancing figures. On the table in front of the bench a ballet girl about a foot in height was placed, the figure being an exact representation of a ballet girl, with all details of costume. By its side was one stripped of all adornments, displaying the mechanical contrivances that enabled it to dance. At an early stage of the case the figure on the bench performed before their lordships, and later a tea tray was procured, on which double figures, consisting of a ballet girl and a soldier, gave illustrations of the value of the inventions.

Mr Aston, Q.C., said that his client had sold 700 gross* of these articles, and he would leave it to their lordships to judge how many gross of babies had been delighted with them.

Lord Justice Lindley said it appeared to him to be a dressed-up top with an adjunct. He remembered spinning a top with a piece of string when he was a boy; it was a good many years ago. The learned

judge then spun a mechanical top that was lying on his table, but the effort ended in the top coming in contact with a pile of law books.
100,800.
24/3/1888

AT the Hammersmith Police-court, on Monday, a boy named Arthur Boughtflower was charged with obtaining cakes and biscuits at the Bedford-park Stores by false representations. The prisoner went to the stores on several occasions, and obtained cakes and biscuits in the name of Mr William Terriss, the well-known actor, residing in The Avenue, Bedford-park. The housekeeper was called, and said she never sent him. She knew the prisoner as a crossing-sweeper at the corner. He was employed occasionally to clean the garden. He had never been employed in the house. Mr Alfred Ross Clyde, the general manager of the stores, said Mr Terriss had a credit account. The value of the cakes and biscuits the prisoner had obtained was about £1. Police-constable 14 T Reserve said he was called to the stores to take the prisoner into custody. In answer to the charge, the prisoner said he had the cakes and ate them. Mr Curtis-Bennett dealt with the case as one of larceny by a trick, and committed the prisoner for twenty-one days, with hard labour.
14/4/1888

MR BALSIR CHATTERTON, who is on tour with *The Mystery of a Hansom Cab*, has been recounting some of his managerial difficulties to a Brighton interviewer. "Take, for instance, the present piece," he said. "One of our initial difficulties was the hansom cab. We naturally thought that we could hire a hansom at Hastings, but what was our consternation on getting to the town on Easter Monday to find that there was only one in the place, and the stage was too narrow to get it on. We hunted up all the mews, and at last came across a dilapidated old vehicle which had just arrived from London. It was in a filthy condition, but the cleaners were immediately set to work, and it arrived at the theatre in the nick of time. We took good care to be on the safe side when we came to Brighton."

EXPERIENCES OF A GERMAN BAND.
The Rev Dr Jessop says: – "We suffer much from German bands, but we have only ourselves to thank. Five or six years ago there was a band of eight or nine performers who perambulated Norfolk, and they came to me at least once a month. Whenever they appeared I went out to them and gave them a shilling, airing my small modicum of German periodically, and receiving flattering compliments upon my pronunciation. These people disappeared at last, but they were succeeded by another band, and a very inferior one, and I took little notice of them. There were seven of these performers, a cornet and two clarionets being prominent – very. However, they got their shilling, and vanished. Three days after their departure came another band. This time there were only four. I thought that rather shabby, but I was busy, did not take much notice of them, and again gave them a shilling. […]

Two days after their departure came a single solitary performer; he had a pan-pipe fastened under his chin, a peal of bells on his head, which he caused to peal by his nods, and a pair of cymbals attached to one of his elbows, a big drum which he beat by the help of a crank that he worked with one of his feet, and a powerful concertina which he played with his hands. He led off with a dolorous chorale in a minor key. It was really more than flesh and blood could bear. "Send him away, Jemima. Send him away, instantly!" The fellow smiled with unctuous complacency. But when he got only twopence, his face fell. "Ach, nein! You plaise, ze professor he geeve one shilling to ze band – I am ze band. He give ze band only twopence. He do not understand I am ze band! You plaise tell him I am ze band!" "No! You're to go away, Master's very kranky!"

Ze band loitered for half a minute, then it took itself to pieces and went its way. But the fellow's hint about the shilling was significant, and led to an investigation. Then it turned out that the band of seven or eight which was going its rounds that year, split itself up when it came into my neighbourhood, and, in view of my shilling, presented itself in two detachments, each of which reckoned on my shilling, and several times carried it off."

MR HENRY COLLARD, the dwarf formerly known as "the pocket Sims Reeves," who has resided in Margate for some years, carrying on the business of a timber and coal merchant, died somewhat suddenly on Friday week. On the previous Monday he was on the jury at the Quarter Sessions, and some amusement was caused by the fact that the juryman who followed him into the box was one of the biggest men in the town – a circumstance which attracted the Recorder's notice. Mr Collard was at business on the Thursday, and when he returned home at night he was apparently in his usual health. During his residence in Margate he has frequently taken part in concerts for charitable purposes, and was very popular amongst those who knew him. He has left a widow and family.

AT Leamington Borough Police-court, on Wednesday, John Shakespeare, who is said to bear a resemblance to the portraits of the "Swan of Avon," and who asserted that he was a direct descendant of the bard, was charged with being drunk and disorderly. The prisoner, who has no fixed place of abode, while in the lock-up threw his clothes into the fire, and they were destroyed. He appeared in court wrapped in a blanket. He was sentenced to one month's hard labour.
21/4/1888

ON Tuesday morning, whilst a cow was being driven down Brunswick-street, Hanley, it suddenly darted in at the stage door of the Theatre Royal, ran frantically round the stage, and was only stopped by getting her head fixed in the window of one of the scenes. It was not without some difficulty she was extricated from her novel position.

AN incident which attracted much attention occurred on Sunday morning at the Deepwater Quay, in Queenstown, in the presence of a number of American tourists. Mrs Birdie Grover, a young lady known as a professional artiste in rifle shooting, had some misunderstanding with the manager of Buffalo Bill's great American show, and hastily left Liverpool on Saturday night for New York in the Arizona. During her passage down Channel she altered her hastily formed plan, and determined to disembark at Queenstown and return to her former avocation. On landing on Sunday morning, however, with her three rifles, the police and Customs officials apparently took her for an Irish-American Fenian disguised in woman's clothing. The rifles were seized, and Mrs Birdie Grover was searched, but nothing beyond the weapons was discovered. She is very indignant at being interfered with, and is doing everything possible to regain possession of her rifles.
28/4/1888

MRS BENNETT is noted for the thoroughness with which she does everything that she undertakes, and in her performance in the part of Eily O'Connor in *The Colleen Bawn* at the Surrey Theatre this week she has not belied her reputation. When she is thrown into the now celebrated tank, in the cave scene, she swims under water for several yards, sinks, rises, and floats across the tank with corpse-like calmness.

A NOTABLE instance of quick work was the exodus of the Roselle-Dacre company from Southport on Saturday last. The curtain fell at 10.25. The company doffed their war paint, changed their dresses, and packed their belongings, which, with two entire scenes, including some heavy set pieces, were carried to the station of the Cheshire Lines Committee, whence a special train steamed out amidst the ringing cheers of a large number of the audience who had followed to see the company depart. Huskisson's Dock, Liverpool, was reached at 11.25, and the steamer for Belfast started at 12.15.

THE performance in the Victoria Colonnade Pavilion, Leamington, when Mr Simpson Webb's circus company visited that town, was interrupted last week by an unusual and amusing episode. One of the special features of the performance was the clever riding of a young lady known as Vera, and, one evening, when she entered the ring on her splendid steed, she was hissed by an indiscreet young gentleman in the promenade. The young lady looked upon this unfavourable demonstration as a great insult, and the ringmaster offered anyone a sovereign who would supply him with the man's name. Thereupon a young man about twenty years of age, son of a Leamington tradesman, stepped forward and remarked that he was not ashamed of what he had done. The young lady at once dismounted and proceeded to the promenade, where she took hold of him by the coat collar, and gave him a sound thrashing with her whip, and only desisted when a member of the audience interfered. The offender then left the building a sadder, but probably a wiser, man. The affair created great amusement.

WANTED, a Novelty. Then book Roselle's Latest. A Child produced from a few pieces of Tissue Paper. Haymarket Music Hall, Liverpool.
5/5/1888

LAST Monday afternoon, as Mr Peter Conroy, the musical director of the Queen's, Poplar, and his partner, Mr James Murray, were riding their tandem tricycle down Hackney-road, the horses of a heavily laden wagon which was standing in the road, became restive. To avoid the vehicle, Mr Conroy steered in to the tram rails, and at the same time a tramcar came rapidly in the opposite direction. The wheels of the tricycle became locked in the rails, and Mr Conroy and his companion, by jumping off the tricycle and pulling it out of the rails, made a narrow escape from being run over by the car, the driver of which had not had time to apply his brake.

MONSTER SERPENT. Suit a Side Show. The Great Sea-Serpent, Twenty Feet long and as thick as a man's thigh. For Sale or Hire. The usual other Stock. WM. CROSS, Liverpool.

WANTED. – Miss Ada Webb, P.S.A., Empress of the Sea and Champion Lady Diver of the World, performs more Feats under Water in her New Crystal Tank than any other Artist. See her marvellous "Monte Cristo" Sack Fête. Has a few vacant dates till July, and after Second Week in October. Apply, F.G. BECKETT, Washington Music Hall, Battersea.
12/5/1888

AN action was brought by Mr Henry Thomas Moore, an artist, at the Liverpool County Court, on Monday last, against Mr Bryant, manager of the Grey Horse public house, Lime-street, Liverpool, for damages for assault and injury to a picture.

The plaintiff's statement was that on March 6th he and Mr Tom Taylor, theatrical wig maker, were in conversation on the subject of a picture which the plaintiff had painted, representing Mr Irving in the character of Hamlet, soliloquising over the skull of Yorick; and that Mr Taylor suggested an adjournment to the Horse Shoe Tavern, in Lime Street, in the expectation of meeting a number of followers of Thespis, and of exhibiting the work with a view to sale. The plaintiff accordingly went to the Horse Shoe, and had been there for about a quarter of an hour talking with some people in the parlour when the defendant came in. According to the plaintiff, Mr Bryant, immediately upon seeing him, made a ferocious dash at him, dealt him several blows about the body, and wound up by putting his feet through the counterfeit presentment of the melancholy Dane. The result to the plaintiff's person was insignificant, but in regard to the picture was disastrous. A work of art, which the plaintiff valued at £25 or £30, was ruined beyond the art of the picture restorer to repair, and rendered in point of fact valueless.

The plaintiff here exhibited the picture, when it was found that the foot of the defendant had penetrated the canvas just above Mr Irving's head, thus leaving the figure of the tragedian intact, but causing irreparable damage to a considerable area of moonlight.

His Honour remarked that the picture did not seem to be damaged in a vital part.

The plaintiff replied that the "tone" had been entirely destroyed, and that he would probably find it impossible to reproduce the same effect.

His Honour gave judgement for the plaintiff for £4 and costs.

MADAME LEONA DARE'S balloon ascent at the Crystal Palace on Whitsun Monday is likely to create a sensation. The huge machine will ascend with the lady suspended from it by her teeth*. The balloon, which is made of Chinese silk and stands 70ft. high, will be under the management of the well-known aeronaut, Signor Spelterini.
*In the event of Madame Dare's teeth proving unequal to the task she was also attached to the balloon by a harness.

WANTED, Ventriloquists and others to Know, that I supply Figures with Electric Illuminated Noses, Ears, &c. Also Cats, Dogs, and other animals with Electric Flashing Eyes in great variety. List, one stamp. E. LE MARE, 28, Coupland-street, Manchester.
19/5/1888

AT the Floral Hall, Leicester, on Sunday night, a pack of performing wolves broke out of their den, and were discovered by three policemen trying to force their way into the street. They had forced a door leading into the corridor, when the policemen armed with sticks kept them back. The lady who performs with them was sent for, and she succeeded in getting them back into their cages.
2/6/1888

AN inquest was held at Cardiff on Thursday on the body of Harriet Elizabeth Symonds, a property woman at a local circus, who died on Wednesday from hydrophobia. On April 8th last she was scratched slightly on the thumb by a fox terrier connected with the circus. Symptoms of hydrophobia appeared on Thursday last week, and after suffering great agony the woman died on Wednesday. The doctor said the deceased's excitement was greatly increased by the disgraceful rowdyism of a mob assembled round the house, who while the unfortunate woman, tied down by ropes to a bed, was writhing in pain, indulged in discordant noises and gesticulations, and refused to disperse. The coroner strongly censured the mob, and said the scenes which from morning to night were enacted in front of the house were a disgrace to an important port like Cardiff and to civilization. The jury, in returning a verdict of death from hydrophobia, endorsed the coroner's censure.
9/6/1888

MR J.B. MULHOLLAND has been giving an interviewer in the North some of his early experiences, among which we find the following: – "I joined a company to tour through the 'smalls' of Ireland, and during this engagement the following took place: – The play was *The Colleen Bawn*, but the hall was most unsuited for the purpose. There was no dressing-room, and, as the temporary stage did not fit close, the space between it and the walls was utilised for this purpose, and the actors and actresses were entombed here until their turn came to go on. This portion was shut off from the audience by two curtains. Well, during the progress of the play, the faithful Danny Man was left soliloquising before the house. 'Ah,' he said, speaking of the heroine, 'my sweet darlin', I would sink into the bottomless pit for ye,' – and he did; incautiously venturing too near the side, he fell with a fearful crash into the before-mentioned chasm, and, worst of all, clutching wildly at the curtains to save himself, he tore them clean

away, exposing a number of gentlemen struggling to get into various garments, some of them being apparently attired for a Turkish bath."
16/6/1888

WANTED, to Sell, Scarf Pin, Demon's Head, carved out of a valuable stone; gold hair, horns, and ears, ruby eyes. Stone changes all colours by day or gaslight. Immense for Wizard or Ghost Show Proprietor. Cost eight guineas; will take four pounds. Address, Box 1,749, "The Era" Office, London, W.C.
23/6/1888

THE absurd and objectionable custom of bouquet throwing has, happily, of late become somewhat obsolete and unfashionable; and we were glad to see that Sir Algernon Borthwick's solitary flowery missile alone marred the excellent effect produced by the good taste with which, at Madame Sarah Bernhardt's first performance of *La Tosca*, floral offerings were dispensed with.
14/7/1888

AT the Marlborough Police-court, on Tuesday, Elizabeth Gordon, a little wizened old woman, rather comically attired, having a hat like an inverted flower-pot, devoid of brim or ornament, was charged with begging in St James's-square on Monday evening. Constable 345 C saw the prisoner at half-past six, when very drunk, catch hold of gentlemen as they were leaving the Army and Navy Club, and ask them for money.

Mr Hannay – What have you to say to this? Prisoner – Why, that it's all a parcel of untruths. Mr Hannay – Then cross-examine him. Prisoner – He says I caught hold of gentlemen, and that is a fib. I had a lot of newspapers, and a gentleman asked me for one of them. I recognised him, ah! instantly, as Mr Barry Sullivan, the great actor. Why, God bless him, I knew him in Belfast. He plays King John, Macbeth, and all those sorts of customers. I said to him one night, "Is it true, Mr Sullivan, you're alive?" He couldn't deny it, because there he was. Everybody knows him in Ireland. He is next to Mr Irving. I don't call speaking to him begging. I've been in the workhouse with that infernal bramkitis. He is a great actor. Mr Hannay – I dare say he is, but what about being drunk? Prisoner – People will say so, you know. They speak to me and make much of me. Mr Hannay – Then you are an old favourite, I suppose? Prisoner – I am always paying, really and truly. If you could send for the theatricals they would tell you the same. I went to the stage door, and a gentleman said, "Come again, missus," and when I went the next time, he told me that the company had gone away. Don't you know Mr Barry Sullivan? I am told his name is in the papers. He is a great actor, a great –. Mr Hannay – I dare say he is, but it appears to me that you mistook the Army and Navy Club for a theatre. Prisoner – Oh, dear, no; there's all the water pipes outside. Mr Hannay – Pay 20s., or go to prison for ten days.

The alternative was preferred.
21/7/1888

MRS A.W. PINERO, as a member of the Society for the Prevention of Cruelty to Animals, appeared at the Marylebone Police-court on Thursday, against two boys whom she had seen, on the previous day, ill-treating a pony in St John's Wood-road. Mrs Pinero offered to pay the cost of sending the pony to the Home of Rest for Horses, at Neasden, to which she is a subscriber.
28/7/1888

THIS week two American actors have taken a London audience by storm. We have seldom seen or heard such enthusiasm as greeted the appearance of Bucephalus and Pegasus, the two fire-engine horses in *The Still Alarm* at the Princess's Theatre. Doubtless, their popularity will continue to increase, and "gushing" ladies will go to the theatre provided, in lieu of bouquets, with wisps of hay and bags of oats to throw across the footlights to these equine "principals." It was a pity that the stage arrangements did not allow the engine also to be brought before the curtain; but why did not the graceful greyhound respond to the calls of "dog" which came from the pit?

WANTED, to Caution Proprietors against Engaging Spurious Scottish Spectacles, "The Gathering of the Clans" (Copyright) is the only Recognised Scottish Military Spectacle before the Public. Beautiful Dresses, Beautiful Music. ALF. DIEY, Glasgow House, 31, St Mary's-street, Southampton.
4/8/1888

WANTED, a Scientific Boxer to Set To with Miss D'Grey. Terms low. Money sure. Will Harry Burns or Percy Logan write. Address, Prof. D'GREY, Post-office, Warminster, Wilts.
11/8/1888

A CORRESPONDENT telegraphs that a banker's daughter living in that town, and having a fortune in her own right, secretly left her home on Wednesday night, and was married at the Bolton Registry Office to a circus clown. Her father arrived too late to prevent the marriage. The newly-wedded couple proceeded to Scarborough for their honeymoon.

ON Monday, at Hamburg, as many as thirteen crocodiles were enabled, through an oversight, to escape from on board a steamer just returned from Africa, whence they had been brought for sale to various Continental zoological gardens. These formidable reptiles are now all in the river Elbe.
25/8/1888

TO THE EDITOR OF THE ERA.
Sir,– It has been reported that Mr Mansfield, as Dr Jekyll and Mr Hyde, employs a trick wig and a rubber mask, or close-fitting skin cover, for his face. Permit me to say that Mr Mansfield's wig is of the ordinary kind, without springs or other mechanical devices, and that he does not use a rubber mask, a skin cover, or adventitious aid of any kind. The transformation in the third act is accomplished by change of facial expression and of bearing, and with such trifling effects of make-up – including the powder-puff – as are employed by every actor. Mr Mansfield throws back his hair, brushes the pallor from his face with a swift movement of the hands, stands erect, and Edward Hyde has given place to Mr Jekyll. I am, Sir, your obedient servant, E.D. PRICE. Lyceum Theatre, Aug. 30th.
1/9/1888

MR RIDER HAGGARD is a successful author, but he cannot be called a modest one. He occupied a private box at the Gaiety Theatre on Thursday evening, and made himself conspicuous by the persistency with which he applauded the adaptation of his own novel "She," and by ostentatiously flinging to Miss Sophie Eye at the end of the second act a huge bouquet. This was bad enough, but what followed was even worse. Somebody having called his name, he advanced to the front of the box and bowed, and bowed in a way that would have won admiration from that great apostle of bowing, Sir Pertinax MacSycophant*. Having finished his bowing, he essayed to speak, and, depising the interruption of the young gentlemen in the gallery who shouted "We don't want no speeches," he proceeded to deliver an address, to give off opinions, and to indulge in predictions that were provocative of something like derision. It is to be hoped that Mr Haggard's impertinent example will not be too often followed. "The play's the thing," and, in the words of that gallery boy, "We don't want no speeches," especially from authors in private boxes.
A character in Charles Macklin's play The Man of the World.
8/9/1888

THE "SUPER" TAKING A CALL.

At the Wandsworth Police-court, on Wednesday, Mr Frederick Harcourt, a comedian, of St George's Hall, Wandsworth, appeared to answer a summons for assaulting William Holmes, described as an actor.

The complainant said he was employed by the defendant to take part in a play at St George's Hall; but, in answer to the magistrate, he hesitated to describe what character he personated and the defendant offered an explanation by stating that he was a "supernumerary."

Mr Plowden – What was the play? Complainant – *The Fall of Khartoum*. At the conclusion of the play the performers were called before the curtain.

Mr Plowden – The delighted audience wished to see the actors? Complainant – Yes, sir, I followed in front of the curtain.

Mr Plowden – You wished to have a share of the applause? The defendant – He was blowing his own trumpet.

The complainant went on to say that after leaving the curtain the defendant accosted him, called him ugly names, and said he would not pay him for his night's work. He replied that he did not care if he did not. The defendant then struck him, knocking him down, afterwards lifting him up and throwing him down again bodily, and with great force. The defendant also kicked him, and threw him off the stage.

In cross-examination, the defendant elicited from the complainant that he asked permission to take part in the "call," but his application was refused. The defendant also asked the complainant if he knew what he would be done to if he had behaved in a similar way at any of the first theatres in London, but did not receive any answer.

Defendant – When I asked you to turn to the left, did you not turn to the right? – Yes.

Defendant – Did I say that if the soldiers were like you, it is not surprising that they were beaten at the Transvaal? – You did.

Other witnesses having been called by the complainant, defendant called Mdlle Gratienne, who said she took the part of Lady Emily Drummond.

Mr Plowden – I thought the play was *The Fall of Khartoum*? The defendant – Yes, sir; but she took the part of the chief character. It is one of the licenses of dramatic literature.

Mdlle Gratienne proceeded to say that she heard loud applause change to a roar of laughter. She went to ascertain the cause, and found the complainant in front of the curtain. The defendant remonstrated with him, but he committed no assault.

The defendant said the complainant violated his commands, and he felt exasperated. The complainant abused him, and he pushed him, causing him to fall on "all fours." He then administered a slight castigation with his toe on him, and took him by the back of the neck and ran him off the stage.

Mr Plowden said there was no real justification for the assault, and fined the defendant the nominal penalty of 10s. The money was at once paid.

THERE was an amusing incident in connection with the opening of the New Theatre, Longton, by Mr Rollo Balmain. In the scene plot of *Hoodman Blind*, a toy horse and wagon for a child is among the list of properties. The property man, doubtless reading his plot hurriedly, reported to the local management that a horse and wagonette were required, and lo and behold! At rehearsal on Monday, a wagonette and pair were ostentatiously trotted up to the stage door.

A COMPANY styled the Anglo-African Concert and Shakespearian company were advertised to give two concerts in the New Rolls Hall at Monmouth, on Thursday and Friday last week. The vicar had promised to take the chair on the first night and the Mayor on the second. In the meantime, however, a letter appeared in a religious paper from someone in Shropshire, impeaching the morals of the proprietor, a big, well-educated African named Fraser, who, it is stated, has studied at Oxford University. The vicar of Monmouth, seeing the letter, decided to withdraw his patronage. As a result, only about thirty persons paid for admission, but the entire programme was gone through, and the singing was of excellent quality.

Troubles never come singly, and, to make matters worse, just before the entertainment commenced a man presented himself at the door with a double bass viol on his shoulder. He said he had come to fulfil an engagement. The dusky proprietor explained that he had advertised for a bass vocalist, not an instrumentalist, but the man had come all the way from Leicester, and there was no means of getting back that night, so he stood his instrument in the vestibule and refused to budge, even though Mr Fraser called him a lunatic. He contended that he was what is technically known as a bass in the profession, and had been promised by Fraser £2 a week salary. The proprietor simply told him to sue him. It transpired that his name is Kilby. He will probably take the darky at his word, but is not likely to get much satisfaction.
15/9/1888

MR DOLPH ROWELLA'S pantomime company have returned to town after a short country tour, and opened at the Temple of Varieties, Hammersmith, on Monday last. Mr William Rowella, who appears with his brother in the above troupe, has been suffering from a poisoned finger for the last week, and a few nights ago he was walking home, having missed the last train, with his wounded digit thrust inside the breast of his overcoat, when a policeman suddenly pounced on him and, pointing to the concealed hand, wanted to know "What he'd got there?" "This," replied Rowella, suddenly pulling out the enormous finger swathed in flannel, and putting it under the policeman's nose. The policeman started back, then recovered himself; but was not entirely convinced of the *bona fides* of Mr Rowella till he had seen him enter his own house, to the gate of which the "bobby" accompanied him.
6/10/1888

IN the amusing comedy called *My Milliner's Bill*, the heroine, referring to the days when she played burlesque, remarks that she was able to keep her dress in a glove-box. A similar receptacle we should say would provide ample room for the costume in which Miss Addie Conyers is now appearing nightly at the London Pavilion. It consists of a jersey extremely short, a pair of tights, and a couple of silver leaves. If Miss Conyers is really desirous of emulating the example of Mother Eve, she should throw the jersey and the tights away, and stick to the leaves.
20/10/1888

MRS KENDAL, during her recent engagement at the Prince of Wales's Theatre, Birmingham, was the recipient of a curious compliment, taking the shape of a glove which some fair owner had split in her vigorous applause of the accomplished actress. The glove was accompanied by an effusion more or less poetical, and concluding as follows:

My hands they met so madly
That my glove was split in two,
And this result of enthusiasm
I send as a proof to you.

WANTED, to Sell, great Attraction and Novelty – Natural Giant's Leg and Foot, splendidly preserved, in large Plate-glass Case, 4ft. by 1½ft. Quite perfect and showing every vein, &c. Also Two Small Skeletons and Three Human Skulls, all in good condition. Fortune to Showman or suit Museum, &c. Price £5, worth £30. JONES, 13, Winding-street, Hastings.
27/10/1888

THE latest novelty in theatricals seems to be a "cycling dramatic company." It is stated that a company of ladies and gentlemen started from Hyde-park Corner on ten bicycles and four tricycles, with one large carrier tricycle for props, dresses, &c. A three nights' stay was made at Hounslow, and from thence the company proceeded to Reading, Bath, Bristol, up North and down again, terminating the tour at Oxford. The tour turned out to be a great success financially and artistically, and it is intended, if possible, to make another and more lengthy tour next year.

10/11/1888

TO THE EDITOR OF THE ERA.

Sir, – Among the various suggestions relative to the phonograph I have not noticed that the extreme utility of this wonderful invention to the acting profession from a certain standpoint has been exploited. It has been well and often said that no man has ever heard the sound of his own voice. Up to the present this has been true, but it is so no longer; but no one seems to have realised what an immense advantage this is for the actor. Bad elocution, indistinct grumbling, mysterious muttering, irritating cacophony of every description, ought now to be impossible. The actor has but to rehearse each new part into the phonograph, constitute himself his own audience and critic, and the modern mumbler – that bugbear of the modern playgoer despair of the modern author – will surely become a thing of the past. Ambitious aspirants, frightened at the sound of their own voices, will themselves condemn their own incapacity, to the great relief of the over-worked critic. Incompetents, professional and amateur, who imagine they can portray Jews, Germans, Irishmen, Yankees, &c., will have their pleasing delusions dissipated. Every actor will be his own elocution master, and, if necessary, executioner. To hire a phonograph at once is the determination of

Yours truly, E. DAVIS PERRY. London, W.

WANTED, Captain Pike and Educated Fish, to send Address to Roderick Stoll, Parthenon Varieties, Liverpool. Very important communications waiting.

17/11/1889

AN amusing incident occurred at the Queen's Theatre, Keighley, last week, during Mr John Lawson's performance in *After Dark*. In the third act the scene is laid on the Underground Railway, where one of the characters is placed across the rails to be decapitated by the approaching express. He is rescued by his friend, who breaks through a hole in the wall of the tunnel just as the express is passing. The bricks on this occasion were thrown too far on to the stage, with the result that when the engine was half-way across it fell down with the stage-carpenter upon it, he having fallen over the bricks. The two carriages followed suit, and the curtain descended upon one of the most amusing scenes ever witnessed.

SINCE "Jack the Ripper" commenced his fiendish work in Whitechapel, threatening letters purporting to come from him have been numerous. One of the latest of these productions is directed against Miss Marie Montrose, a member of Wyn Miller's *My Sweetheart* company. The company was appearing last week at the Alexandra Theatre, Sheffield. On Thursday a postcard was delivered to the theatre bearing the address "To Tony, Alexandra, Sheffield." It was placed in the usual rack, and Mr Augustus Cramer, who was playing Tony, on coming down to the theatre at night, took possession of it. He found it to be a communication bearing "Jack the Ripper's" signature, and expressing a desire to "do the Whitechapel wonder" for Miss Montrose. A rough drawing of a murderous-looking knife had also been made. The postcard was immediately placed in the hands of the police, but as yet no clue to the sender has been discovered. A good deal of indignation has been expressed in the town. On leaving the Alexandra on Saturday night Miss Montrose was presented by a few admirers with a splendid set of Sheffield scissors in a plush case, and also with several penknives of Sheffield manufacture.

WANTED, to Sell. Jack the Ripper captured by Ally Sloper*. Life-size Figures. Suitable for Fairs. FEAR, 55, Old Market, Bristol.
*A red-nosed, top-hatted cartoon character featured in the paper Ally Sloper's Half-Holiday.
24/11/1888

ON Wednesday last Mr J.W. Cardownie, the champion Scotch dancer, when leaving the Star Music Hall, Bermondsey, in company with Mr Tula (of Tula and Miaco), was pounced upon by three plain clothes constables and one in uniform, and arrested as "Jack the Ripper." After examination of his bag, the turning over of his stage properties, and the production of his medals, the police apologised and let him go.

SMILER, SMILER, SMILER, the Quaintest Quadruped in Creation, the Donkey that makes the best-trained Horses blush, introduced by his trainer, E.R. DAINEZ, JOHN HENRY COOKE'S ROYAL CIRCUS, EDINBURGH. Disengaged for Panto, through misunderstanding.
1/12/1888

MESSRS. LEAHY AND O'BEIRNE have been advertising for a principal baritone for grand opera, and have received the following reply, which we print verbatim et literatim, from an aspirant who hales from so far north as Durham:

Dear Sir, – I see you are advertising for a singer or two so I take the oportunity of writeing I may tell you that I am a most splendid Baritone or high set voice either I have comand of two voices I can gow down to G but I am more better at Hight. I sing some songs in C and some in F but I get nearly any Hight there has been a few Gentlemen of late heard me sing and they seem all to say that I am fullish for not to try and get into an opery I have had some practise a chorus singend but I have not a first clas understanding of the music but it would soon come to me if you could only try and have a place for me I would not look for mutch pay for a while if we could mannidge to live I would be ever so mutch oblige I have such a notion of opery singing I can not send my foto as I have not one at present but if you like I will get on and send this weak my Hight is 5ft 7 stout dark and I may say I am a joiner and I would willingly help the carpenter or anything for a while or help with Baggidge you might think about it for me and I can reach F nicely I sing I dremt I dwelt in its original kee you might let me know please I will join for a small sum to get into it your obedient servant

The notion of a principal baritone in an opera company helping the carpenter or assisting with the "baggidge" is truly delightful, and suggests infinite possibilities in the way of adaptibility in "principals." Messrs. Leahy and O'Beirne would only require a tenor who would work the limelight, a bass who would take a turn at scene-shifting, a soprano who would not object to showing people into their seats, and a contralto not above presiding over the refreshment department in order to be able to open a theatre of their own with a very economical staff salary list.

WANTED, Crowds of Intelligent Beings, Dec. 20th, to Hear Edwin Wright's New Songs and Edwin Drew's New Readings. French Chamber.
8/12/1888

TO THE EDITOR OF THE ERA.
Sir, – What do you think of the enclosed as an example of atrociously bad taste? These bills have been sent out by the provincial company playing Dr Jekyll and Mr Hyde. To the credit of the local manager in whose theatre I found the bill, he refused to allow it to go out in his town, but they have been issued broad-cast elsewhere. It is this kind of thing which puts weapons into the hands of the enemies of the stage. Yours obediently, AN ACTOR WHO RESPECTS HIS ART.

THE WHITECHAPEL MURDERS. – Much has been said in the Press about the impossibility of such a character as Mr. Hyde having ever existed – in effect, that the author's imagination has carried him too far away in the domain of fiction. The strange facts that have lately startled not only the metropolis but the whole world, appear now to give some foundation for what a few weeks ago was thought so improbable. These wholesale murders, the handicraft, most probably, of a single human, though to all appearances demonical, fiend, are fully realised in *The Strange Story of Dr Jekyll and Mr Hyde*, which was produced in London a few months ago, and on its appearance on the boards of the Lyceum Theatre created as much excitement as the sad reality is now causing throughout the world.

AT the Bow-street Police-court, on Monday, William Butler and Thomas Irving, two young men, were charged on remand with stealing some towels, bottles of scent, and pomade and other articles, the property of Messrs Rimmel. Mr Arthur Newton prosecuted, and Mr Burnie appeared for Irving. Both prisoners were engaged by Messrs Rimmel, and had access to their stores. They were arrested in consequence of a communication made to the police by the landlady of 48, Tennyson Street, Lambeth, who had seen Butler come home dressed in women's clothes. The police went upstairs to where the prisoners slept, and were there denied admission for nearly half an hour. When they were admitted they found a quantity of ashes in the grate, which looked as though a woman's dress had been burnt. They also found a woman's mantle, trimmed with astrakhan, and some women's wigs. The prisoner Irving accounted for his possession of some scent by stating to the police that he was sent nightly to the Empire Theatre by Mr Rimmel to scent the ballet. They boiled the scent in the dressing-room. Mr Bridge, after hearing other evidence, remanded the prisoners, admitting Irving to bail.
15/12/1888

THE Crystal Palace pantomime, *Cinderella*, will include a stag hunt, with live stages, dogs, and horses. This forms part of a grand *ballet d'action* entitled "Autumn Leaves," with dresses emblematic of forest trees and hedgerow fruits, carried out with great accuracy of form and tint, several of the effects being produced with hand-painted satin. The dressing of Cinderella for the ball is treated in a special manner, and her carriage, to be illuminated by electric light, will be drawn by cream-coloured ponies.

A NOVEL mode of dealing with the female high hat nuisance in theatres was employed at the Savoy Theatre the other evening. There were a number of ladies in the amphitheatre with hats which prevented the "gods" from getting a good view of the stage. They therefore handed down a paper, on which a request to the ladies to remove their headgear was written in a large round hand, and which was passed from hand to hand along the front rows. Some of the ladies at once took off their hats; and, in the next interval, another paper was sent down in the same way, thanking them for their kind and obliging conduct.

WANTED, by Fred. Davis, the Black Cough Drop, and Kate De Vere, Burlesque Actress, to warn a certain Nigger from singing my Song entitled "Put my father's whiskers on a plate." So beware.

WANTED, Proprietors to Look Out for the most Marvellous, Sensational, and Original Performance ever seen – the great Balloon Race, Balloon Race, Balloon Race, Balloon Race. Two men hanging by their teeth under two Balloons. Look Out, they are coming. Look Out.
22/12/1888

WE received from Col. H.J. Sargent, the manager of the Jodrell Theatre, a ticket for a stall for Miss Patti Rosa's first appearance in London in *Bob*. Across the ticket was printed, in bold type, the words: – "This ticket must not be sold." We wonder whether Colonel Sargent considers a gratuitous insult to the critics a good way of predisposing them to take a favourable view of Miss Rosa's performance? We are sure, however, that they did not visit upon the innocent head of the *debutante* the ill-manners of those responsible for the issue of these insulting vouchers.
29/12/1888

10
1889
"I AM 302 YEARS OF AGE"

ON Dec. 28th, at the Kingston-on-Thames Borough Bench, John Clements, a tailor, was charged with being drunk and incapable. Evidence having been given against him, prisoner said that he came from Macclesfield, where he had been in a lunatic asylum for four months. He came down to Euston-square on Sunday, and as he could not ask for a job he had several drops of beer given to him, which went to his head. Clements was described as having been "leg drunk," and as he did not give the police any trouble he was discharged. Prisoner thanked the magistrates, then informed them that he was a ventriloquist, and in the asylum where he had been he had frequently amused the other patients with his "sketches." Turning round, Clements conversed with a man who was supposed to be on the other side of the screen which was behind him, and also with another supposed to be outside the court. The magistrates did not object in the least, in fact they, together with the various police officials, reporters, and others in court, indulged in hearty laughter. When the man had left the hall one of the magistrates remarked that it was not often that they were entertained there by a ventriloquist.

IN the course of some amusing experiences narrated by an actor the other night was the following very characteristic Scotch trait. It is usual for his company on tour to leave a town on the Sunday with any suitable train between twelve and three. But when he asked his Glaswegian landlady for his bill before leaving, and held out the money to her, "Na, na," she said, with a deprecatory uplifting of her hands, "I canna tak your money on the holy Sawbath. Jest pit it doon on the mantelshelf!"
5/1/1889

A FATAL accident occurred at the Grand Theatre, Glasgow, on Saturday night, during the performance of *Babes in the Wood*. Robert Potts, aged thirty-seven, principal flyman, overbalancing himself, fell twenty-two feet from the flies upon the stage with a sickening thud. He alighted on his head and died immediately. Miss Rose Lee* was the sole occupant of the stage at the time of the accident, and was singing a love song, which she bravely continued; she also stepped to the edge of the stage so that the light would be away from the prostrated form of Potts. As only a few persons witnessed the accident the excitement amongst the audience speedily subsided.
The unfortunate singer was in fact Miss Ada Beminster.
19/1/1889

TYPE-WRITING now forms so important a part in the production of piece that anything in connection with its development is interesting. Mrs Marian Marshall recently invited a number of ladies and gentlemen to an "At Home" at her Type-Writing Office, 126, Strand, to see the new invention called the graphophone used in combination with the type-writer. With her feet on the treadle of the graphophone, which is worked as easily as a sewing machine, and the tubes in her ears, a lady listened to a message

which she committed to paper by means of the type-writer. By this means a dramatic author, in the solitude of his study, may dictate his inspired periods at any pace he pleases to the graphophone, and afterwards send the cylinder to be copied direct from the type-writer. The guests assembled included several notabilities, and much interest was expressed in the combination of the two inventions.
2/2/1889

AN amusing incident occurred at the Avenue Theatre, Sunderland, on Monday. In an interval of the performance of *True Metal*, by Mr Pitt Hardacre's company, Jerry Twaddle's donkey was sent before the curtain, at the end of the third act, to receive its share of applause. When it got in the centre of the stage, it laid down and would not move; and two carpenters had to be sent on to drag it off.
9/2/1889

AUGUSTE CHEETHAM HARDY, thirty-five, a tall, powerful-looking man, describing himself as an actor, and professionally known as Fenwick, of 19, Arthur-road, Holloway, was charged before Mr Horace Smith, on Monday, at Dalston Police-court, with being a lunatic wandering at large. Constable 298 Y found the prisoner in Hornsey-road at nine o'clock that (Monday) morning wandering about with only his shirt and trousers on. When spoken to he said he came from Sodom and Gomorrah, and that he was a pillar of salt. Asked what he had to say, the prisoner made a rambling statement. He said his mother cursed him when he was a boy, but that curse was removed when he was at Northampton. He would go to the scaffold walking firmly, but if he were put to death there would be the most awful storm that ever raged.

Mr Smith told the man kindly that he must go to the workhouse, and tell the doctor there what he had told them now. The prisoner looked up in surprise and said "Oh, then, I'm not going to be hung now?" Mr Smith – No. Prisoner – I thought I was on the scaffold.

Mr Smith then directed that the prisoner should be taken to the workhouse, and he inquired of Inspector Holland why a man so manifestly insane should be brought to the court and placed in the dock and accused of no other crime than not being able to look after himself. A powerful man like the prisoner might have resented being brought to such a place in a very unpleasant manner.

Inspector Holland said the man was brought up before a magistrate in accordance with the Commissioner's orders, but he would represent the magistrate's remarks to the Chief Commissioner.

A STARTLING incident occurred at the Theatre Royal, Oldham, on Monday evening during the performance of *My Sweetheart*, by Messrs Miller and Elliston's company, in the scene between the Doctor (Mr George Herbert) and Mrs Fleeter (Miss K.M. Neville). The wind blew one of the pit-doors open, and the cold current of air caused someone to shout "Off side!", a familiar football term. This was mistaken by the audience for "fire", and in a moment nearly every one in the place was on foot, and making a rush towards the doors. Mr Herbert and Miss Neville, with great coolness and presence of mind, at once stepped towards the footlights, and begged the audience to be seated, while Mr Courtenay with promptitude appeared by their side, assisted to restore order, and averted what might have proved a very serious disaster.

ON Tuesday evening, after Mr G.H. Chirgwin had left the stage of the South London, the curtain in coming down fell upon his violin, which he much valued, and completely crushed it.
16/2/1889

ON Saturday, at Westminster Police-court, Elizabeth Sinclair, aged forty-five, a thinly-clad, wretched-looking woman, in evident ill-health, was charged with begging in the vicinity of Victoria Station. Police-constable Gray, 339 B, said prisoner was stopping gentlemen on that day (Saturday), and asking for money. She exhibited a small brown loaf (produced), and said that was her prison fare. She went into a public-house, where she asked for a piece of cheese to eat with her "prison loaf." She also stated that she had no money, but at the station 3d. was found on her, and she asked the inspector, whom she appeared to know, to make it up to 4d.

Prisoner – The inspector knew me when I was in a very different position in the West-end. I've come down in the world, and going before one of the magistrates at Marlborough-street was my ruin. Mr d'Eyncourt – Where do you come from? Prisoner – I came out of gaol this morning. The constable said I was drunk, but I was only selling lights* in a public-house. It was not much harm to ask the inspector for a penny. Only a few years ago I was taking fifteen guineas a week as a serio-comic singer, and married a gentleman who was an officer in the army. Unfortunately for me I one night met a man – I thought he was a gentleman – after I had done my turn on the stage. The man paid for champagne, and made me presents, including two rings, which it turned out afterwards he had stolen from a gentleman he was nursing, and the exposure in the police-court ruined me. I am ill, and getting old now, and while I was in prison this last time the doctor had to paint my chest with iodine. Mr d'Eyncourt – Go away this time; but remember, if you are found begging again you will go back to prison**.

The woman thanked his Worship and hurriedly left the court.

*Matches.
**The following week Elizabeth was found lying drunk in Wardour Street and sentenced to twenty-one days in prison.

WANTED, to Sell, Two Paintings of Hairy Albert. Cost £10; will sell for £4. As good as new. Would like to hear from Harry Newey. Address, F. FARRAR, 3, Tebut-street, Rochdale-road, Manchester.
23/2/1889

WE regret to report the death, by a very sudden and painful accident, of Miss Helen Daly, wife of Mr Frank O'Grady. Whilst knitting in her dressing-room during the performance of Eviction at Macclesfield on Monday last, she stooped to reach an article out of a basket, and the end of one of her needles caught on the edge of the table. The other end penetrated her chest, entering her lung, and causing her death shortly afterwards.
2/3/1889

A TALL, well-dressed person, who answered to the name of Harriet Muir, described as an actress, was charged at the Marlborough-street Police-court on Wednesday with being disorderly by appearing in male attire in Hemming's-row, at half-past one o'clock on Tuesday afternoon. The prisoner blushed when entering the dock, and then faced the magistrate with eyes downcast and a smile. She wore a black coat and vest, fashionably cut trousers, a deerstalker hat, and a white scarf round her neck.

Mr Hannay (to Gaoler) – Did you say Harriet Muir? The Gaoler – Yes, sir. It's a woman in man's attire.

A Police-constable said that when on duty in Hemming's-row, he was called by an officer from the St George's Barracks to take the prisoner into custody. He was told that she was a woman in man's clothing, and that she had been trying to enlist for a soldier. He took her into custody, and great anxiety was shown by the large crowd to catch sight of her as he was taking her to the station.

Mr Arthur Newton said that he appeared for the prisoner. It was an extraordinary case, and the circumstances were these: the prisoner left her home four years ago, and from that time to the present she kept herself respectably by acting upon the stage. She was the only child of her father, now a farmer at Christchurch, in New Zealand. Until recently she had been performing at Bristol, but being out of employment she thought the best thing she could do would be to come to London. On Saturday night she took up her quarters at Anderton's Hotel, and and on Monday morning she repaired to the docks for the purpose of procuring a berth as under-stewardess on board a vessel about to sail south. It was found that she had not had sufficient experience in waiting, and she returned to the hotel somewhat dejected and disheartened. The next thing she thought of doing was an extraordinary one – she determined to try and enlist as a soldier, but that failed also.

There were some persons in the City to whom she was related, and they had assured her that, if the magistrate would let her go, they would see she was properly clothed and sent out by the next steamer to her father. He (Mr Newton) would suggest that she should be allowed to remain with Sergeant Brewer and Police-constable Marlow, the gaolers, both married men, until the afternoon, when no doubt money would be forthcoming, and a respectable lodging provided for her. She would not repeat that sort of conduct again, and he hoped the magistrate would think that what he had suggested would be the best thing that could be done for her.

Mr Hannay – If she had enlisted she would have found herself in a very awkward position indeed. Is there anyone here from the barracks?

Sergeant-Major Kelman, of the recruiting department, stepped forward and said the prisoner presented "himself" or "herself" at the barracks on Tuesday and asked to be enlisted as a soldier. Witness looked at her, and seeing that she blushed, and that her features were not exactly those of a man, he had his doubts, and told her to remain until the surgeon could see her. The doctor saw her, and was satisfied that he was a she.

Mr Hannay – Is there no question of sex in that long string of questions which you put to would-be recruits? Sergeant-Major Kelman – No, sir.

Mr Newton – The word "him" goes all through them.

Mr Hannay – Really, I don't see that much harm has been done. Her conduct has been ridiculous, no doubt; but I think I will allow her to be put back, and perhaps her friends will appear in the meantime.

The prisoner smiled and retired.

9/3/1889

MISS ELLALINE TERRISS had made to her the other day by her father, Mr William Terriss, the present of a very handsome pony and trap. On Monday, as she was driving by herself in the neighbourhood of Kew, the animal took fright at the approach of a contingent of the Salvation Army, and, running away, dashed up a bank on one side of the road, and wedged the carriage in a gap between the end of the gate and the hedgerow. From this unpleasant and dangerous position Miss Terriss was rescued by two labourers, who came to her assistance; and, luckily, the young actress escaped with only a very severe fright.

MISS ADA CAVENDISH being out of town at the time of the recent Dogs' Home matinée was unable to assist in the entertainment, but she has sent as her contribution to the institution two hundredweight of dog biscuits.

AT the Westminster Police-court, on Friday, March 8th, Harriet Muir, a tall, good-looking, well-dressed young woman, with close-cropped hair, was charged, before Mr d'Eyncourt, with stealing on the 4th inst. a coat, vest, trousers, socks, belt, braces, a collar, tie, hat, boots, and overcoat, value £3 10s., the property of Mr George Johnson, musician, of 5, Park-place, Battersea. Mr Arthur Newton defended. […]

The prosecutor, a young man, deposed that on Monday night, between eleven and twelve o'clock, while walking in Victoria-street, Westminster, he met the prisoner casually, and got into conversation with her. They had refreshments, and afterwards, at her invitation, he accompanied her to 37, New Peter-street, where she lodged. He recollected drinking a glass of ale, but remembered nothing else until six o'clock the following morning, when he woke up in bed, and to his great surprise found his clothes, hat, and boots gone. The young lady's clothes were left, but of course they were no good to him. He now identified his property, which, with the exception of the overcoat, was produced by the police.

Elizabeth Howell, landlady of 37, New Peter-street, said the prisoner came to lodge there about five weeks ago, describing herself as an artist's model. The witness knew nothing of the circumstances under which Mr Johnson came to her house, and was astonished on Tuesday morning, as she was sending her children to school, to hear a male voice calling out from the defendant's room. The prosecutor was in bed and regretfully explained that he was not in a presentable condition, as he had nothing left but a flannel vest. [...]

Mr Newton said her history was really a most romantic one. When the prisoner was a very young child her father left her with friends in Scotland, and proceeded to New Zealand to seek his fortune. When she was sixteen she ran away, and she had kept herself ever since. She had been a chorus-girl in the Drury-lane pantomime of *Puss in Boots*, and more recently she was on the stage at Bristol. [...] After she met the prosecutor she conceived the idea of "borrowing" his clothes to get on board a ship to take her to New Zealand, where she hoped to find her father, who was now a wealthy man. Afterwards she tried, under circumstances already made public, to enlist, not being aware of the formalities a recruit had to go through. She was sorry she had inconvenienced the prosecutor, but hoped that he would forgive her. He (Mr Newton) proposed that she should be remanded for a week, and then, if friends were able to report that her passage was paid to New Zealand, he trusted that his Worship would see fit to discharge her.

Mr d'Eyncourt remanded her for a week, and said he would consider what course to take

WANTED, to Sell, Case of Wax Heads of the Whitechapel Victims (Seven in Number), quite new, also Boy Gill, murdered at Bradford, life size, £12. W. HOLMS, 3, Tebutt-street, Rochdale-road, Manchester.
16/3/1889

AT the Manchester Police-court, on the 15th inst., before Mr Headlam and the other magistrates, Charles Manners, one of the principal vocalists in the Carl Rosa opera company, was summoned for using threatening and abusive language towards Francis Hubert Celli, another of the principal members of the company. Mr W.K. Taylor appeared for the complainant.

In opening the case Mr Taylor said that he appeared in support of the summons which had been taken out against the defendant, in which he was charged with having, on March 2nd, threatened to commit an assault on the complainant. The case was a serious one, and the proceedings had been taken with the full sanction of Mr Carl Rosa.

On Saturday night, March 2nd, the company gave a performance of the opera *Maritana*, and in that opera Mr Celli appeared as Don Jose, Mr Manners taking the part of the King. In that opera he had to sing a song at the end of the second act. At the conclusion of the song Mr Celli had to approach him and to address him. Instead of replying in the proper words, Mr Manners turned abruptly round, with his back to the audience, and, hissing, made use of very abusive language, and threatened to knock Mr Celli's brains out. He then used the proper words of the opera. Defendant subsequently repeated his abusive language, and threatened to "rip" complainant up. The result was that complainant was seriously affected. When afterwards asked what he meant by his conduct, defendant replied that Mr Celli had come on stage too soon, and had stopped the applause, and shaking his fist over his head, threatened to take it out of him for doing so. He also asked Mr Celli to only just touch the hem of his coat and see what he (defendant) would do for him. He was in a violent state of rage; indeed, he was a man of almost uncontrollable temper. Mr Celli, on the other hand, was a peaceable man, and said, "I'll take no notice of you." Defendant replied, "You only say that because you think I can't thrash you until the performance is over." Mr Barton McGuckin, another member of the company, hearing the noise in the wings, called for it to cease.

In this opera the part of Mr Celli finished before that of Mr Manners, and, seeing what was Mr Manners's state of mind, the former gentleman went to his room to dress with the object of leaving the theatre before Mr Manners had concluded his performance. Whilst he was in his room Mr Manners rushed in, and, "squaring" himself up in a fighting attitude, said, "Strike me, and we'll finish this business." Mr Celli declined to do so, and Mr Manners thereupon left the room, saying, "I'll do for you yet." Unless Mr Manners could be restrained from carrying out his threat, complainant was in fear of meeting him, as he had to do almost nightly on the stage. […]

Mr Manners having repeated his statement as to his having been willing to apologise and pay the costs before the case was called on, he was bound over in his own recognisance to keep the peace for six months, and pay the costs.

ONE evening last week at the Grand Theatre, Glasgow, a slip of the tongue occasioned great amusement among the audience. The play was *Madame Midas*. In the last act Madame says to the intruder in her drawing room, "Who are you? Pierre?" to which the reply should have been, "No (throwing off disguise), your unworthy husband, Randolph Villiers." By a curious mistake, however, the actor in this instance announced himself as Randolph Churchill*. This lapse created a wonderful effect among the audience, and also among the artists engaged in the scene, who found a little difficulty in terminating it.
Lord Randolph Churchill, politician and the father of Sir Winston Churchill.

WANTED, Professionals in every line to see the Greatest Picture-treat in the World, the only Life Portraits extant of Shakespeare and Daughter*. Shakespeare Hotel, Huddersfield. Proprietor, SHAKESPEARE HIRST.
The portrait attributed to Adam Elmsheimer, was supposedly painted during Shakespeare's alleged visit to Rome with his daughter Susanna in 1608. Needless to say, it was a forgery.

WANTED, to Sell. A Mount St Bernard Dog, with Six Legs. Alive. Thirty-two Inches high. Apply, after Six or before Ten, 2, Custance-street, Nile-street, Hoxton.
23/3/1889

THERE was a panic at Russell's Theatre of Varieties, Maryport, on Saturday night. The building, which is by no means a small one, is chiefly composed of wood. On Saturday night it was packed full, the majority of the audience being colliers and their sweethearts and wives. Soon after the performance commenced the gallery began to sway to and fro. This naturally caused some alarm, but a few reassuring words from those on the stage restored to some extent the confidence of the audience. A few minutes later, however, a very ominous crack was heard, and the people in the gallery made a frantic rush for the doors. Mr Russell, the proprietor of the theatre, entreated the audience to keep calm. His appeals were to some extent effectual; but soon afterwards one side of the building totally collapsed. Several women fainted, and were trampled upon. Cries of "Fire!" were raised, of course increasing the excitement. Several persons were badly bruised and otherwise injured.

WANTED, Managers to Secure this Great Novelty, the Brothers Hanlon, the Crying Babies, the only Two. Required, Six Nights April 1st by Brothers Hanlon, Crying Baby Mimics and Lightning Change Artists. Wire, 71, Northgate, Bradford. Agent, F. Westgate.
30/3/1889

A WELL-KNOWN dramatist, when rehearsing recently a not too amusing piece, thus addressed his leading comedian: – "My dear boy, be good enough not to gag, please. Speak my lines, and wait for the laugh." The actor answered, "Yes; but my last train goes at twelve!"

A FUNNY incident occurred on Tuesday last at the Paragon during the interval between the two scenes of *On Guard*. By some mistake the signal bell for raising the curtain was touched before the scene was properly set, and the curtain rose half way, disclosing a man carrying a tombstone under each arm, and others pushing the church, which is a solidly built structure on wheels, towards the front of the stage. This unrehearsed effect caused a good deal of merriment.
6/4/1889

ROSCO, the King of Pork, is still on Earth and meeting with success everywhere. A great success with Circus Busch, Warsaw; also the biggest success ever known with Performing Pigs in Moscow. My latest Novelty, the Talking Pig. I am called and recalled Nightly for my Champion High Stilt Act. Kind regards to all my Friends. Address, CIRCUS SOLOMONSKY, MOSCOW, RUSSIA.
13/4/1889

MR ROBERT COURTNEIDGE*, who has been playing Pepin with Mr. Charles Wibrow's *Girouette* company, recently had the misfortune to poison his feet through wearing coloured tights in that opera. After struggling through his part for several nights in great agony, Mr Courtneidge had to absent himself on Saturday at Nottingham, but managed to play on Monday night in Leicester, after which, by medical advice, he resigned his part in order to give himself a complete rest.
*The father of actress Cicely Courtneidge.

MR NORMAN KIRBY, operatic vocalist and teacher of music, West Hartlepool, had a remarkable adventure with a burglar on Sunday night last. Returning to his home in Scarborough-street shortly after twelve o'clock, he was surprised to find in possession of his establishment a strange man who was leisurely packing up for removal a quantity of silver plate and other goods collected from various parts of the premises. Mrs Kirby, who had retired for the night, heard someone moving about the house, and also go upstairs into one of the bedrooms adjoining her own, but concluding that it was her husband she took no notice, and the burglar was about to take his departure with the plunder when Mr Kirby suddenly came upon the scene. The fellow was then on his knees in the back sitting-room coolly packing up. Upon seeing Mr Kirby, however, he made a dash for the open door, where he was promptly seized by Mr Kirby, who gripped the rascal by the throat and forced him into a chair.

The amusing part of the affair now comes in. Finding it was no use attempting to escape, the fellow began to plead for mercy, and ultimately assumed a quite friendly attitude towards his captor. He expressed his deep regret that he should have caused any inconvenience to anyone, and when Mrs Kirby and the servant were aroused ingeniously suggested that as it was not safe at that time of the night to send the females out in search of a constable, he should be permitted to wait in the house while Mr Kirby himself went for an officer. The good-natured professor was vastly tickled at the suggestion, and, as he stated afterwards, would not have been surprised to have heard the impudent rascal propose to go and fetch a policeman himself. Needless to say the fellow's suggestion was not entertained. But an officer was brought all the same, and this very obliging burglar, who gave the name of Thomas Walker, and said he belonged to Liverpool, was subsequently taken before the local Bench of Magistrates, and committed for trial.

WAX-WORK. – The Wax Head of "Jack the Ripper," carefully Modelled from Sketches published in the "Daily Telegraph," Furnished by witnesses who had actually seen him, also a Wax Head of Mary Jeanette Kelly, his last victim. Apply, Reynolds's Exhibition, Liverpool.
20/4/1889

THE latest instance of risky realism is furnished by Mr Richard Mansfield, who puts special vigour into his fighting scenes, and encourages his enemies to play up to him. Accordingly, we learn, the standard bearer at the Globe the other night delivered a vigorous cut, which King Richard failed to parry, and the result was such as would have shocked the audience extremely, had he not kept his back turned and signalled to drop the curtain. Mr Mansfield has guarded himself against a repetition of this particular accident, it is said, by making his wig sabre-proof.

DR ARNE'S setting of "When daisies pied" in *Love's Labour's Lost* was recently sung in a northern suburb at a school-room concert, where the price of admission was covered by the purchase of a book of the words. The line "And lady-smocks all silver white" must have offended the prudery of the worthy programme compiler; for with the righteous spirit of another Bowdler he left Nature and Shakespeare out of the verse, his emendation of the text reading "And ladies dressed in silver white." "Lady-smocks" was much too shocking! What would poor Mrs Grundy say? That dear old lady would never dream possibly that lady-smocks is the fanciful name given to a pretty flower of the genus Cardamine, and does not refer to underclothing!

IT may not be generally known to professional Freemasons that Unthan, the marvellous performer who was born without arms, is one of the craft. At the Paragon last Saturday Brothers Barwick and Eaton put him to the test, and not only did he prove himself a proficient craftsman, but he also gave all the grips accurately with his right foot. It would interest and surprise a masonic brother to see Unthan give the signs, which he does satisfactorily and clearly in a manner that is, of course, entirely his own.

AT the Marylebone Police-court, on Thursday, Alfred Honeychurch Roberts, otherwise Roberts Honeychurch, residing at Tolmer's-square, Hampstead-road, was summoned for on April 17th assaulting Julia, his wife. On the complainant being sworn she gave her surname as Roberts. The husband, however, said her name was Honeychurch. The wife adhered to her statement, and an altercation ensued between the witness and the defendant. Eventually the complainant said Roberts was the name they were known by.

She said she was engaged on the stage. Her husband had ill-used her for years. On the night of the 16th he broke a photograph, and while she was putting it together the next morning he entered the room and struck her several times with his fist. Since the summons had been issued he had turned her out of the house, and she had to take refuge in the workhouse.

The defendant said the cause of all "the bother" was the wife having had a photograph of herself taken in stage attire. The photograph was not a very decent thing for a married woman to carry about with her to show to men. (He produced the photograph, which depicted the complainant in tights.) The complainant said she had to get her own living, and the photograph was necessary for professional purposes. The defendant said that was all nonsense. He was, he might say, born in the theatrical profession, and his sister, who had been an actress for many years, would tell the court that a photograph such as he now produced was quite unnecessary. Mr Cooke remarked that it seemed strange that such a photograph should be necessary for professional purposes. He asked the complainant if she had any engagement at the present time. The complainant said she was on the stage at Drury-lane Theatre, but her engagement would end on Saturday.

The defendant told the magistrate that his wife simply did as she liked, and if he asked why she did this or that she replied that it was no business of his. She was in the habit of coming home late at night and lying in bed all the next day reading 2s. novels. She said she was in ill-health, but the people in the house had remarked that she could not be very ill judging by the dinners he took up to her. She neglected his home. He had even to wash her stockings after she came home late, because she pretended she could not do it. She had got mixed up with some other women who had got rid of their husbands; but he did not want to leave her. The complainant said she was anxious for a separation.

Mr Cooke ordered the defendant to be bound over in £20 to keep the peace for six months, and he advised the parties to separate for a time if they could not agree.

27/4/1889

IT is not often that a man rebuts a serious charge by proving that he has been a convict, but such was the case with Albert Wardle, in the Nottingham Police-court, on Saturday last. He was accused of stabbing, on the 23rd ult., a man in the upper gallery of the Grand Theatre, Nottingham; but proved an alibi by

evidence which substantiated the fact that he was at the time the offence was committed upon the stage engaged in representing one of the convicts in the performance by Mr J.A. Atkin's company of Arthur Shirley's drama *The Grip of Iron*.
4/5/1889

ON Saturday night, shortly after ten o'clock, a serious accident occurred at the Albert Hall, Jarrow, which for the last three months has been used as a music hall, under the management of Signor Durland, of Sunderland. It seems that a large net had been suspended over the pit, and a number of lads were running a race along the net. The event caused great excitement, and a considerable number of persons were bending over the gallery to see the result of the contest. Suddenly the front of the gallery gave way, precipitating about a hundred spectators into the net. About thirty yards of the gallery fell, including a heavy iron rail which is used as a protection. Fortunately the net protected the people in the pit from the mass of debris, and also had the effect of breaking the fall of those who were thrown down. A scene of the greatest excitement ensued, and many people were believed to have been killed. It transpired, however, that the accident was not attended with any fatal consequences, although several persons were conveyed to the Memorial Hospital in an insensible condition, and, on examination by Dr Smellie, the house surgeon, were found to be suffering from concussion of the brain. [...] The event caused the greatest excitement in the town, and shortly after the accident Elliston-street was rendered impassible in consequence of the large number of people assembled outside the hall.
11/5/1889

BROOKE'S Great Monkey Show, which is to be held at the Alexandra Palace on the first of next month, promises to be a novel and exciting exhibition. The proprietors of the celebrated "Monkey Brand" soap have hit upon the ingenious method of advertising their commodity and amusing the public at the same time. At least a thousand specimens will be gathered together in the palace, where they will have full space to disport themselves in a tropical temperature in the spacious conservatory. Amongst the numerous prizes which are offered is one for the finest monkey, the *bona fide* property of a professional entertainer; another for the best performing monkey, similarly owned; and a third, for the finest monkey, the property of an organ-grinder. We are informed that for the delectation of those for whom monkeys have no charms, a variety of other attractions will be provided in the palace and grounds.
18/5/1889

FOR some time past a "masher" has been doing everything in his power to obtain admission behind the scenes at the Croydon Theatre. Last week, during the performance of *The Ruling Passion* by Mr Lawson's company, this individual was so importunate in his entreaties that it occurred to some of the staff that it would be a good idea to give him an experience which should cure him of his curiosity. He was admitted during the Hyde Park scene, and invited to join the crowd upon the stage. When he saw the "real rain" begin to descend he attempted to retire, but was promptly seized from behind by several carpenters, and held firmly in the downpour in the full view of the audience. After he had been sufficiently rained upon to damp his ardour for stage exploration he was permitted to depart, a wetter and, let us hope, a wiser man.

ON Tuesday last, at the Darlington Borough Police-court, a youth named Charles Harkless, belonging to Sunderland, was charged with stealing a gold watch and chain, the property of John King. The facts of the case were extraordinary, as it appeared from the evidence that Harkless, who is only sixteen and the son of well-to-do parents, got into his present unenviable plight owing to an infatuation for ladies of the ballet. In February last Messrs Milton-Rays' pantomime *Forty Thieves* appeared at the Theatre Royal, in which the lady of the young gentleman's heart was employed. He took lodgings in the town, representing himself as holding the exalted position of baggage master to the company, and towards the

end of the week, in order to keep his inamorata in chocolate bon-bons, he appropriated the goods and chattels of a fellow lodger. Prisoner's company was shortly afterwards in particular request by the minions of the law, but he was not to be found until last week, when he was discovered wandering about Bristol in a most pitiable and distressed condition. The Bench took into consideration the prisoner's youth and the pleadings of his parents, who were prepared to forget and forgive, and let him off with a fine of £5 and costs.
25/5/1889

WANTED, a Play for a Soubrette Actress. Must be full of fun and pathos, and without the slightest approach to coarseness or vulgarity. Authors please address, Box 2,109, care of "The Era" office, 49, Wellington-street, Strand.
1/6/1889

MR WYBERT ROUSBY met with a serious accident on Tuesday morning. He was bathing on St Clement's sands, Jersey, and for that purpose had hired a bathing machine, which was taken some distance down the beach. The waves were breaking with some force, and finding this he ordered the machine to be taken back a little distance. Before this was done, however, a huge wave caught him and dashed him with much force against the machine. The result was the Mr Rousby's right shoulder bone was dislocated. He managed to get into the machine, but could not afterwards move. His condition being discovered, he was placed in a cab and driven home. Dr Thomson was then summoned, but finding the case a serious one, he called in the assistance of Dr A.C. Godfray. Chloroform was administered, and the bone was then replaced in its socket.

MR BRANDON THOMAS, proceeding along the Embankment to Terry's for the matinee of *Sweet Lavender* the other day, saw a lot of little urchins crying on the steps of Cleopatra's Needle. The cause of their sorrow was a poor little dog which was drowning. Mr Thomas instantly threw off his coat, dived into the water, and brought the little animal safe to land. Taking a cab he rode to the theatre, and, divesting himself of his wet clothes, proceeded to act the stern old father in Mr Pinero's play, and happily was none the worse after his ducking for a dog.

TWO boys named Bright and Chandler died on Wednesday morning from burns sustained in a fire at Pain's firework factory at Mitcham on Tuesday. The lads were mixing purple light in No. 5 shed, and the composition ignited, causing a great blaze, but no explosion. The two boys were severely injured, and the shed in which they were working was burnt out.
8/6/1889

GENTLEMAN, 6ft., dark, striking appearance, age thirty-four, private means, good all-round sportsman, athletic, and linguist, travelled man of the world, belonging to exclusive clubs at home and abroad, but caring little for society, would like to go in double harness with a Lady of congenial tastes and lovable disposition. Must have means sufficient for her own use. The most honourable secrecy guaranteed and photo returned. Write, ANGLO-PARISIAN, care of Brown, Gould, and Co., 53, New Bond-street, W.
29/6/1889

MISS LOUISE MOODIE met with a curious mishap during one of the rehearsals of Mr John Uniacke's new play, *The Marquesa*, which has been in active preparation at the Opera Comique for the last fortnight. As the Marquesa Miss Moodie has to put a glass, supposed to contain poison, to her lips. The stage had been set in an "impromptu" manner, and to represent the glass of laudanum the property-man, in his haste, had put a cup containing some very powerful cement with which he was repairing some small items. As soon as the cement touched Miss Moodie's mouth, she, of course, put down the cup; but not before her lips had become literally "sealed," and so strong was the adhesion of the cement that it was some time before she again obtained "freedom of speech" and could continue the rehearsal.

A NOISY demonstration of the "gods," which took place at Mr Arthur Roberts's matinee at the Avenue Theatre on Monday last, culminated in a regular chorus, the time of which was marked by a "fugleman," which consisted of the words, "One, two, three, four – take off that *hat*!" It was not, however, mere exuberance of animal spirits or wanton rudeness which led to the disturbance, but the irritating interposition between the "god" and the stage of a remarkably large straw hat ornamented with poppies, which was worn by a lady who was seated in the very centre of the amphitheatre, and who refused to remove it in spite of the "voice of the people" thus peremptorily expressed during every interval of the entertainment.

WHILE the de Rosa troupe were travelling recently from Wakefield to North Shields the carriage-lamp burst, severely scalding Miss Jessie Herbert's foot, and it will be some time before she will be able to appear. Great excitement was caused by the train being stopped, and great kindness was shown by the station-masters at Harrogate and Thirsk, a special carriage being put on. All the members of the company were splashed with oil, and were unable to appear at the Gaiety in the evening.

MR T.J. OSBORNE, of Old Market-street, Neath, was the subject of a strange adventure at the Bridge Hotel, Llandrindod Wells, on Friday afternoon, 28th ult., about half-past three o'clock. Mr Osborne was preparing to leave for home by the afternoon train on that day, when a full-grown African lioness dashed in through the open window. Mr Osborne seized a chair to defend himself. At this instant the animal's keeper and a staff of men appeared on the scene. The keeper warned Mr Osborne not to stir. With as little delay as possible the keeper and his assistants made their way to the room with the necessary appliances for recapturing the brute. With some difficulty they succeeded in throwing a sack over the animal's head, after which she was firmly secured with ropes . It was found that the lioness had made its escape from Wombwell's menagerie, which was located on a plot of ground near the Bridge Hotel. *6/7/1889*

MISS GRACIE WADE, one of New York's pretty actresses, has sprung into celebrity by bringing a suit against a cigarette firm for libel. This firm took a portrait of Miss Wade and attached it to the body of a skirtless ballet dancer; then turned the combination into a chromograph, and gave it to the public. Miss Wade says that the face is hers, but that it is scandalous to represent her with so little drapery, and that she had never authorised any firm to misrepresent her in this style.

THE Botanical Gardens at Edgbaston, a fashionable suburb of Birmingham, afford an absolutely ideal theatre for pastoral playing; but Mr Ben Greet on the occasion of his previous visits has been singularly unfortunate in regard to weather. This year the elements have been more propitious; but not wholly so. One old lady when booking her seat declared that rain should not prevent her from seeing the show; but she was in great fear of lightning, and stipulated that the seat she booked should not be near a tree!

WE are pleased to notice that the Midland Railway Company, who are generally foremost in everything that may be calculated to conduce to the comfort and convenience of their passengers, have commenced to run third-class carriages fitted with lavatory accommodation. This will be a great boon to long-distance travellers, and in the case of theatrical companies on tour, who often have to spend half their Sundays on the train, the advantages of the innovation will be obvious.

RING a ting ting! Hello! Who's there? The readers of *The Era*. What do you want? We want them to know that we are now on the telephone, and that our number is 2634. Yes! All right. Thank you. Good day! Don't forget, 2634.
20/7/1889

TO THE EDITOR OF THE ERA.
Sir, – The enclosed is a copy of a letter sent to Mr Winterbotham. I sincerely trust that you will publish it. Yours truly, JULIE SEALE, Alhambra Theatre, July 25th.

To Mr Winterbotham, M.P.
"Sir, – At a meeting of the ballet ladies of the Alhambra, Lyric, and Empire Theatres I was requested to forward to you the following resolution, which was carried unanimously: – 'We have heard with indignation and disgust your statement that "the majority of ballet-girls end by becoming street-walkers." We deliberately tell you that this statement is a cruel and cowardly untruth. We challenge you to prove it is true, or publicly withdraw it. It is a disgrace that anyone professing to be a gentleman should thus libel women who are earning their living by an honourable and useful calling. If we were men we should know how to deal with you; as it is we despise you.'
"Signed, on behalf of the meeting, JULIE SEALE."

IN the train coming home from the Music Hall Sports on Tuesday last, the wife of one of the competitors (who carried off several of the prizes last year, but was less fortunate on this occasion) was heard to remark, "What a disappointment. Joe's won nothing to speak of, and I've been for the last two days shifting the furniture to make room for the prizes."

ON Saturday afternoon a well-dressed woman attracted a crowd round the Green Man pond, Leytonstone, by throwing her umbrella, mounted with silver, far out into the water, in order to show off the qualities of a large retriever dog which accompanied her. The umbrella, open, and sodden with mud, and heavy with water, remained just visible above the surface, the retriever refusing the "fetch." The valuable umbrella was given up for lost, when the tiny black and tan terrier which figured so conspicuously as the "Demon Dog" in the last pantomime at the Theatre Royal, Stratford, suddenly appeared on the scene, being instantly recognised by all the juveniles present.
    Plunging into the water, to the astonishment of the crowd, the tiny animal made five desperate attempts to move the umbrella before she succeeded in getting it "under weigh." Three times she sank from exhaustion between the middle of the pond and the shore, but each time reappeared with her teeth in the "gingham," with which she struggled on until, amid excited cheering, she laid it at the feet of her master, who enjoys some reputation as an amateur animal trainer. Unseen by the gentleman, the owner of the umbrella, with unpardonable thoughtlessness, again threw it to the spot whence the poor little "demon dog" had just rescued it. This time it sank altogether, but not before the terrier had seen it, and had again made for it. She plunged and dived until it seemed certain that she would be drowned, for it appeared impossible to induce her to leave the spot without the umbrella. Eventually she was with great difficulty decoyed ashore, whereupon her owner expressed to the umbrella-thrower his gratification at the final loss of her property.
27/7/1889

WANTED, Known, Miss Lily Marney, the Only Female Irishman, at present appearing Nightly, Folly, Manchester. A very successful artist – Vide Press.
3/8/1889

AT Bloomsbury County-court, on Tuesday, his Honour Judge Bacon had before him the adjourned case of Maltby v. Cleaver, the hearing of which provoked considerable mirth. The plaintiff is an Army tailor, carrying on business at 8, Hanover-place, Regent's-park, and the defendant described himself as a popular song-writer and a general *littérateur*.

Some four months ago he called at the plaintiff's shop and ordered some clothes, including a velveteen coat and waistcoat, the entire cost of which was to be £10 16s. The clothes were made and sent home, but when the messenger found that he could not get paid, he brought the clothes back again. On the last hearing of the case the defendant informed his Honour that his notion of the law was that unless the clothes were delivered to his residence there was no delivery, and therefore the plaintiff could not succeed in his present action. His Honour said that unless there was a contract to give credit a tailor was perfectly entitled to keep his clothes until he got his money, and he ordered the defendant to go to the plaintiff's shop and try on the clothes. When the case was resumed it was stated that the defendant had not done so, and his Honour said there was no alternative but to have the clothes tried on in court.

Mr Cleaver, having taken off his coat and waistcoat, made an imperious gesture to the plaintiff. His Honour – You should not treat your tailor as if he were a mere slave! The velveteen coat defendant declared was "skimpy," and, addressing his Honour, he said he knew what the law on the subject was. There was not only the question of the clothes fitting, but there was also the question of style. No one could force him to take things which he objected to on the latter ground. His Honour – That is for me to decide. It is easy for a man who has a quarrel with his tailor to find fault with the clothes. Defendant – You do me an injustice. His Honour – I do not think so. Defendant – It is an old adage, "Those who wear the shoe know where it pinches." His Honour requested defendant not to make speeches, but to get into the top coat, which he did, declaring that it was too tight in the chest. The learned Judge – If the clothes were delivered up to you would the money be forthcoming? Defendant – Not at present, but within a week if they were altered to suit my taste.

Having tried on the waistcoat Mr Cleaver declared it to be too short. His Honour – No, it is not; where is your hip-bone? Defendant – here. His Honour – That's not where your hip-bone is! Defendant – I declare to your Honour that that (indicating the spot with his thumb) is where my hip-bone is. His Honour – Nonsense, that's not the top of your hip-bone. Defendant – Surely I ought to know. Will your Honour take the evidence of the usher on the subject?

His Honour, in the course of an elaborate summing-up, said he was of the opinion that the clothes fitted very well. Of course, as to the contention of the velveteen waistcoat not being long enough – of course if a man wants to cover the whole of his stomach with velveteen he could do so; but, unless he gave a special order for it to done, the tailor could not reasonably be expected to do it. There would never have been any dispute at all about the clothes if it had not been that the defendant got hold of a false notion of the law, and imagined that a tailor was bound to deliver his goods before he got paid. That was not the case, and showed that "a little learning is a dangerous thing." His Honour gave judgement for the plaintiff for £10 16s. and costs, the clothes to be given to the defendant and the money to be paid in a week.

THE practice of giving bouquets as a testimony of admiration for stage favourites seems to be going out of fashion, but surely vegetable marrows are not a convenient substitute. Four of these gigantic esculents ornamented the top of Miss Nellie Richards's brougham at Deacon's the other evening. They were the gifts of an admirer from the country.
10/8/1889

THE death scene of poor Jess, in *Hoodman Blind*, is as sad a stage spectacle as the theatre-goer wishes to see; but at the Prince of Wales's, Birmingham, a night or two since, it assumed an air of comicality. The stage-picture represents the Thames Embankment, and Jack Yeulett apostrophises the stream so that there shall be little doubt as to its identity. The "river," thanks to cleverly arranged perspective, goes from the level of the stage up to the Houses of Parliament. The other night, when Jess was in her last agonies, and when between her and death there was little or nothing, a black kitten walked over the river amid the roars of the house – strange accompaniment to a death scene – crossing the Thames successfully on foot. A local joker says that, as the time of year at which Jess died is not stated, the

Thames may have been frozen over, and young pussy's successful attempt to cross it not so extraordinary after all.

MEDLEY, the mimic, tells a yarn of how, some years ago, having taken a house in the north of London previously vacated by a doctor, and not having taken the precaution to plug the speaking tube, he was awakened the second night after moving in by a loud ringing at the door bell, and, on starting up, by a guttural voice from the vicinity of his pillow exclaiming, "Will you come round at once to Mrs Smith, up the Green-lanes, she's werry bad, and the nurse is there."
24/8/1889

WANTED, Responsible Managers to Know Sanger's Midgets are Genuine. We do not dress up two little boys and show them as man and wife. Fried fish hawkers and amateur Showmen, please take notice of this. Sorry to hear you have lost so many Jubilee Coins, but I suppose business is bad when Genuine Midgets are about. No open dates. North of England to follow. Sanger's Midget Exhibition, Oldham. Splendid dresses and costly jewellery.

"THE CURATE" company had a very narrow escape last Sunday night from being in the accident that occurred to the Scotch Limited Mail. They missed the connection with the mail at Stafford by about two minutes, and were sent on to join it at Crewe, where they found it lying on the platform with several carriages telescoped and one of the engines standing nearly on end. After a long delay a fresh train was made up, and the company arrived in Scotland several hours late, but in safety.
7/9/1889

WANTED, to Sell, Frog's Dress, complete. Magnificent Head. Also Set of Sleigh Bells. ESMOND, 209, Isledon-road, London, N.

THE cockatoo is a knowing bird, and an inquiring one, as was proved on Wednesday evening during the performance of Miss Ellen Marvelle's feathered pets at the Oxford. One of them not relishing restraint, perched on a guy rope fixed to the Dillons' trapeze apparatus, and made the pianist aware of its presence. Later on it flew through one of the ventilators, but returned and made a general tour of inspection around the building. The bird was not captured until the following morning, when it was secured and returned to its owner.
14/9/1889

ACTING MANAGERS get many presentations, but it has been left to Mr W.F. Morton, of Mr Pitt Hardacre's *True Metal* company, to be the recipient of nearly half a hundredweight of a well-known soap. It was a mystery at first to find a reason for the gift till a letter from the makers came to hand, when it was found to be in return for an unintentional advertisement gag. Such advertisements are undoubtedly very valuable, but if managers are to take advantage of them to get extra profit and drag in So-and-so's soap, &c., in a serious piece, the much talked-of decline of the drama may be fairly said to have set in.
21/9/1889

DIFFERENT plays have different effects, and different playgoers have different ways of manifesting their emotions. We repeatedly have to tell of some honest rough who, seeing a villain on the stage, puts into practice the treatment said to be recommended for strangers in the colliery districts, and heaves half a brick at him; now and again we have to report the gallant effort of some British tar to descend from the gallery to the rescue of beauty in distress behind the footlights; but not until now have we had to report so strange a result of seeing a play as that which attended a visit to *The Golden Ladder*, on Wednesday, at the Southend Alexandra Theatre, where an old lady, in her emotion, shed three of her front teeth, which were not discovered until the attendants went to clear up things on the following morning.

MISS BESSIE BELLWOOD was the recipient of a curious "floral offering" at the Gaiety Theatre, Glasgow, on Wednesday. Some young men in a private box threw a cauliflower at her at the end of her third song, and the fair artist endeavoured to return it in the same manner. The managers caused the offenders to be expelled, and then drew aside the curtain of the box to show that it was not occupied. Miss Bellwood burst into tears, and was unable to respond to the encore accorded her.

ON Friday afternoon Miss Finney, sister of Professor Finney, the champion swimmer, following in the wake of Larry Donovan, dived over London-bridge. Of course, the act was an illegal one, and on that account the arrangements for the performance were kept secret. Beyond the customary gangs of loafers, no one was about at the time. It was decided that Miss Finney should leap from the first arch on the Middlesex side at 2.45, and punctually a small skiff containing Dave Godwin, the oarsman, and Professor Finney, pushed off. A number of steamboats and tugs were passing at the time, and it was not until three o'clock that the signal was given to the fair diver. The course, so to speak, being clear, one male friend took her broad-brimmed hat, and another her long ulster, the lady immediately leaping on to the coping stone. She was attired in a tight-fitting, dark blue, navy jersey. After pausing for a few minutes to take her bearings, she dropped upon the projecting stone, a couple of feet below the parapet, and then dived down, striking the water beautifully. The whole business occupied a few moments only, and before the loafers could realise what had happened, she was striking out for the boat. On reaching it she waved her hand to her friends, and was rowed to the shore none the worse for her immersion.

MR W.B. MOSELEY, the well-known impersonator of the great Napoleon at St Helena, threw himself out of a window at his lodgings at Paris-street, Lambeth, last week, and is not expected to recover*. The act is attributed to a fit of mental aberration.
*Mr Moseley made a full recovery, and claimed that the accident occurred "during a fit of somnambulism".
28/9/1889

WANTED, Ugly Petite Comedienne, as Contrast to Magnificent Comedienne, for Duologue (London). Vocal ability important. Edwin Drew, 124, Gower-street.
12/10/1889

AN elephant belonging to Sanger's Circus, which on Monday was at Accrington, escaped on that morning and wandered into a co-operative store. A police-constable was summoned, and found the animal busy among the biscuits and jam. He had evidently enjoyed a good breakfast, and had become frolicsome, scattering the onions and other light commodities left and right. His keeper was communicated with, and the elephant was taken back to his quarters, offering no resistance. The same elephant was on Thursday morning discovered in another burglary at Chorley. While the circus paraphernalia was being packed up, he slipped away in the darkness, and forced open a grocer's shop in the High-street, where he demolished a whole cheese, two boxes of biscuits, and other goods, valued, with the damage to property, at £10.
19/10/1899

SCENE – Pit of Grand Theatre, Leeds. First Pittite – "Take off your hat. I cawn't see Mrs Langtry." Second Pittite – "She doan't want such as you to see her!" First Pittite punches Second Pittite's head. Both turned out. Neither see Mrs Langtry!

SPEAKING the other evening at a Birmingham chapel, the Rev Nicholas Knight propounded the idiotic theory that no man could play Mephistopheles for 300 nights without injuring his moral tone, nor could he imagine it to be possible for any woman to act Margaret for 300 nights without suffering in moral health.

2/11/1889

AT the Lambeth County Court on Tuesday, before his Honour Judge Powell, Q.C., the case of Henderson v. Egerton was dealt with. It was a claim by a servant girl against Mr Frank Egerton, a comedian, of 131, Lower Kennington-lane, to recover the sum of 16s. 8d. for wages due. Mr W.H. Armstrong, solicitor, appeared for the defendant.

The plaintiff stated in her evidence that Mrs Egerton went away from home for five weeks, and left her to take care of the baby. When Mrs Egerton returned, she told her to go at once.

Mr Armstrong said the defendant was a comedian, and his wife was accustomed to go away with him to the provinces. In August they went away, leaving the child under the care of the plaintiff.

The plaintiff, in cross-examination, denied that she was in the habit of stopping in bed until twelve o'clock in the day and neglecting the child. Mrs Merchant, the next door neighbour, had not remonstrated with her for neglecting the child.

Mr Armstrong said the defendant was a comedian of some standing, and would not have contested this matter had he not had a good reason.

Mrs Merchant said she formerly lived next door to the defendant's. During their absence she frequently heard the piano going, and the plaintiff boasted that she could nearly play "God Save the Queen." She went into the house repeatedly, and saw the condition of the child. It was grossly neglected. The house was stinking from top to bottom.

Dr F.W. Farr said the child, which was suffering from measles, was in a very neglected state. The plaintiff said she had treated the child properly, and thought the clothes ought not to be taken off while the child had measles.

Mrs Egerton stated that when she came home she found the house in a dreadful state and the child very much neglected. She said to the plaintiff, "Sarah Henderson, I give you one hour to clear out of this house."

His Honour gave judgement for the defendant.

9/11/1889

VERY recently in Bristol, when Joseph, in *Joseph's Sweetheart*, was proving his "moderation" in the matter of love for the charming Fanny by kissing her several times, an enthusiastic and much-mashed West Countryman in the gallery caused roars of laughter by shouting, "Gi'er another one vor I!"

MADAME PATTI is entertaining a party of friends at Craig-y-nos Castle, among them being Mr Percy Harrison, a member of the firm of Messrs Harrison of Birmingham, who will for three years after next spring be her sole entrepreneurs both for concerts and opera, as far as this country is concerned. Madame Patti will leave her Welsh castle on Tuesday, and proposes to sail on Wednesday next by the City of New York. The prima donna's baggage comprises upward of thirty enormous trunks, containing, besides her stage costumes, some concert dresses calculated to excite the envy and admiration of American womanhood, more than half a hundredweight of the particular sort of cocoa which she prefers, and a quantity of grapes from the conservatories at Craig-y-nos. Before quitting London Madame Patti presented Mr N. Vert with a valuable scarfpin of catseyes and diamonds in token of her appreciation of that gentleman's excellent management of her concerts at the Albert Hall and elsewhere.

A DISGRACE TO THE PROFESSION.

At the East Dereham Police-court, on the 15th inst., Edward Francis, alias Brown, a member of Captain Dudley's comedy and burlesque company, was charged with stealing a crocodile skin cigar case of the value of £1 1s., on the 9th inst. The company had been performing at the Theatre during the week, and on Saturday prisoner went to the shop of Mr Thomas Bulmer, tobacconist, &c., ostensibly for the purpose of purchasing a cigar case, and having looked at some asked to be supplied with some tobacco. Whilst the assistant was serving him he managed to slip the case into his pocket. The article was missed soon after prisoner had left the shop, and information given to the police. The prisoner being suspected, a search was made amongst his property, and the case found in his box. The police also found several silk handkerchiefs and a pocket book which prisoner had stolen from various shops in the town and which were identified by the owners. He had gone to the different shops on the pretence of purchasing and succeeded in carrying the items away. Prisoner pleaded guilty, and was sentenced to two months' imprisonment with hard labour.
16/11/1889

WANTED, Good Set of Impaling Knives, immediately. Address, WHITE, 59, Thesiger-street, Grimsby.
23/11/1889

A CONSIDERABLE amount of damage has recently been committed on the statuary at the Crystal Palace, and the authorities have experience much difficulty in capturing the offenders, but on the 9th inst. the official in charge of the Greek Court detected two young men breaking some of the figures. One of these was summoned last week before the Penge divisional magistrates and fined 20s. and 9s. 6d. costs, and the other*, who is the son of well-to-do parents residing at Herne Hill, was to have appeared on Tuesday to answer the charge of wilfully damaging "Centaur Tamed by Cupid," it being alleged against him that he broke off Cupid's arm. The defendant did not appear, however, and as it was stated that he had not been home since the summons was issued, the Bench granted a warrant for his apprehension.
*The runaway vandal was the 18-year-old son of a clergyman, and was later fined £5 and 20s. damages.

MRS LANGRY'S CORRESPONDENTS.

Mrs Langtry has a great deal of correspondence, and some of the letters she receives are very funny. We give several specimens. The first is evidently in answer to an advertisement:

honored madem
  seeing your advertisement in paper for a dresser i beg to say i can do for you i could make you up having done same for myself in a called back co which failed i am 302 years of age hoping to hear from you
am yours
trooly

A stage-struck lady writes from Cornwall as follows:

Dr Madam,
  I humbly beg to opoligise for taking the liberty of writing to you. Having the pleasure of seeing your Advertisement has regards taking the St James's Theatre London I beg most Affectionately to ask if I might join you in the Play, As I am highly delighted in it and have had several years in the profession, I would send Photo if needed. Should feel happy to hear from you by return! Yrs Most Obedient, ------

The last is from a firm of saddlers and speaks for itself:

Madam,
  Seeing you are about to appear in the favourite play "Twixt Axe and Crown," and having made the Saddle used by Mrs Rousby when she played in "Joan of Arc" at the Queens Theatre, Long Acre, and we perfectly understand the kind of Saddle that is required we should feel it a great honour to take your order for the saddle &c. Yours respectfully, ------

AN ACTOR'S HOAX.

Jack-in-the-Box company appeared at York Theatre Royal last week. Certain members of the *corps dramatique* had old friends in this city of spires, and their visit was the occasion of much pleasurable social intercourse. After the performance on Saturday evening, two gentlemen of the company were invited to the house of a mutual friend to meet a couple of well-known citizens, one connected with medicine and the other a distinguished member of the Civil Service. The guests got home to their apartments before the milkman arrived, the party having previously arranged to meet at a certain hostel at 1 p.m. that day. Only two, however, kept the appointment – the host of the previous evening and one of the members of the company. Inquiries being made for the remaining member, the actor replied, "Oh! Haven't you heard the news?" "No," was the answer. "Oh, poor So-and-so and his friend Mr Blank are missing. Two hats and an eyeglass have been found on the bank of the River Ouse, near Skeldergate Bridge, and it is feared that they have fallen into the river." As a fact, the gentlemen were "missing," because they had never appeared since the early morning.

There was great consternation at the prospect of the pair having met with a tragic end in the river, and the news of the mysterious disappearance of an actor was not long in spreading over the cathedral city. The manager (who was in on the secret) looked very sorrowful, and said it was a sad termination of the visit, and he would have to make fresh arrangements to fill the part at Grimsby (where the company opened on Monday night). The landlord of one hotel was so anxious that he sent a messenger to the station to see if Mr So-and-so turned up for the train! There were also a score of other people there, all of whom expected corroborative evidence of the tragic end of "poor So-and-so." But when, a few minutes before the train steamed out of the station, the unfortunate actor (who was totally unconscious of his "tragic fate" which had created so much sensation) strolled calmly into the station puffing a cigarette, many minds were relieved. So many people said that they were glad to see that he was "all right," that he was impelled to ask what it was all about, and when the manager broke it to him that there was a rumour that he had been the central figure of an unfortunate incident with which the coroner would probably have something to do, he saw at once that somebody had been playing a joke at his expense. It was only on Monday night that York was reassured, and settled down to its accustomed peaceful existence.

30/11/1889

WANTED, the Profession to Try One Pot of Una's Electrified Hair Producer, for the Hair, Eyelashes, Eyebrows, and Whiskers. The Circassian Secret. The Greatest Wonder Ever Unearthed. Post free, 2s. 3d. per Pot. Apply, UNA and Co., Blackpool.

14/12/1889

ON Tuesday, at the London County Sessions, before Sir P.H. Edlin, Thomas Pearce, aged twenty-nine, described as an engineer, but who, when given into custody, said he was a fruiterer, and resided at Stangate-street, Westminster-bridge-road, was indicted for violently assaulting Thomas Clayton and Henry Sealey, doorkeepers at the Royal Aquarium Theatre, on Monday, the 24th inst., and causing them grievous bodily harm during the progress of a boxing competition. Mr Arthur Hutton prosecuted, and the prisoner, a tall, powerful man, who pleaded not guilty, was represented by Mr Purcell.

Mr Hutton, in opening the case, described the conduct of the prisoner as violent in the extreme. At about half-past eight o'clock on the night in question, he, with about twenty of his associates, forced their way into the Aquarium Theatre without paying a farthing, and assaulted the prosecutors in a most brutal manner, causing very severe injuries.

Thomas Clayton, an elderly man, said he was gate-keeper at Kempton-park racecourse, and he lived at Sunbury. On the 2nd of this month he was engaged to take the checks at the stall entrance at the Aquarium Theatre, and he saw the prisoner and several of his companions forcing their way past some other check-takers, and they succeeded in getting into the stalls. Witness and his friends received several blows and kicks in the struggle. As soon as they got in the prisoner and his companions commenced "blackmailing" gentlemen.

The chairman – You had better tell us what he did. Witness – He went up to one gentleman I know, named Coborn, and said something to him, and he gave him 5s., and told him to be quiet. He then went to another named Blacklock, who also gave him 5s., which the prisoner turned over in his hand, saying, "Only 5s. Make it gold; there is a lot of us boys here." During all this time the prisoner was using bad language, which could be heard all over the house. About nine o'clock he came to where witness was standing, and struck him a violent blow in the mouth, saying, "Take that." Witness's lip was cut. At that time two black ladies, sisters, were on the stage boxing.

The Chairman – Black ladies? Witness – No; half-caste.

Mr Hutton – What did you do? Witness said he was obliged to put up with the blow. As the prisoner continued to make a disturbance, the manager ordered witness and some other of the employees to remove him, and witness in consequence proceeded to evict him.

Mr Hutton – You mean "eject" him; remember we are not in Ireland.

Mr Purcell - "Chuck out" they call it at Westminster.

The Chairman – You had better not interrupt. Mr Purcell – I did not intend that observation to reach your Lordship's ears – only my learned friend's.

Examination concluded – The prisoner and some of his companions came back and struck witness another blow in the face, causing his jaw to swell, and nearly breaking it. He was knocked down, three of his teeth knocked out, and he was badly hurt all over his body. He then became insensible, and did not remember anything more until he found someone washing the blood from his face. During this time witness received the injuries the prisoner was cursing and swearing that he would murder him before he was done with him, and urged his companions on, saying, "It's all right, there's no police."

Henry Sealey was proceeding to give corroborative evidence when the prisoner, acting under the advice of his counsel, withdrew his plea of not guilty and pleaded guilty to the charge.

A long list of previous convictions was then proved against him, including a sentence of five years' penal servitude and thirty lashes with the cat for robbery with brutal violence.

The Chairman passed sentences amounting in all to twenty calendar months' hard labour.

Upon hearing this the prisoner's wife screamed out "Oh, God bless you," and was assisted out of court in a fainting condition.

WANTED, Purchaser for the Latest Illusion, a Lady Burnt to a Skeleton in full view of the audience. The Lady stands on a small round stool in full view, and is then set fire to. E.J. DALE, 10, Cursitor-street, Chancery-lane, E.C.
21/12/1889

11
1890
THE DEAD WOMAN JUMPED TO HER FEET

AN ACTOR'S CARVING.

AT the Warwick Borough Police-court, on Monday, before the Mayor and other magistrates, Mr Augustin Knight, a member of Miss Janette Steer's dramatic company, was summoned for having damaged the stonework of Guy's Tower, Warwick Castle, on March 12th, by cutting certain letters and figures upon it. Defendant did not appear, and the service of the summons was proved, Miss Steer's company appearing last week at Coventry.

Mr Lloyd Chadwick said – I appear for Lord Warwick in this case, and I will ask the Bench to allow me to make a few remarks upon it before I proceed to call the witnesses. It may appear at first sight perhaps that this is rather a trivial charge, but I think when all the circumstances are considered it will be seen that it is not so. If the damage had been done to a modern private house even then it would have been sufficient to have justified proceedings being taken, but in this case, when the building is a grand historical ruin like Warwick Castle, of which not only this town, but all England is proud –

The Mayor – Not a ruin.

Mr Lloyd Chadwick – Well, I will say historic relic. I say when it is a case like this, it is most important that such a building should be preserved. Every stone of such an ancient structure is in itself a feature of interest, and adds to the historic value that attaches to the place, and any damage that may be done to a building of this kind is a very serious matter. As the Bench are aware, through the kindness of Lord Warwick, visitors are allowed to pass through the Castle, and view the splendid collection of art treasures and historical relics which it contains, and every year many thousands of persons flock to it for that purpose. Among other building shown is the tower called Guy's Tower, and in consequence of the number of steps leading up to it, visitors are allowed to have access to it unattended. For a long time past damage had been done to the walls of this tower by the carving of names, &c., on it, and this having, of course, caused great annoyance to Lord Warwick, notices have been put up warning visitors that if such practices were continued the tower in question would be closed to the public. In spite of these notices, however, which the evidence will show that he must have seen, the defendant further defaced the stonework by cutting an inscription on one of the battlements of the tower. I need scarcely point out that his lordship is, of course, anxious and bound to protect his property against injury of this character, and I shall ask the Bench to mark their sense of the defendant's conduct by imposing a substantial penalty. Perhaps I may mention, if the Bench will allow me, that a letter was received from the defendant on Saturday stating that it was not possible for him to appear in answer to the summons, to which a reply was sent to the effect that the summons would not be withdrawn, and that he must either appear or an application would be made to hear it in his absence.

The case was then proceeded with *ex parte*.

Mrs Eva Knight – who is no relation to the defendant – said that she was visiting the Castle with a party of friends, and she saw the defendant on Guy's Tower, in company with a young lady, who was found to be Miss Nita Rydou, a member of the same company as defendant. He was carving his name and hers on one of the battlements, and when they saw they were discovered the young lady "blushed and looked ashamed." Witness informed the commissionaire of what she had seen.

Sergeant White, the commissionaire, deposed that he was spoken to by the last witness, and he went to the defendant on the tower. Defendant admitted carving the letters, which represented his own initials and those of the lady, and the figures 90, and said he did not think he was doing any harm.

Mr Gregory, house steward, said the stone could not be replaced under £1, apart from the historic value.

The Bench imposed a fine of £4, including costs, £1 12s., and damages, £1.

22/3/1890

MADAME PATTI'S treatment by the audience at M. Kuhé's concert at the Albert Hall, on Wednesday, was simply disgraceful. Suffering from a severe cold, she was obliged to refuse to comply with any demands for the repetition of the songs which she substituted for certain selections from *L'Etoile du Nord*. Then an uproar uprose, which nothing, for the time, could quell. M. Kuhlé appeared on the platform, but the disturbers would not hear him, and he had to sit down. M. Hollman began a violoncello solo, but it was drowned in the din, and he departed in disgust and despair. It was not until the malcontents had partially exhausted their energies that Madame Patti was permitted to sing a song by Tosti. We have frequently expressed our dislike of the "encore nuisance." The persisted endeavour to force a singer to repeat an air is on a par with the greed which would ask for two coats for the price of one, or demand a couple of hats instead of a single head-covering and for the same amount of cash. Encores do harm, too, in another way. They cloy and satiate the hearer with a particular tune; and prevent him coming to hear it on another occasion. We congratulate Madame Patti upon her firm, spirited, and succesful resistance to a shameful and unwarranted attempt at extortion.

17/5/1890

AN amusing scene took place at the Theatre Royal, West Bromwich, during the performance of *Hans the Boatman* on Saturday night, the comedy scene in the first act between Hans and his sweetheart Gladys (Miss Edie Casson) being interrupted by the appearance of a telegraph boy, who had deliberately walked on the stage and handed a telegram to the lady, saying he would wait for the reply. He had been told at the box-office that Miss Casson was on the stage, and evidently believed it was his duty to deliver the message.

24/5/1890

THERE are certain gallery customs concerning which it may with truth be written that they are more honoured in the breach than in the observance. This, however, may not be written of a custom which prevails in the gallery of the Gaiety Theatre, Dublin, whenever the Carl Rosa company happens to be in the possession of the stage. The company's patrons, from the stalls upwards, are nothing if not musical, and the gods invariably wax so enthusiastic that they seem determined to fill up the whole evening with harmony. Accordingly, between the acts they organise a concert on their own account. Two, and sometimes three, songs are given by volunteer vocalists, and are, as a rule, listened to with the most respectful and appreciative interest. The late Mr Carl Rosa in this way, upon the occasion of his last visit to Dublin, discovered a very fine voice while seated with his wife in one of the private boxes. Directing an attendant to find and bring to him the possessor of the same, he was disappointed on discovering that he was a piece of deformity, of dwarfish proportions, being in height not more than 4ft. 3in. Operatic heroes, of course, are not built that way, and the impresario, ever on the look out for talent, had to confess with regret that his "find" was not so valuable as he had hoped. It should be added that so

admirable is the management of the house by the esteemed lessee, Mr Micheal Gunn, that the impromptu concerts referred to are never attended by disturbance.
6/9/1890

THE Taylor dramatic company touring in America had a curious experience recently. The play was *Camille*, and Miss Irene Taylor, who was the heroine, had just died in the final throes of consumption, when some women in the audience tittered. Immediately the dead woman jumped to her feet in furious indignation. She pointed savagely at the offenders, and said witheringly, "Any woman who would laugh during such a scene as this is utterly devoid of every sense of refinement or delicacy of feeling. She is totally lacking in the sentiments of common humanity, and could not appreciate any dramatic art higher than that of the donkey in *Uncle Tom's Cabin*." After which fierce invective Miss Taylor lay down on the stage again, and deliberately went through the entire death scene once more before a hushed and respectful audience.
4/10/1890

ON Tuesday Mr Selden, a tradesman carrying on business in King-street, Hammersmith, waited upon the magistrate, at the West London police-court, with several of his neighbours, to request his interference to suppress a nuisance existing in that thoroughfare. He stated that King-street was a very narrow and busy throroughfare, and there was a show, or what was called a "penny gaff," in an ordinary shop without sashes. The showman caused a crowd to collect in the street extending into the road. Mr Plowden – Is the show indecent? The Constable – I can't say. There are some supposed Zulus.

Mr Plowden – They wear the national costume. Mr Selden told the magistrate that a fat boy formed part of the exhibition. He was disgustingly fat. Mr Plowden thought the applicant was getting on dangerous ground, as some people were obliged to be fat. However, he granted a summons for obstruction.
15/11/1890

INDEX

BICYCLE BELLS: musical, 38
BIG SHOWY GIRLS: wanted in Edinburgh, 109
BLACKMAIL: rife in Birmingham, 3, 4
BOUQUET: attached to string, 40; causes fire on stage, 10; composed of Bath buns, 72; Fairy Queen insulted by lack of, 56
BOUQUETS: custom of throwing becoming unfashionable, 115; trundled across stage in wheelbarrow, 40; vegetable marrows not a substitute for, 134
BOXER, female: opponent/doorman sought, 75; wants scientific boxer to set to with, 116
CAB TOUTS: dirty and intoxicated, 20
CAMEL: fails to turn up for dancing lesson, 68; sits on keeper during pantomime, 39
CANE-BOTTOMED CHAIR: causes death of theatre manager, 57
CAT: given funeral at Drury Lane Theatre, 88; makes surprise appearance in play, 22; runs after Hamlet, 42
CHECK-TAKER: trousers ripped by jet ornament manufacturer, 81; violently assaulted by gang, 140
COFFEE URN: fatal injuries inflicted by, 22
CONCERTINA: novel use of by dancing teacher, 18
CONJOINED TWINS: require pianist, 51
CONJURER: accidentally kills boy in audience, 28; falls down cellar, 91; falls through trapdoor, 78; struggles with audience member in rabbit fracas, 64; suicide by tourniquet and poker, 6
COSTUMES: historically inaccurate, 36; non-arrival of leads to hilarity, 28
CROCODILES: escape into River Elbe, 116
CURTAIN: rises at inopportune moment, 127; resented by footmen, 13; crushes violin, 123
DEERSTALKER HAT: jumped on by husband of insulted actress, 17
DOG: confused with Duke of Teck, 6; declines to take curtain call, 115; incurs fine for owner by following him into park, 104; infects property woman with rabies, 114; interrupts performance of *Faust*, 47; invades stage and is thrown to prompter, 103; poisoned by vet's assistant, 71; retrieves umbrella from pond, 133; surprise appearance in *Fidelio*, 39; shot by comedian, 76; survives attack by savage mastiff, 19; successfully treated for worms, 100
DONKEY: disengaged for pantomime, 120; ecstatic to be on stage, 24; falls off piano into orchestra pit, 81; not vicious, 80; takes curtain call and refuses to leave stage, 123
DONKEY (mechanical): rescued from theatre fire, 73
DONKEYS: take part in beauty contest, 72
D'OYLY CARTE, Richard (impresario): objects to illegal performance of *Patience*, 45
DRESS IMPROVER: causes actress' death, 58; musical, 98
DR JEKYLL AND MR HYDE (play): rubber mask not used in, 116; suggestion for enhancing character's transformation, 95
DWARF: punches racist heckler, 72
ELEPHANT: goes on burglary spree in Lancashire, 136; remains used as hall-porter's chair, 110
ELEPHANTS: attempt to break into ale and porter store, 108; play instruments and take part in farce, 101; rob greengrocer's shop, 33; run amok in Kentish Town, 48; tricycles wanted for, 78
ELEPHANT MAN: to be shown on the Continent, 59
FAT WOMAN: not really a woman, 91
FIREWORK FATALITIES: 38,131
FISH: educated, 119; prefer electric light to gas, 23
FOOTBALL TERM: causes near-panic in theatre, 123
GAS: powers new type of organ, 64
GAS CHANDELIER: rashness of attempting to light cigarette from, 2
GERMAN BANDS: ruin private secretary's concentration, 89; divide to maximise profits, 111
GIANT: narrowly escapes lynching after assault, 98
GUN: barrel explodes, 11; exchanged for fan at Wild West show, 101; fails to go off three times in row, 69
GUYS: damaged at Alexandra Palace, 33
HAGGARD, Rider (novelist): lack of modesty, 116
HAIRY ALBERT: paintings of for sale, 124
HANGMAN: enjoys pre-execution night out, 33
HANSOM CAB: difficulty of obtaining on tour, 111

PIGEONS, PERFORMING: have nerves of steel, 99

PIKELETS: cause of misunderstanding in Preston, 93

PRINCE ALEXANDER: entertains audience with whistling song, 92

PRONUNCIATION: cut-glass accent unsuitable for Shakespeare, 35; gentleman desires assistance with, 13

PUBLICAN: vandalizes portrait of Henry Irving, 113

RAT: falls from flies during performance, 78

REEVES, Sims (singer): competes with noisy steam engine, 43; refusal to give encore causes near-riot, 79

RECITALIST: overestimates popularity of Tennyson play, 60

RICE, UNBOILED: mixed with silver spangles for rain effect, 43

SALVATION ARMY: causes closure of Darlington theatre, 81; cheers theatre accident, 32 contingent of frightens actress' pony, 125; defrauded by "converted" tight-rope dancer, 37; fails to crush theatre-going in Cardiff, 13

SHAKESPEARE, alleged descendant of: appears in court wrapped in blanket, 112

SHOWMAN: disappoints youthful audience, 17; moulder's wife elopes with, 59

SINGER: not allowed to perform Irish character songs in pub, 54

SMOKER: responds violently to acting-manager's rebuke, 49

SONGWRITER: refuses to pay tailor for clothes, 133

SPANISH FLY: as hair restorer, 58

SPITTING: deplored in Glasgow, 2

STAGE ASPIRANTS: odd letters from, 120, 138

STOKER, Bram (theatre manager/novelist): wife and child narrowly escape death in shipwreck, 91

STUDENTS: cause pre-arranged disturbance, 41

SUPERNUMERARY: insists on taking curtain call, 117

TELEPHONE: taken advantage of for wrong purposes, 32; utilised by *The Era*, 133

TELEPHONE TRANSMISSIONS: *Faust* from Manchester, 42; live opera in Paris, 22; opera from Liverpool to Queen Victoria during visit, 73; *Patience* from Savoy Theatre, 38

THOMAS, BRANDON (actor/playwright): rescues drowning dog, 131

TINGLE TANGLES (sleazy continental music halls): unfit for decent British girls, 66

TINY TIM: not to be confused with Little Jim, 16

TOMBSTONE COACH: overturns at high speed, 101; used at Liverpool wedding, 100

TROWBRIDGE: to be avoided at all costs, 31

TWO MACS (music hall act): Berlin waiters misunderstand hatchet trick, 75; house of burgled, 84

TYPEWRITING: combined with early dictaphone machine, 122

VENTRILOQUIST: fails to entertain children, 102; gives impromptu performance in court, 122; has six figures, 20

"VOCAL OWLS": resemble tarred and feathered poodles, 43

WILDE, OSCAR: fails to captivate lecture audience, 41

WOLVES, performing: attempt to escape in Leicester, 114

YORICK'S SKULL: found in Runcorn ashpit, 11

ZULU: larcenous transvestite, 10; objects to being touched with wet finger, 65

ABOUT THE AUTHOR

Julia D Atkinson was born in Bradford, West Yorkshire, in 1960. She was formerly a critic for the British Theatre Guide. Her ground-breaking article *A Name Not Just Now Familiar to Ears Polite:* The Importance of Being Earnest *and* Lady Windermere's Fan *on Tour, 1895-1900*, was published in the July 2015 issue of *The Wildean: A Journal of Oscar Wilde Studies*. She now lives in York.

From the same author in the "*Comic and Curious Clippings From the Legendary Theatrical Paper* The Era" series:

A Complete Somersault Into The Orchestra: 1870-1880
Fairies In Cabs: 1890-1900
Crocodiles In The Green Room: 1900-1910